A Soul's Journey

The Essence of a Spiritual Path
Towards the Transpersonal

A Soul's Journey

The Essence of a Spiritual Path
Towards the Transpersonal

Lindy McMullin

Talking

Whoever holds the talking
stick has within their
hands the sacred
power of words – but
only the one must
who holds the speak the
stick may truth about
speak personal
understanding
and experience

Stick

First published in 2014 in Great Britain by
Talking Stick
an imprint of Archive Publishing
Dorset England

For all our titles please go to:
transpersonalbooks.com

A CIP Record for this book is available from
the British Cataloguing in Publication data office

ISBN 978-1-906289-27-0   (Paperback)

To contact the author, please visit her website
www.quantumgreece.com

Printed and bound by
TJ International Padstow UK

PREFACE

Each of us carries our own back story and family history and while we are living our way through it we find it hard to see what is happening, let alone do anything about it.

Every now and again a way-shower emerges who, through their own experiences and endeavors, is able to shine their light for the rest of us to see a little more clearly.

This is a truly facinating, yet harrowing, tale of four generations, each attempting, in their own way, to make sense of their lives but oblivious to the consequences of their actions, related here to us by a woman brave enough to share the depths of her personal process to help others find their way home.

Ian Thorp
The Alchemy Centre
August 2014

CONTENTS

FOREWORD

The Soul is a concept science does not recognize. Nevertheless it is an important aspect of being! To define Soul is impossible; either one believes it exists or not. I liken it to a drop of honey vibrating at a very high frequency, radiating forth beauty from its original being. Soul is something I know, and cannot separate from Spirit. They are one and the same; I believe Soul guides us and in my case has walked up mountains and down into valleys with me, reflecting aspects of self, leading me to a Transpersonal Perspective.

Carl Jung speaks about the ineffable nature of dreams and visions; this ineffable nature is what embodies Soul. I grew up in vision with Soul, but it was not only Personal Soul that guided me, but Universal Soul, with depth and many layers. It is only in unravelling mysteries that we begin to know it, and yet, in the end, discover how numinous and ineffable it remains, no matter how hard we try to understand it.

My decision in writing this book is to re-discover Soul; to peel away at layers hiding it from sight, and to uncover its essence and intrinsic nature through being and becoming. It is also to help those on a similar journey to find Faith, Courage and Light in the depths of their own internal darkness. The spiritual seeker must learn how to dance with the shadow aspects of self; to seek out depth and pledge allegiance to heart, for in the end result, when all the fabric has been torn away, Soul stands naked and unashamed, urging us forward through life.

There is an unseen thread of pure essence keeping this universe alive and in place. Macrocosm and Microcosm unfold in a dance of the spheres, pulsating gently as a Universal Heartbeat. To hear the beat of one's own heart is easy, but to hear the beat of the Universal Heartbeat is not.

Each life is a unique journey! We must of necessity delve deep down into the subconscious, look at the many archetypes hidden from sight, embrace those shadow aspects of self that hinder us from uniting within, and then wait in silence for essence to manifest. Essence, like a precious drop of nectar, is within. It is part of Source, and yet some of us only touch its surface in our dreams; others delve a little deeper; and those who are stirred, traverse the barren nights of the Soul, the destined paths of the Mystic, the Saint, the Shaman and the modern day Spiritual Pioneer, for the road is long and hard. Eventually, however, we hear something calling us deeper and deeper into the heart of existence – we hear the heartbeat of Mother Earth, Father Sky and that of the Universe, in a celestial hymn that takes us into the heart of Love, Hope and Compassion.

Each path we tread, each calling to Spirit, is unique and necessary for evolution of our personal being and becoming in all life, both seen and unseen. The extraordinary depths one can descend into are often reminiscent of the archetype of Persephone, mourned for by her goddess mother Demeter, descending into the underworld so she can become queen.

What greater gift of life can the human be given, than that of re-birth?

I think about Demeter and Persephone, the crone-maiden, the mother-daughter, the giver-receiver, who becomes the giver again, in a long cycle of birth, death and rebirth. I see Persephone, enchanted with the beauty of a flower she stands gazing at, a reflection of her inner being, enter Hades, the underworld. Driven by circumstance, her own deep inner psyche throws out shadows and shatters aspects of self she needs to govern, to hold, caress and finally transform, before she can rule. The pomegranate seed reminds her that in order to live in both worlds she needs to descend periodically, to reflect on the need to integrate the beauty and grace of exceptional experience. Living in three worlds – the exceptional world of the upper realms, where Demeter resides; the middle world, where mother and daughter meet; and the lower world – her Myth helps explain the Transpersonal Perspective of altered states of consciousness.

Birth, the precursor of experience, teaches us to take our place in society and come to terms with knowledge that one day, we too shall have to greet the face of Death. Consciousness will question whether or not we have obeyed the rules of life, and those of re-birth. If we are lucky, we will feel whole, ready to become part of a Greater Whole. We are seekers of life, death and re-birth, as were the ancient Gods and Goddesses of ancient times, for we carry their sentiments within us. With Demeter and Persephone, I place Pandora.

Prometheus, the folk hero, rears his head up. As archetype, I call him Forethought, and his brother Epimetheus, Afterthought. The all-giving Pandora, joined in matrimony to Epimetheus, emerges to open a vial that will unravel the depths of Shadow, with its many faces.

Afterthought questions, with wonder, if it is at all wise to open a vial bringing so much suffering? Forethought wonders if life, perhaps, should be lived only on the surface? Hope, trapped and alone, manifests into freedom to ponder on destiny! Sometimes there is no choice but to follow the unique path we have been given! Perhaps the warning not to open the vial, an echo from that ancient time, is to make us realize that once we have, there is no turning back. Plunged into the depths of Hades, taken to the heights of Olympus, we will take vows, receive blessings, and walk a path through the middle world, to a deeper understanding of who we are. In learning to listen to the rustling leaves in the oracle of everyday life, watching nature, we become high priests and priestesses of an ancient world, blessed with the kind of sight that sees no pain, and the kind of listening that hears no harshness. All that is left at the end of a long dark night of the Soul are lessons deepening understanding of self.

Entangled in the web of destiny we learn how to become, but not before we have faced our Demons. Learning is the gift of birth, death and rebirth, this and an invitation to re-address symbols that myths extend towards us. Through giving and receiving, we connect with the essence of life, finding the shattered remnants of the Soul we need to put back together. This is the hope we carry: to touch the beauty and grace of our innermost being.

I look out of the window. Fortune has carried me to Istanbul; the city of seven hills lies at my feet. Like a jewel it stretches forth, reminding me of the time I knew how to fly. I watch seagulls, catching fish from the glistening Bosphorus, plucking them out of the water, and swallowing them whole. I know I must remember and honour what has brought me this far, as I get ready to deliver a seminar. I have become Priestess and Hierophant, looking beyond broken dreams and into the heart of men, women and children who walk a path to no man's land, longing for freedom of Soul. I am healer of self, a Demeter and a Persephone. I am a Transpersonal Therapist and yet a tiny grain of sand in an enormous expanse of universe. Sometimes, called upon to assist others in need, I become a gardener ready to rake leaves that settle around the beauty of a rose, without damaging it, for I follow laws of Soul. I delve into the world of Soul, recognizing the mirror in me, and the mirror in others, reflecting beauty, grace and light, but darkness too.

I look around me. There is a small table in the corner of the room, where I often sit to meditate. I have covered it with a cloth and placed on it a quartz crystal, an amethyst stone, a white feather, water in a bowl, and a candle, which I light. A solitary, flickering flame draws me into stillness, and I close my eyes. The universe throbs somewhere in the depths of being. Light pulsates, streaming from my fingers, as I feel the soft brush of a feather between my closed eyes. The top of my head tingles, as Light pours into me. Bursts of colour fill my mind, and inevitably I go back, back to the moment when my life took a turn; to the time when Spirit spoke and Soul awakened within me, trying to answer my deep resounding cry: "WHO AM I?"

I am a three-year-old girl, lying in bed at night. The moon sheds light through my bedroom window, as I find myself drawn to patterns of darkness and light, dancing through trees outside my bedroom window. I am fascinated with them and they, invariably, are fascinated with me, for they beckon and I cannot resist them. Soon, I lose form, and feel vibrations taking me from one world into another. Stars rush past and I soar, flying through space. A portal appears before me, haloed in such brilliant white light, it blinds! Brilliant conglomerations of colour every now and then enfold, giving me the strength I need to move beyond the portal, hungry for Love. The portal, however, remains closed.

This is when I awake, unable to breathe for great sobs that wrench at my being; I do not like this world and want to go home! I do not appreciate having been sent here, as I have memories of another world! I find my way back the next night and next, but the Universe will not open to me! I cannot go home! Somewhere in the recesses of being, I discover a passport, a spiritual passport, with stamps of many lifetimes I cannot let go of. I know how to fly and I fly, only to find myself in space, empty and dark. I seek this darkness, hungry and thirsty for the elixir I know exists, and must find. I settle into this space to look out. I get used to darkness and am surprised, for I recognize I am in a wood – a wood between worlds, where I have found peace! Every night I stare at a spot on the ceiling, facilitating my entry into deeper states of lucid dreaming. I travel to the wood, no longer afraid I have become a grain of sand in an endless universe, for I am not alone. No older than I, but infinitely older in wisdom, he comes to me, a young child with fair hair and blue eyes; a boy who holds my hand, soothes me, and teaches me how to see in the dark.

Shortly before my fifth birthday, he motions for me to follow him out of the wood. My time of learning is over and we walk, he leading, I following. We come to an enormous tree, its gnarled roots buried deep, and he speaks, his words piercing both heart and mind, but soothing my Soul.

"I will always be there for you!" he says, turning to go.

I see how smooth his path is, as he takes his leave towards the West. I look at my path, which lies towards the East. There is a garden, where the rose bushes have all withered. They no longer bloom, and I fight the darkness pulling me towards them. I cannot escape this destiny, for I have asked to touch Light; I have been shown the way!

He leaves me to return to the world I have been born into. Tears stream down my face, for I hate Earthly existence. I cannot go back into the wood and the spot on the ceiling has faded for I can no longer fly; I have lost my wings!

On Earth, I pore over books and spend long nights staring up at a star-filled sky, wondering where Truth is? I know beyond a doubt I need to make my way back to the stars, for I have been abandoned to Earth, and cannot touch Sky; unless I learn to move beyond duality, and the shadows that dance on the window of my mind, I will not find freedom! I pray, calling out to those beings I know live in the Universal Sky, asking for forgiveness, for I am sure I have done something terrible to have been shut out like this! I know I must while away long hours in nature, drawn to butterflies, dragonflies and shiny, green apples that silently drop off apple trees, leaving small indentations in the rich grass. I must find my way back to the Adam and Eve of my existence and give myself over to Earth, so I may feel I belong once again.

Hidden in a garden, Mother Nature speaks to me. I sense spirit folk, and feel their wings vibrating softly, so it becomes a paradisiacal garden, where life continuously moves in spirals and circles. I feel like an alien, come from a plane light years away, and although I still hanker to go home, I accept exile. I draw a veil of light around me, learning more and more about the world I love so deeply. I begin learning about a Father who came down through a Son bringing Spirit, but I believe I am a daughter amongst sons because I know Him as a daughter! I pledge allegiance to someone who has suffered so greatly, whilst hanging from a cross, so enter His Heart and Mind to understand His pain. I cannot accept He dies to forgive me, but rather believe those who kill Him are to blame!

This does not help me love those who live on the Earth – I cannot understand them at all, and I often sit beside Him, with adoration, for I know He loves me with all His heart. He sometimes reads to me and this is how I fall asleep, imagining I live with Him, although I know these imaginings are different and come from mind. Those that come from heart go back in time, to where I sit among daughters listening to Him, accepting what He says, for he is my Master! I speak to Him silently, far more than I speak to people on Earth, struggling to find balance and then one evening, I find myself in space that brings vision!

I stand in the ruins of a temple, dressed in a long white gown. A black knight, riding a black horse, thunders towards me. He wants something I hold to my heart. I am surprised to see I hold a Golden Book I know is precious, and belongs to me, for it has been given to me. His voice is clear as he comes towards me, threateningly.

"Give it to me!"

I back away from him, crying, because I cannot part with my book. I repeat over and over again that I can never give him the book because it is mine. Sobs wrench at my heart that flutters in growing fear as he carries on towards me. I stumble backwards when suddenly two arms lift me off the ground. The arms enfolding me bring warmth, warmth belonging to the realms in my wood. Safe in the arms of Love, that sweeps me up and holds me, we gallop off on a white horse. This white knight takes me to a beautiful, stone abbey and helps me off the horse. We walk inside. I find myself standing at a round table and my attention is captured by what lies on it: an extraordinarily beautiful golden chalice, which sends off a halo of brilliant light that mesmerizes. I feel a profound sense of honour and duty as I stare at the chalice.

I watch the white knight lift the chalice and drink from it. He passes the chalice to me, and I raise it to my mouth. Everything explodes at once; immense warmth, like the glow of a gentle fire, runs through, igniting my heart. I am free and yet chained to the destiny of my life, as written in a Golden Book. It has given itself over to the cup and yet I know it is still there, hidden in the depths of my being. I have been given a taste of it, a sweet elixir that has cleansed me with beauty and grace. I am lost and yet found, unable to find words to describe how I feel. Instead, I find a path I must tread, for I have touched this perfect light to make a rose garden bloom. It will not be an easy life, because I know nothing at all, and yet Light has been given to me; I carry it in my heart!

I am Persephone, no matter how old Demeter has become inside of me, for all her wisdom. As I gaze at the beauty around me, the ground opens beneath me and I plunge into the very depths of Hades, for if I am to master Hades, only then shall I reign as queen. I live in Hades for the cycles of ebb and flow; I live on the Earth looking for cycles of Love and Light; I live in Heart, for it is only here that I shall begin to discover the gentle balance between the three worlds.

I receive a gift – and I must cherish this gift! I must acknowledge the Master who has given me the gift of Light; I must be grateful and remember that everything is as it is, for I have asked to be given the grace of Life. I know now, I must move forward and yet this entails going back to my roots, to that which may eventually answer the question "Who am I?"

CHAPTER ONE

When we seek out darkness, therein to find light, we offer ourselves to a magnetic force that carries with it all negative thoughts and wishes that have been carried on through generations of time. If we can, we learn to use prayer as a means of protection, but sometimes it is not enough. We need to consciously understand the world of opposites before we can move beyond it.

The Curse

Do human beings create their own destiny, or are they influenced by unseen forces? This question has haunted me and still I have no clear answers! What I do know, however, is that we come into this world carrying a bag. This bag holds, amongst other things, a spiritual passport, and this passport decides where we travel to and what becomes of us, because it is our personal Book of Life. I believe, however, that the negative thoughts and emotions that lead to curses, inevitably create thought forms that grow to enter space where we are at our weakest. This is the shadow that must be overcome, for it is part of our destiny that we manage to overcome it!

In my family, curses were all too frequent! My grandmother Maria from my mother Kaya's side of the family, cursed my sister Jackie, telling her she would bring dead babies in an apron to Kaya, because she was angry. My grandmother Johanna of Dutch descent, who gave birth to my father Edward, cursed him and his unborn children when he left home at the age of sixteen and abandoned her. My mother Kaya told my sister Jackie that if she got married when she was twenty, she was dead as far as Kaya was concerned and Vaia, my ex-mother in law of Greek descent, cursed me the day I got married, hoping I never had children! No doubt, there were strangers who cursed fortune and fame as well, due to jealousy and rage. Inevitably, darkness seeped into our lives, hurting us, healing us, but also blinding us to the fact we were all tied by some unseen thread that would eventually bring the dawn of a new era. I had no idea it would all come together in a castle in Northern Ireland in 2014.

Death was an aspect that always haunted my mother, Kaya. From the time she could remember, Kaya was afraid of people dying and leaving her behind; she always awoke, terrified, the night before someone left this realm for the next, or before something happened that would change lives. She believed she had been cursed by this gift of foresight and her fear of the unknown created wounds that ran deep within her psyche. She was unable to embrace her gift.

Kaya was born to Maria and Mihail in Belgrade in 1922. She claimed to have come from a royal bloodline and her childhood, although pristine with the beauty and grace that wealth brings, was sadly filled with fear and loss. Her father Mihail was strict and never forgave her for being a daughter, unable to carry his name. An only child, Kaya found herself surrounded by austere governesses and a fraught mother, Maria, who constantly fought with her tyrant husband who was unfaithful to her. Whenever her parents argued, which was frequently, Kaya would huddle in Maria's wardrobe, wrapped in soft mink, shaking with fear. Her ability to recount these moments with rich imagery brought emotions that settled into my mind and heart, because they depicted life that was tragic, yet beautiful at the same time.

My grandmother Maria was a well educated young woman, born in Czechoslovakia. Her upbringing had been warm and simple, giving her every opportunity to become a lady. When she graduated from school to enter university, she became one of the first Suffragettes to claim equal rights in a man's world, but it also took her away from her many siblings and the father she had hardly seen whilst growing up. She was studying medicine in Vienna, when she met the tall dark-haired man who swept her off her feet. Mihail had finished studying pharmacology and he proposed before Maria had finished her studies. Blinded by love, she followed him to Yugoslavia, as it was known then, to become what appears to be his prized possession. She lost part of her spirit, like many women do when faced with a man who looks at them as a subject, because her husband's explosions kept Maria trembling. Finally they led to fear of being suffocated so completely that she lost her zest for life, and longed for freedom.

Mihail appears to have been a perfectionist with good social standing and his determined efforts to maintain his growing fortune often took a toll on his ability to relate to those around him. Everyone was supposedly afraid of him and Kaya was often made to kneel on cobbles in the courtyard until she fainted and was brought in by the butler, whenever she displeased her father. Maria would twist a handkerchief in her hands over and over again, whilst dabbing at a tear that escaped every now and then. Her mutterings sang to the wind, *"What to do…oh what to do?"*

I had great difficulty listening to my mother describe these events, because anger welled up inside of me and I wanted to shake Grandmother Maria who, it appeared, had not changed. I was born when she was in her early seventies, and I often thought her inner strengths became weaknesses; although she had always wanted desperately to break free, she was still tied to her destiny.

Kaya, as any young girl would, needed to escape from the confines of daily life. She was an excellent student who had private tutors who taught her a number of languages, how to play the piano and how to excel in whatever she undertook to do. She learnt how to embroider and all the necessary graces of a young woman who would one day take her place in society and yet she longed for freedom and joy. Both mother and daughter hankered after the same things and neither could see the other's reflection.

At the age of sixteen, Kaya was drawn into the arms of a young man who was poor and from a much lower class than she was, but who fired her gentle heart. Intent on finding some semblance of happiness, they secretly met on the banks of the river Drina in the small village of Loznitsa, sharing dreams of a future that only exists in the imagination of the young, blinded with love. Although she often managed to escape from her governess and prying eyes of the many staff who worked on the estate, one day a curious neighbor saw her and promptly informed Maria. Maria knew it was only a matter of time before her husband found out. She would be blamed, so she made plans to marry her daughter off to Masha, a pharmacist in his mid-forties. Maria knew that even though he was an older man, her husband at least would be relieved by the fact he was wealthy; he could settle with the knowledge his fortune was safe. She coached Kaya to consider this arranged marriage as a form of release from her strict upbringing, underlying the fact she would be helping her mother too. Kaya was torn in two, as any young adult would be who is made to feel responsible for her mother's freedom, and trapped at the same time.

Being an only child was not easy and Kaya doted on her cousin Risto. Risto was four years older than her and lived in Zvornik, a small town close to Loznitsa. Kaya's Aunt, Angelina, loved inviting her over on weekends because she knew how strict her brother Mihail was. She had tried talking to him on numerous occasions, but no one could persuade Mihail to change his ways. Their father Vladimir often argued with Mihail because he disapproved of the way his son treated his wife and daughter. There were times when his hand held so tightly to his cane, as he faced his son, that Angelina, Mihail's sister, often thought her father would have a heart attack. When she invited Kaya to stay for a week in Zvornik, it was after a particularly explosive moment when she had challenged her brother with the shocking news that had reached her ears: he had bought a flat for one of his mistresses! She suggested taking Kaya in for a week.

It was the summer vacation when Risto and his sisters made plans to have a party for their cousin, and as my mother spoke about it some years later, she left out the most important details of that summer. I include the story here, although this was a secret Mother took with her to her death. I found out about her first love only then, when I found his letters.

Kaya was taken shopping to Belgrade the day before the party by her aunt, who bought her a beautiful black dress that hung in folds around her slim body and a pearl comb for her short, curly hair. Mihail had insisted Kaya wear her hair short, as though he wanted to force her to be the son he hankered after.

Plans for the party were underway and a local band was hired for the occasion. Dragan and Kicho had been invited to play guitars and, eager to make an impression, Dragan had taken extra care with his appearance that evening. Dragan was not tall, but had beautiful blue eyes. He chose a dark blue jacket and light blue shirt, enhancing his eyes. He did not see Kaya as he began playing, but she saw him. Later, as he stood laughing with a friend he stumbled slightly, bumping into her. She looked up at him with such admiration, and asked him when he was going to dance with her? His heart was beating, because she was so beautiful, and she did not realize what was breaking inside of him! She was of a different class than he was, but he knew he could not let this chance go, even though he wondered if he had a chance at all! They danced and for a moment time stopped. It seemed as though she was melting in his arms and Dragan held tightly onto her. No amount of reason could part him from her; not the curious glances Risto was giving them or his friend Branko's stare. When they finally broke apart and Branko told him he was mad, he was already locked in the dream of how he would see her the following day.

So their romance had blossomed. Kaya always insisted that when he returned from Rashnik where he worked, she would be waiting, so they could walk together, hidden from those who disapproved of him. The meetings were stolen moments, Dragan always afraid they would be caught. She was brave though, and so, for six months, they met, falling deeper and deeper into the spell of love that covered them. His mother had met Kaya, and loved her dearly, but worried about such blatant class difference. Dragan loved her with all his being, unable to think about differences, because he felt they were one!

I met Dragan when he was in his eighties, and yet he recalled every detail of his meeting with Kaya. Listening to him was like listening to a poet singing the sad tones of a love song, for it was evident Dragan still loved her, no matter that he had a wife and grown children. As Dragan's story unfolded, it was easy for me to imagine Mother, who had died the year before on Dragan's birthday, as she prepared for her wedding to Masha. She had never shared this part of her tragic story with me.

My imaginings saw Kaya standing in front of her mirror, prior to her marriage to Masha.

She looks at the beautiful, white lace dress that has been carefully fitted over the previous weeks. For a moment she closes her eyes. She can feel Dragan's arms around her and yet it becomes painful to think of him. How can she ever tell her father she has fallen in love with someone as poor as Dragan? She shivers. Her father would kill her if he knew! She realizes how terrified the thought makes her feel, so she opens her eyes and thinks about Masha.

Masha had been courting Kaya for a week before she allowed him to hold her hand. His fingers had caressed her hand roughly, and she had quickly withdrawn it. He had frowned and tugged at his dark moustache. Then he had laughed at her and when she had looked into his eyes, she had seen a dark desire that sent shivers down her spine.

Looking back at her reflection in the mirror, she allows herself to think about her wedding night. A sob catches in her throat and at that moment her mother comes into the room.

"Don't you look pretty," Maria says softly. "Your father has at last relaxed and he is taking me to Vienna after your wedding. God knows how long it has been since he even looked at me! My child you have made me very proud and happy."

Maria walks over to the window and draws back the shades.

"Your father has booked the church on your seventeenth birthday. It can be a double celebration" she says smiling.

Kaya's hand catches at her throat as she turns towards Maria. She wants so much to plead, to talk about Dragan, but the dreamy look in Maria's eyes stops her. She smiles, turning her head away so her mother does not see the tears that fill her brown eyes. The young, poor man, who has given her his soul, she buries deep within her heart, allowing the memory to steal part of her spirit. Perhaps this is a deep, unfulfilled desire that class and fortune has to pay; it will cost more than she can ever imagine.

Three weeks had gone by since Dragan had seen Kaya and he was worried. He had not seen Risto either to ask where his cousin was, so he decided to take a cake his mother had baked to her Aunt Angelina. He was surprised when she answered the door, because he had expected their maid to. Taken aback, he politely gave her the cake and asked how they all were.

"Oh we are so well!" Angelina replied. "Kaya is getting married on Saturday, on her seventeenth birthday, so we are all busy. Please do thank your mother for the cake!"

Angelina took the cake and said goodbye to Dragan. For a moment she wondered if he had fallen in love with Kaya, but quickly suppressed the thought. She decided he must know about the wedding and that the cake had been sent as a gift; it made her feel much better! Dragan felt the blood draining from his face as he quickly turned around, mumbling a wish for happiness. The door shut behind him and he stumbled along the road and around the corner, where he suddenly bent double and began sobbing uncontrollably. His friend Branko found him there an hour later. Branko took him home, sat him down in the small kitchen and tried to make out what Dragan was saying. He poured a glass of pear liquor for them both and then another. He told his friend how he had warned him this would happen, but Dragan would not stop crying. He was sure Kaya was being forced into the marriage and he felt completely powerless. His despair was so complete that for the next two months, he refused to leave the house. He wrote her a letter, asking her why she had not told him. When they met for the last time, she cried in his arms, asking for forgiveness, explaining she had no choice but to follow what was expected of her!

Kaya had moved out of her parents' mansion and was now mistress of her own house. Her marriage to Masha had been elaborate. A beautiful reception had followed and then a whirlwind honeymoon on the Dalmatian Coast. Masha was a considerate lover who was quite taken at first by his young wife. He lavished presents on her and encouraged her to make changes in the house he had clumsily furnished. When she fell pregnant five months after their marriage he was a proud father-to-be who invited over four hundred guests to Banja Koviliacha to celebrate. When he came home one day to find the doctor in his study, he was eager to find out how his son was doing. He was convinced his wife would give him a son, but the doctor looked at him with a stern frown. He very curtly informed Masha that Kaya had miscarried and that she had been rushed to hospital with a serious infection.

"Did you not see the signs you have been carrying an infection?" he asked brusquely. "Your wife may never fall pregnant again because of your indiscretion!"

Masha, only concerned about his own health, immediately asked the doctor what was needed to treat the infection. He called Maria and told her that her daughter had miscarried, deliberately leaving out the details and comforted his wife by telling her he was devastated, but they would have other children. When Kaya started crying and told him about the infection he told her she was delirious and she should never repeat such terrible lies!

When Mother related this story, I saw how many times she had slipped back into this pattern of her past, burying certain memories in order to survive and heal. At the time it was very apparent this would become a pattern that could not serve her; it would manifest later in her life as illness!

It was a slow process and when Masha started travelling for days on end, she knew he was seeing someone else. She tried talking to her mother, but Maria reminded her men were like that – after all hadn't her father done the same thing! Trapped in a loveless marriage, Kaya became listless and the only thing that saved her from falling into deep depression was the news, eight months after her marriage, that war had broken out.

It was August 1939 and the German army had invaded Poland. Tensions were rising and Masha continuously arranged dinner parties, where he could discuss the situation with friends. He had dismissed the miscarriage with a shrug and then settled down to work. Yugoslavia had become increasingly pro-German over the previous years and the Prime Minister Stojadinovic had resigned.

Maria had come to dinner one Sunday with Mihail. Maria was a short lady, with brown hair and a vacant look in her eyes. She was always well-dressed, walking beside her tall, grey-haired husband, who was aristocratic in his demeanor, having taken after his father, Vladimir. Both were very concerned with the turn of events. Maria worried about the breakup of Czechoslovakia, whilst Mihail, who was a major in the army, worried about impending war. Everything was hanging by a thread, so Kaya tried to be attentive, slowly coming out of her listlessness.

On the 27th March 1941, Masha did not come home. He sent Kaya a telegram to tell her there were riots in Belgrade and that General Simonic had led a coup, overthrowing the Regency and the Government. He urged her to go back to her parents' home and wait for him there. Lucille, her governess, packed her things and the chauffeur took her to the estate she had grown up on. Maria was fraught and clasped Kaya, wailing. Kaya tried to calm her mother down, and here was another pattern, where daughter became mother, spilling over into areas where there were no boundaries!

News that came on the 17th April was chilling: the Axis forces had attacked Yugoslavia! The royal family and government had fled to London and Mihail was sent to a camp in Hammelburg. The German army occupied the mansion where Kaya had been raised, but arrangements were made for Maria, Masha and Kaya to live in the West wing.

Maria and Masha began to stay up late in the evenings, huddled over a radio in the cellar, listening to the BBC. Kaya had acted as lookout for the first two weeks but then grown bored and angry, so she started playing the piano in the drawing room, to calm her growing worries something terrible would happen to them all. Pieces of Chopin and Mozart filled the air with promise and German soldiers often smiled and nodded to the music as they went to and fro. One of the officers was particularly drawn to the young girl, who played so beautifully.

Hans was in his late twenties. He was tall and handsome in his dark uniform. His blond hair was short and he had the most incredible blue eyes that often held Kaya's gaze. They started going for walks in the evening and soon, Kaya was under his spell. Masha did not seem to notice and she persuaded herself she was doing something to keep them all safe.

It was Sunday evening. Kaya had taken her usual walk with Hans and he had kissed her for the first time. Her body had trembled as she had responded to the kiss and after he said goodnight to her, she had stolen down the stairs to the cellar. Masha and Maria were huddled over the radio and they did not see her. Masha had his arm around Maria's shoulder and for a moment, Kaya wondered if her mother was having an affair with her husband. She tiptoed back upstairs and had a long bath. She would give herself to Hans, she decided, when the time was right.

Kaya was convinced her affair with Hans was part of an innate desire to protect her mother. It was also an act of defiance against her husband, who had betrayed her, and whom she obviously did not love. That night she fell into a restless sleep and when she awoke it was to the sound of soldiers shouting and the noise of a jeep leaving in a hurry. She fell back to sleep, to awake again well past nine. She disdainfully noticed Masha had not come to bed, so she especially took notice of her appearance that morning. Her chin up in defiance, she swept down the stairs in search of Hans.

As she was looking for him, Kaya suddenly realized how important her own life had become. She was struggling to help her grandfather Vladimir oversee his saw mills and console her mother. She was shocked her father had been taken to Germany as a prisoner of war; although she had always feared him and often hated him, he was still her father. Torn by the sudden surge of love in her heart, she struggled not to cry.

When the German army had first occupied most of their home, she had tried to be cheerful, always pointing out to her husband and mother how lucky they were they could still live there. Instead of fearing the soldiers, who were so neat and handsome, she enjoyed watching them and greeting them openly, recalling how her father had forbidden her to talk to anyone of the opposite sex. She wondered what he would do if he saw her, but then her thoughts turned to her mother and Masha. They certainly seemed far more suited to each other and this just made Kaya more determined to pursue her tall and handsome soldier of war.

The autumn leaves had blanketed the ground and the sun had barely risen. Two soldiers were outside carrying a metal crate to a jeep parked in the driveway. Kaya made her way to the small pantry that served as a kitchen. Lucille was sitting at the table and jumped up as she came in. There was a heavy awkwardness in her behavior as she began to prepare breakfast. Kaya walked outside. She raised her hand to block out the sun and saw Hans striding towards her. She smiled at him but her smile froze, as she could see tension in his face.

"Let's go to my office," he said in a low voice.

She had never been into the library that had once been her father's since they had taken over. She sank into the black leather chair and looked up at the bookcases around the library. The books were all leather-bound and carefully arranged in alphabetical order. She had read so many of them and for a moment she felt her throat constrict. Hans sat down opposite her, at her father's mahogany desk with beautiful engravings on either side, looked at her and cleared his throat.

"Something happened last night after you went to bed. We were having dinner and I sent the cook down to the cellar for some wine. Kaya, he found your mother and husband listening to the BBC and reported back to me! They have been arrested and as you know, the penalty is death."

Kaya froze. She knew their lives now hung by a thread that could very easily break. She looked at him with pleading eyes and he drew her close. As she stood in his arms, she fought to keep the tears back and allowed her stiff body to mould against his. This was her complete surrender!

Hans immediately arranged for her to visit her husband and mother. Kaya felt the bitterness choke when Masha told her to do whatever it cost to set him and her mother free! Suppressed anger and pain bubbled up inside her heart as she stared at her husband. He looked back at her tauntingly, with a challenge she knew she could not ignore. Her mother's slumped body, as she sat in the corner of the cell where she was being kept, broke something inside of Kaya!

Kaya told Hans she would give herself to him completely and begged him to help her mother and husband. He arranged for their release and, in exchange for their freedom, Hans took Kaya with him to Germany shortly thereafter. A week before they left Loznitsa, a neighbor spat at Kaya in the street, calling her a whore; she was deeply troubled by the accusation. Unable to deal with the many emotions that threatened to emerge, she tried to create a different future. Deep in her heart, she felt her husband had betrayed her completely from the moment he had laid eyes on her. She had been betrayed by her mother over and over again and yet Kaya could not blame Maria. She identified with the woman who cried, when she had told her she was leaving for Germany. In her own eyes, Kaya had simply been following the man who had done everything to support her, by saving her mother and husband; the fact he was an SS officer and that she had betrayed her nation was something totally blocked from mind. She was young, and the young do not always understand the true ramifications of war! In order to cope, she began to choose what information she paid attention to and which she dismissed as dangerous to her sanity!

Mother was not always able to recount her story in sequence. Often there was fear in her eyes as she spoke about the past. She reminded me of a very brave woman, and I only saw her courage at the time she spoke about her past. I was unable to be a child then, because I had already been introduced to a divided world. I sensed she was very unhappy, but had no way of knowing I would take on the apparent guilt she felt, the subtle nuances that would carve my future as a seer and healer, nudge me into the world of the Mystic and Spiritual Warrior, and teach me so much about life.

CHAPTER TWO

The act of living one's destiny includes a series of stages far beyond our understanding, the objective of which, it seems, is to take us back to the path of our personal legends. Drawn by an unseen thread, we often find ourselves in a labyrinth looking for the key to our freedom.

Bondage

Germany gave Kaya an opportunity to begin studying medicine – something she had always wanted to do. When they arrived in Leipzig, Hans took her to his parents' house. They lived in a modest three-bedroomed terraced house that was close to the city center. Hans' mother was a tall woman, with fair hair and sparkling eyes, and his father a rather nondescript man who worked closely with the Führer. Kaya hardly saw him but she liked Frau Renate, who welcomed her in. Renate felt sorry for the thin girl who clung onto her son's arm, especially when she realized he had not yet told her he already had a wife and young daughter. Renate heard the sobs one night and then her son's soothing voice promising he would get a divorce. Frau Renate thought about the girl her son had married, when he was twenty, because she was pregnant! She thought about Kaya! Her hands lying in her lap were tied by an unseen cord. She knew the situation was difficult but dared not interfere, so did what was necessary to support her son and the young woman he had brought into their house, as much as she could.

Kaya began medical studies at Leipzig University and went to the local hospital daily, to learn the practical aspects of becoming a doctor. Her flair for languages had her speaking fluent German in no time and she started learning Italian, whilst overseeing a group of prisoners of war. Life had taken on an idyllic pattern, where war was almost forgotten, and Kaya began to fill out and look more beautiful than she had ever done. Hans and his father saw to it there was always good food on the table and Hans often brought her silk stockings and perfume. Frau Renate gave her beautiful fabrics and she began to sew dresses for herself, becoming an expert seamstress. She had only once glimpsed Hans' wife, when she had come to see his mother. Kaya decided she was not very pretty and when Hans told her he had never really been happy with her, and had only married her because of the child that had come so unexpectedly, she began to relax more and more. It was as though the war was a shadow that appeared on a wall, which had to be avoided at all costs. What remained of importance were the daily nuances that brought feelings of belonging! It was essential that Kaya ignored what was happening in the world, and yet it was obvious she absorbed a great deal of guilt during this time. It remained buried in her subconscious!

Over the next two years, Hans brought Kaya news about the Yugoslavian Partisan resistance movement and their successful guerilla warfare. She had had no news about her mother or Masha, but Hans assured her they were fine. He told her he was not sure what would happen if the Partisans managed to expel the Axis from Serbia, but Kaya was unable to deal with this future.

One evening, as she had just finished making a velvet jacket for Hans' mother, she was surprised when the door opened and he tiptoed inside, looking over his shoulder. He quickly shut the door and placed a finger on her lips.

"Kaya, I love you with all my heart but something terrible has happened. I have to leave; I am being sent to the Russian Front."

He clutched her, as she began to sob. Fear gripped her as he explained it would be better for her if she went to stay at the hospital.

"My father thinks these orders have something to do with you! The Führer does not take kindly to foreigners and we think my wife may be involved. My darling I will come back to you! The war will soon be over and we will be free. Please be strong!"

Kaya began to pack her suitcases, trembling. She carefully checked her jewelry was safe in the pocket of her handbag and clung to Hans.

"It won't be for long my love. I am so sorry! I will write to you," he told her. "I love you and please don't worry. My mother will come and see you whenever she can. Here is my ration card. You can use it to get food outside the hospital. I love you Kaya! I will come back to you."

That night, in a narrow bed at the hospital, Kaya cried herself to sleep. She woke in the morning and began to work with fervor. This was the only way she could forget her pain! Her life had slipped away from her, and she was unable to think about life in Serbia. She dared not think about her future and that was when the fear came. Three days later, convinced something terrible would happen, Kaya received a call from Frau Renate. At first, Kaya could not make out what she was saying. The woman was sobbing uncontrollably and eventually she understood; Hans' train had been blown up on the way to the Russian Front!

For the following weeks, Kaya walked around the hospital in a daze. Like an automaton she did what was necessary, but her brown eyes were filled with deep despair. The loss she experienced became unbearable, so she had to find a way to escape! Huge black circles framed her eyes that held sorrow, making her face look drawn and she seemed unable to connect to reality. She was only nineteen, so when Pino, one of the prisoners of war she tended to, began to talk to her about escaping, she suddenly snapped out of her despair.

Pino had been planning with a group of his friends to escape into Czechoslovakia and asked her if she would accompany them. Although she did not seem to understand what he was saying, there was a flicker of hope in her eyes. It was two days before they planned to escape in a Red Cross truck that he grabbed hold of her whilst they were walking outside, and kissed her fiercely on the mouth. She responded to his kiss and the tension in her body seemed to leave as he spoke to her. He told her of their plans and she quietly agreed to go with him. Events of the past were neatly buried deep within her, as she told him they could go to her mother's sister Aida in Czecho-slovakia. To Kaya, Pino had become her savior!

The evening they escaped, Kaya began to pray. She felt a silent strength carrying her through the dark night as they huddled in the back of the truck that was carrying supplies across the border. She bit her lips until they bled when she heard the German border guard ask questions about the supplies, and when she felt the butt of his rifle against her leg as he lifted part of the tarpaulin, covering them. They were huddled down low behind boxes of medicines, cramped and cold. Only when they were on the road again did she dare breathe.

She was pleased she had listened to Maria's stories about her sister Aida. Aida lived in an old castle her husband had inherited from his grandmother. Kaya knew it would be an ideal place for them to hide, but when they finally left the truck, Pino's friends did not want to go with them. They knew it was dangerous for them to split up, but Pino insisted he wanted to stay with Kaya. They hid in the fields the following day as they made their way to Kalinov.

Czechoslovakia had already been liberated by the Red Army, supported by Czech and Slovak resistance. Kalinov was a small village near the Dukla Pass and when they finally arrived, Kaya was close to collapsing. Her aunt and uncle immediately took them in, although it was difficult for Kaya to tell them what had happened. They gave her a big bedroom overlooking the back gardens and she slept for two days. It took her a week to fully recover and in the meantime Pino began to make plans for their escape across the border and into Italy.

Kaya had given Hans' ration card to her aunt, as she knew it would help them all stay alive. At the back of her mind she recalled the love she had shared with Hans, but dared not think about his death. She knew in order to survive she had to bury him in her heart, where she had buried Dragan. She helped her aunt clean potatoes and carrots and often stayed up late at night, listening to stories about Maria when she was young. Again, the war seemed to have faded – until the morning the Russian army surrounded the castle.

The Russians were convinced Kaya's aunt and uncle were harboring an SS officer called Hans. They had traced the use of the ration card and when they found Kaya there, they were sure she was a spy. She told them she had stolen the card but they did not believe her! Kaya spoke perfect Russian, as it was one of the languages she had learnt with her tutor Professor Roshenko. She pleaded with the officers who finally agreed to release her aunt and uncle. Pino had hidden in the cellar when he had heard the commotion, but she had been picking fruit when she first realized soldiers had surrounded the castle, which stood on a small hill on the outskirts of the village.

Kaya was taken down to headquarters where she was told that, in order to prove she was not a spy, she would work for the Russian army as a translator. She was taken to a camp with German prisoners of war and forced to go around the camp, asking for valuables. With a gun in her back and a helmet clutched to her chest, she told German soldiers and officers to give up their watches and rings.

Day in and day out, she translated for the Russians and slowly Kaya began to lose innocence. She heard the cries of soldiers, when they pleaded with her not to take their valuables. One soldier in particular touched her as he told her he could not give up the watch hidden in his sock – the watch that belonged to his grandfather. Kaya stared at him but then pointed to his sock.

"They will kill me if I don't do what they want!" she replied dully.

Days turned to weeks and it seemed as if Kaya had switched sides so many times she could no longer remember who she was. She was close to having a breakdown when her uncle told her Pino had finally made plans necessary for their escape. He made it clear she was to disappear on her way home and that she only had two hours to find Pino and follow him. He told her he would contact the Russian commandant to ask for her whereabouts, because they could not risk becoming implicated in the escape.

Kaya took only her personal papers and jewelry with her the following day, when she reported to headquarters. They were in her bag, and she tried not to pay attention to it. She especially did not take her bag with her when she went to the camp, but when she returned that afternoon she picked it up, put it across her shoulders and went to her bicycle. She cycled up the road and held her head down. Her muscles were aching as she pedaled fast along the path that took her towards the castle. Suddenly she looked over her shoulder and then veered across the road and into the woods. Her heart was pounding as she cycled to the place her uncle told her Pino would be waiting.

She dared not open her eyes after she had been covered with a dark blanket, and baskets of vegetables had been placed on top of her. She could hardly breathe and was only conscious of the sound of the truck's engine. She fell asleep and when finally she awoke, it was to hear Pino tell her they were at last safe! They sold some of her jewelry to buy clothes and a train ticket and at last they were on their way to Bari.

Once again it appeared Kaya had floated from one scene to another, vulnerable and gullible. It was strange no one had worried about using Hans' ration card, and it was as though destiny was playing its hand, placing her at the gates of duality, trying her, as she faced the soldiers, demanding they hand over those items that held sentimental value! Kaya transferred all her feelings of guilt onto the Russians, who she later claimed had done so much harm, and yet had seemingly escaped criticism of the world!

That evening, Kaya tried to keep awake but the movement of the train sent her to sleep. She had taken her new coat off and forgotten she had put her soft leather jewelry case in the pocket. She clutched onto her bag, aware the train was cramped and anyone could steal it! When she awoke in the morning she looked for her coat, but it was not on the seat beside her. It was only when she reached into her bag to look for the jewelry that she realized what had happened. Kaya was devastated! She had taken the best rings, bracelets and necklaces her father had given her, which were worth a small fortune. Her mother had given her a diamond ring and earrings, which alone, would have kept her for a number of years. Maria had given her the papers she needed to sell them for a good price on the black market, and now she had lost everything. She cried for the rest of the trip! Nothing could console her and inadvertently she realized her fate lay in the hands of the Italian who had helped her escape Germany.

When Kaya arrived at Pino's family home, she was again drawn and listless. Pino's parents, overjoyed to see their son, were curious about the young girl who came with him. Pino's three sisters shared their clothes with her and took her for long walks. They treated her as if she was a princess and she quickly became accustomed to her new lifestyle. She read about the bombing of Leipzig and tried not to think about Frau Renate.

The Partisans had expelled the Axis from Serbia and they had denied supremacy to the old government of the Kingdom of Yugoslavia. Marshal Josip Broz Tito had been elected to lead the new communist state as Prime Minister and Kaya shuddered to think of her family's wealth that would be lost to the communists.

She wondered what had happened to her father. Hans had arranged for her to visit him in Hammelburg but during their meeting he had been so tired that he had asked no questions. He had simply signed a piece of paper giving her power of attorney over his affairs and finances, and now she realized she had lost everything! She tried slowly to forget about the tragedies, as her relationship with Pino progressed. He told her he wanted to marry her, but when a British officer flashed a smile at the hospital she had started working at, and told her she was mad to stay in Italy with a brood of children hanging from her skirt, she made up her mind. She would go with them to London, where she would start a new life! Steven helped arrange for forged papers that had her born in Poland.

When she told Pino she was leaving him, Kaya had been living in Italy for a year. He stood staring at her aghast. His sisters pleaded with her and his mother sobbed. Kaya carefully took her small suitcase and walked out of the house to the jeep waiting for her in the street. She tried to apologize and to explain why she could not stay any longer. She told Pino she would always remember him, but felt stifled living with his family.

When she finally settled in Britain, she was alone, apart from a group of Polish friends who had traveled with her, as part of the Red Cross, across the borders. She was given a grant to carry on her medical studies but when Anita, the young Polish girl she had traveled with, told her it was unfair, the fear came.

Conscious her past was a heavy burden and someone might realize her papers were forged, she became very fearful. Desperate for news about her parents, Kaya at last managed to contact Maria. Mihail had returned after the war, a broken man. He had asked Maria for a divorce and moved to Belgrade. Maria told Kaya the properties had been confiscated, and that she had been forced to sell her porcelain and Chinese vases. She told Kaya how much she had suffered at the hands of the partisans because of Hans. She warned her daughter never return to Serbia, because she had a code name and had been sentenced to death! Kaya knew she could not risk anyone finding out about her past.

She told Anita she could have the grant and immediately moved out of the room she shared with her. She was grateful when she found a job as a seamstress for a wealthy Jewish furrier, Samuel Cohen, and moved into the small flat upstairs. She had always been good with the needle and even though it was difficult to sew the fur, she managed. On her days off she went for long walks in Hyde Park, holding her body and trying desperately not to think. It was there one afternoon, as she sat on a park bench, she noticed a young man sitting on a bench opposite. He was reading a book in German and memories came flooding back.

She asked him about the book he was reading. Ziegfried was startled at first but he invited the young, attractive woman to share his bench. He had a soft melodious voice and told her he was half German and Jewish. He was in his early thirties and was an accountant. His love of Chopin, Mozart and his philosophical yearnings captured Kaya. He spoke about everything so passionately that he gave her back a yearning to live. They met every day in the park and often shared sandwiches for lunch. Kaya was conscious of the poverty she faced living in the small flat above the furrier, and was reluctant to invite him there. She felt ashamed and he could sense it! Instead, he asked her if she would do him the honor of spending Passover with him in his modest two-bedroomed house in Kensington Gardens. The romance blossomed and seven months later they were quietly joined together in matrimony. Kaya could finally close the door on her past, sealed with this marriage. She was happy and hoped they could build a future together. She still worked because it was important she feel independent, even though it was not easy for her! She followed the Jewish faith rigorously, knowing somewhere in her heart this was necessary, because it eased some of the pain.

When she missed her first period and then a second, she told him the news with quiet concern, because she was worried about the added financial burden a young child would bring. He assured her they would manage.

Kaya worked until she was eight months pregnant and then

resigned. She still kept up her friendship with the Cohens who had taken her in, and when she gave birth to a healthy four-pound boy, they came with a large bouquet of flowers. Kaya decided to call her son Paul, and Ziegfried doted on him. They were managing financially and as she prepared meals and looked after her son, she often thought back to her life when cooks and butlers had taken care of her. Her mother had moved to a small house she had managed to buy in Loznitsa, and Kaya often thought about Maria and how responsible she felt towards her.

War was over and people had been horrified with the terrible war crimes that had been committed, but Kaya could only remember the soft embrace and the help Hans had given to her. She often sat singing in German to Paul and never thought about the strange and tragic circumstances that had taken her from Hans to Ziegfried. It was as though she had no past, for it always cast a shadow over her, and she was petrified of the future!

Paul was six months old when they decided to have a dinner party. The Cohens had been invited and some colleagues of Ziegfried. It was a simple dinner that allowed Kaya to relax and recall happier moments, but the following day Ziegfried woke up with an excruciating headache. By lunch time he could hardly walk and Kaya rushed out to take Paul to Sheila Cohen, who promised to look after him. Shaking, she went back home and called for an ambulance! Kaya accompanied her husband to St. Michael's hospital where he was admitted for tests. She sat waiting for the results, twisting a handkerchief in her hands, her body tense. The doctor called her in to his office two hours later.

"I'm afraid your husband has less than two months to live," he said quietly. "He has a brain tumor that is inoperable. I am sorry!"

Kaya knew she was going to faint. She began to sway back and forth and closed her eyes. As she slumped in the chair the doctor ran to her. From far off she heard the sound of a train blowing up and Hans screaming. The screaming soon became her own voice and as her eyes fluttered opened, she gratefully took the sedative being offered to her.

Kaya only went home to change her clothes and get clean pajamas for her husband. Ziegfried deteriorated rapidly and most of the time he lay on his side staring into space. Kaya sat beside him, pleading with him to get better. Sheila was still taking care of Paul and Kaya had not seen her son since Ziegfried had collapsed. Three weeks later Ziegfried was dead!

Kaya lay on her bed rocking. Ziegfried's best friend from work organized the funeral and she stood shaking throughout the service. She could not believe life had been so cruel to her! Choking memories of her life began to seep into her consciousness and once again she was close to having a breakdown.

Three days after the funeral, she went to speak to Ziegfried's employers. She knew she was entitled to his pension, and even though it was too soon to think about money, she knew had to survive. She was graciously received, but sensed an awkwardness coming from colleagues who had been so warm and caring only three days before. Ziegfried had left a will with his wife as beneficiary, but he had also left some of his personal effects to his mother. Kaya had never met his parents and asked the accountant Peter if they had been contacted. He assured her they were doing all they could.

When Kaya left, she went to Hyde Park and sat on the bench where she had met Ziegfried. He had not spoken to her about his family in Israel and she had never thought to ask him. She realized how little she knew about his past and wondered whether his parents would come to England. That afternoon she went to see her son. She clasped him to her but the pain was so deep, she told Sheila she was still unable to cope. The woman told her not to worry! Paul was in good hands but she urged Kaya to see a doctor. Kaya left, tears streaming down her face, and stopped at the local pub where she sometimes ate with Ziegfried. She knew some of the locals and tried to smile feebly. She went to a small table in the corner and ordered wine. She was shaking so badly, she thought the alcohol might warm her. She did not like drinking, but it was her only option. She hadn't been eating properly for days and the wine soon made her feel dizzy.

She started crying again and was grateful when a young British officer handed her a handkerchief. He looked at her earnestly and asked what was wrong. Kaya told him her story. Yet another

Samaritan had come to assist her, when there was no one else she could turn to!

Kaya had amazing charisma. Not particularly beautiful, she was striking and elegant and in this elegance carried her sorrow, reflected in her almond-shaped eyes. Her mother Maria and her father Mihail had entertained lavishly when she was young, so she had learned how to behave and prided herself in being a lady.

David seemed a kind, gentle man. He listened to Kaya's story and took her home. He gave her his telephone number and promised to call her the following day, to see how she was doing. Kaya appreciated his concern and that night she lay in bed staring at the picture of her husband, until sleep finally came. In the morning, true to his promise, David called her and the next and next. They arranged to meet again the following week and she woke on the morning of the day she was to meet David, with the sound of a bell ringing in her ears. She jumped up pulling on her dressing gown and ran to the door. She looked through the window and saw the accountant from Ziegfried's work standing outside. She opened the door, ushered him inside and apologized that she was still in her dressing gown. She made him a cup of tea and went to get dressed. She came back into the living room and sat down.

Peter Gosh was a small man. He appeared even smaller in the large green armchair that seemed to engulf him and looked nervous. He kept on tugging at his moustache and for a moment he reminded Kaya of her husband Masha.

"I am sorry I came so early," he said apologetically "but it was imperative I see you. Mrs Klausner, there is no easy way to tell you this, so I am going to come right out and say it. Your husband has left a widow and two small children in Israel. They are his true beneficiaries!"

Kaya stared at Peter! What was he saying? Who was a widow?

"I don't understand what you mean," she said. "Who is a widow with two children?"

Peter looked back at her. He did not know how to explain to her, her husband was not her husband! He had hardly slept the night before. He had contacted Ziegfried's parents to tell them of their son's death and had been shocked when Ziegfried's father had started crying and talking about his two grandchildren who now had no father. It had taken him a full thirty-five minutes to ascertain that his colleague had never divorced his young Jewish wife, who lived with his two children in a kibbutz in Israel. He got up and moved to sit beside Kaya.

He had never really liked her, and had not liked the fact she had come to the office so quickly, to ask about money. However, he began to warm towards her. She had lost weight and looked no more than twelve. Her face was pale and her dark eyes filled with pain. He cleared his throat and laid a hand on her shoulder. He quietly told her what he knew. He did not expect her reaction that took him by surprise.

Kaya jumped up and began to shout out in Serbian. She picked up a vase and smashed it against the wall, then an ashtray, smashing it as well. Moreover, she turned on him.

"Get out of my house! You never liked me and now you are here telling me lies. Get out! Get out!" she shrieked.

It took every bit of courage to stand where he was and take hold of her arms.

"I am not lying," he shouted back. "The house is not yours. Nothing is yours and I am sorry – I am truly sorry!"

She broke down then and wailed, as she kept hitting him against his chest.

"The bastard lied to me! He lied to me!"

Her face was contorted and he did not know what to do. He wanted to go back to the office, to forget the entire story, but could not leave her in the state she was in. She collapsed against him and began to heave. He laid her on the couch and ran to get water. He saw a bottle on the dresser and took out two small pills. He did not even know how he managed to get her to swallow them, and an hour later when she was asleep, he let himself out of the house. He would call her later to make sure she was alright. He felt sick and for a moment terribly sad. He thought about his own wife at home; what it would do to him if she died and then he found out they were never really married! Peter did not go back to the office. Instead, he found himself walking rapidly to a flat on the outskirts of Kensington Gardens, a flat his wife often went to, to have beautiful lace underwear made by a very talented, middle-aged Polish woman called Yolande. He had to help because he felt responsible in a way. He could not imagine why, but he felt sure she had sensed his dislike of her.

It did not take long for him to persuade Yolande to take the young woman in! He knew Kaya had been sewing fur coats and when he explained the circumstances of her life to Yolande, she immediately offered to give her a job.

"She can stay at the boarding house," she said in her heavy accent. "The owners are friends of mine and I will ask them to offer her a good rate. Bring her here tomorrow afternoon!"

Peter thanked Yolande and went back to the house that afternoon. He knew she would still be sleeping, so he leaned heavily on the bell and then banged on the door, until Kaya finally woke up and let him in. He explained he had found her a place to stay and a job. She stared at him and only nodded. He made her a cup of tea and some toast, and told her he would come to get her the following afternoon.

That evening David waited for Kaya to arrive at the pub they had met at. When an hour had gone by and she still had not appeared, he called her. She answered the phone groggily and he immediately paid for his drink and left. He drove to her house and knocked at the door. She almost collapsed into his arms. She clung to him, as she told him what Ziegfried had done to her. She begged him not to leave her and to help her pack. He poured her a brandy and together they packed her belongings in two pigskin suitcases he found in the closet. That night, he held her in his arms as she fell asleep. She looked like a child who had been abandoned and he felt himself drawn to care for her. The following morning when she awoke she told him about her past in Yugoslavia, and about the great tragedies that had come, one after another. She told him about the baby the Cohen's were looking after, and he found himself crying with her.

When Peter came to the door that afternoon, he was surprised to find David there but relieved someone was with her. He took them to Yolande who graciously invited them in and Peter left, never to see Kaya again!

Yolande spoke briefly to David and then ushered him out. Kaya was still clinging to his arm but Yolande told her kindly.

"You have time my child. Now you must rest. I will take you to the boarding house later on. Come now, say goodbye."

Kaya tried to resist for a moment, but then she let David go. She felt betrayed, betrayed and angry! She was tired and wanted it to all go away. All she could think of was that she wanted to be saved – saved by David. Instead the Polish woman was steering her into the back room and down some stairs to the workroom.

"I only sew by hand my dear, and you will do the same. Look at this beautiful underwear. Here look, this is your size. You can have it. Come now let's have some tea. Tea always makes things better."

She placed some lace underwear in Kaya's hand, as if the gift would cheer her up. Kaya followed Yolande upstairs. She pushed the lace underwear into the pocket of her suitcase and sat down. She was exhausted and her body was trembling. The tea was warm and there was a hint of lemon in it and brandy. At first she gagged, but then she drank the tea. The brandy warmed her and she lay back in the chair. Yolande covered her with a blanket and soon Kaya was asleep. She dreamt Ziegfried was standing in the doorway. He looked at her for a moment and then turned away. She tried to follow, but two children began to crowd around him. She saw Masha looking at her! She knew he had not divorced her either, but she would not think about this! She awoke her heart pounding! Yolande was busy making soup in the kitchen. Kaya looked around Yolande's flat.

There were two big chintz armchairs and a small glass table. There was a pin cushion and a small thimble on it, which she picked up and slid on her finger. She thought about her small son. How was she going to feed him? Yolande had told her how much she would be earning downstairs, and it was just enough to pay for the boarding house. How was she to eat and to feed her son? She got up and went to the kitchen.

"Please, can you take me to the boarding house? I am really tired."

"But you must eat something! Your clothes are hanging on you!"

"Please?"

Kaya's voice was almost strangled as she begged Yolande to take her to her new home. The woman looked sharply at her and shrugged her shoulders. There was a strained atmosphere between them as they lugged the heavy suitcases to the boarding house. When Kaya saw her small room she burst into tears. She sat on the bed, her shoulders drooping. Yolande watched her. It was so obvious the young woman was used to luxury, but there had been a war and she would have to make do with what she had!

"I will see you tomorrow," she said to Kaya. "We begin at eight thirty so don't be late!"

She left and shut the door softly behind her. Kaya got up and began to unpack. She placed her medical books on the window sill and her clothes in the cupboard. They did not all fit, so she folded some and left them in suitcases which she pushed under the bed. She went into the shower and let the water soak into her skin. She towel-dried her hair and put on her dressing gown. She went back into the bedroom and looked at the clothes in her wardrobe. She had been wearing black and suddenly she began to take out all her black clothes, dumping them on the bed. She got out her suitcase, took out the dresses she had folded and stuffed the black ones into the case!

She chose a soft grey dress that hung to her ankles. It had a small embroidered black design on the left shoulder, and she put flat black pumps onto her feet. She brushed her hair, added some powder to her nose and pinched her cheeks. She took her raincoat and handbag. Taking a last look around the room, she shut the door.

She walked to the Cohens' house five blocks away. The wind blew her hair which was now a little longer, and she buried her hands in the pockets of her raincoat. At last she arrived at the Cohens. She was happy to see Paul, but looking at him, he only reminded her of the man who had betrayed her. She told Sheila what had happened. Sheila kept on shaking her head.

"I can't believe it," she said in her strong Jewish accent. "He seemed to be such a nice man. Why lie and marry you?"

She looked at Sheila.

"I can't afford to keep Paul," she said. "Can he please stay a little more with you?"

Sheila did not have children and Paul had brought light into her life. She was happy to play with him, feed him and she felt very sorry for Kaya. There was an awkward silence when Kaya told her she had found a job. Sheila thought Kaya would ask to come back, which would have made it much easier for her to see her young son frequently, but she realized the young woman was not even considering it! For a moment she felt a shiver run down her spine! Kaya did not look normal. She was neither angry nor hurt but seemed to have become someone else. She was distant and almost detached and Sheila was concerned. She put a hand on Kaya's arm, trying to reach the woman who appeared to have locked something up inside of her.

"Of course," she said immediately. "You don't have to worry about Paul. I will look after him for as long as you need me to!"

Kaya quickly got up and barely glancing at the baby asleep in his crib, she said goodbye to Sheila and left. Over the next few weeks that turned into months, she carefully sewed underwear, knowing she was doing a good job, but kept to herself. When she finished work, she usually met David at the pub and they sat chatting or going to the occasional film. She was comfortable with David and they began to visit Paul together. It was just after Paul's first birthday that David invited her to lunch with his mother.

Doreen was an extraordinary lady. Having spent a number of years with her husband in India, she loved entertaining. She was tall, regal looking and the moment she set eyes on Kaya she could tell the young woman had come from a good background. This was a match she would support, although she wondered how long it would last. She knew her son was a womanizer and yet he seemed totally captivated by the young foreign woman he told his mother he wanted to marry. When he placed the fine diamond ring that had belonged to his grandmother on her finger later that evening, she felt a glow in her heart. Perhaps at last life would be good to her, and she could forget the past! Forgetting was important to her! Had she begun to analyze things, she would have had to look at herself honestly in the mirror; she would have wondered about Masha, and the fact she was still married to him. Instead, she buried the memories deep within her psyche, refusing to consider her feelings. She was sure he must have signed the divorce papers.

They found a small apartment close to Doreen's and Kaya moved out of the boarding house. David told her it was time for her to take Paul back and they went together to tell the Cohens the good news. Sheila was devastated.

"But you can't take him back," she said. "Not now! We have grown to love him! You are going to get married and what kind of a life will you have, with a small child you hardly know? Let us keep him, Kaya. We will give you money to start your new life!"

Kaya stared at Sheila. Was she suggesting she sell Paul? For a moment she thought about the money, how she could put it away as security, but then it was too ridiculous to imagine!

"No," she said. "I can't sell my son to you! Please Sheila I am grateful you have done so much; you can see him whenever you want to, but he has to come home to me!"

They took Paul home that afternoon. He cried himself to sleep. He did not seem to be happy in his new home and Kaya was unsure most of the time what to do with him. She took him to David's mother, but Doreen seemed to shrink away from the child she suddenly discovered Kaya had. Yolande told her she could bring him in to work, but it was not easy. David looked after him most of the time but could not do everything. Kaya began to regret not having left Paul with Sheila, but then she had an idea.

"Why don't we send him to my mother in Serbia? She will be so happy to see her grandson. It wouldn't be for that long. You could take him!"

It seemed to be a reasonable solution and David readily agreed. They started making enquiries at the consulate to get papers for Paul to travel, and a week later, Kaya and David were married at the registry office. They had a quiet ceremony. David's brother Keenan was there as well as Yolande, Doreen and her sister Nicky. The Cohens had been invited but they did not come. Paul stared at everyone during the service and only cried a little at the end. What thoughts went through Kaya's mind only she knew, as she married David!

The consulate had told David it would take time but eventually, five months after the wedding, Paul got his travel documents. Paul was close to his second birthday when David took him to Serbia.

Kaya waved to them from the window until they were long out of sight, and then sat down on the couch and closed her eyes. She had not told David she had missed her period. She was certain she had fallen pregnant and she was pleased she could rest, knowing her son would be taken care of. Her mother had been ecstatic when she had sent her a telegram to tell her she was sending Paul to her. Maria could not wait to see her grandson!

Everything had once again fallen into place and Kaya let out a sigh. She opened her eyes and looked around the cozy flat. She had sewn beautiful cream curtains that hung in the living room, and cushions to match. The room was cozy with gold, brown and orange fabrics. Doreen was pleased when she had seen how Kaya had decorated the apartment, and had given them a beautiful Indian throw over, which looked exotic on the sofa. Kaya jumped up and went into the study. She would start making curtains and cushions to make the study a beautiful children's room. When she had given birth, she would tell her mother to bring Paul back. It would be good to see her mother and then maybe they could move to a bigger home. Kaya dreamed of a life that would finally take shape and bring her happiness.

CHAPTER THREE

At the beginning of time, out of the chaos, a fine blueprint of existence begins to evolve. In each and every seed, there is a map containing the form and characteristics of birth, flawless like a diamond. The diamond reflects who we are. People acting as reflectors are very often blinded to the beauty that lies in their innermost being.

Freedom

Kaya felt good as she made plans over the next few weeks and when David returned from Serbia, she had prepared a wonderful meal. She looked rested and the glow of pregnancy had made her hollow cheeks fill out. They had veal with mushrooms and sautéed potatoes and when David told her she looked ravishing, she told him she was with child. David nearly choked as he sipped at his wine but he pulled her close. It was all a bit sudden!

On the way back from Serbia he had thought about taking her on holiday to the Isle of White to celebrate their marriage. Now, there was a baby coming along – another child. He was taken aback but then warmed to his wife's excited voice. He knew his mother would be happy, so he decided it was probably the right time to settle down.

Over the next months, Kaya blossomed. She went for long walks with her husband and often visited with Doreen and Nicky. She tried to write to her father, but he told her how disappointed he was in her. She had always been a disappointment to him, and it still hurt. She knew he was living with one of his mistresses, Georgina, and that he no longer spoke to Maria. Even the fact her son was with his grandmother had not warmed Mihail's heart. Every now and then she received a letter from her mother, who told her how Paul was growing and how he could recite small passages from the Bible.

Maria had, after the war, turned to the church for comfort. Kaya could not imagine why her mother was teaching the Bible to her son, but she persuaded herself it would all work out in the end. It was becoming much easier not to face reality!

Her cousin Risto came to England to visit her and told her about his three children, Zorana, Brana and Branko. She asked him about Dragan, and learned he had been a prisoner of war in the Alsace Lorraine area for four years, during the war. It was difficult for Kaya to hear this! She tried not to think about the young man whom she had understood so completely, and who had loved her so deeply; it was too dangerous to think of him!

Risto told her Paul was growing and that he often played with Branko, Brana and Zorana. When he left, she gave him a small teddy bear for her son and a present for her mother. She felt sad as she watched him walking down the street with his small case. She wondered if they would ever meet again!

As time slowly brought her closer and closer to the birth, Kaya clung more and more to David, feeling insecure and afraid. Memories of her last pregnancy and birth would not leave her. When at last the day came for Kaya to give birth, David and his mother were with her. They encouraged her and held her hand until she was wheeled into the delivery room. Two hours later, Kaya looked down at her beautiful daughter and smiled softly.

David went out that night to the pub and got terribly drunk. He kept on telling everyone he was a father and the following day, surfaced around lunch time. He went to the hospital and peered at Kaya from behind an enormous bouquet of flowers. He had a sheep-ish look on his face and she laughed.

"Come," she said softly, "Come and meet Jackie."

David smiled and went over to the basinet. Jackie was beautiful and she clutched onto his fingers, as she kicked robustly.

"I will have to teach you how to play football, with those robust legs!" he whispered gently as he picked her up. Kaya watched the tenderness between them and smiled. For the first time in her life she felt a sense of peace in her heart.

Jackie was simply a delight. She hardly ever cried and was a beautiful baby who grew over the next few months, bringing much pleasure to both her parents. Kaya was still breastfeeding her, but then she got an abscess. She went to hospital and had to place Jackie in day care. Doreen found her Mrs. Perry, a delightful lady, who took care of Jackie for the week Kaya was in hospital. David picked Jackie up every evening and dropped her off the following morning. It was an ideal situation and when Kaya returned home she was still weak so she left Jackie with Mrs. Perry.

It took her two weeks to recuperate and when at last she took Jackie back, she agreed to take her to Mrs. Perry twice a week. She wanted to go back to work at Yolande's, so it seemed a perfect solution. Kaya was happy and when David got a job in the film industry, she was relieved. They could at last move to a bigger home and she could bring Paul and her mother to England. David was busy and came home at all odd hours of the night, but Kaya did not mind. She had food ready in the warmer and he always told her how much he had missed her and Jackie.

Jackie turned one and then two. David stayed at home more and in general life was good. Even Doreen was surprised to see her son was so settled. She often invited them for lunch on Sundays, to her comfortable home near Oxford.

They went that summer to the Isle of White and Kaya could at last relax, because she was happy. When Jackie turned three, Kaya told David she was thinking about asking her mother to come and visit with Paul. David told her they could all go to the Lake District, but when Maria replied it was not suitable for them to visit, Kaya was almost relieved.

She settled into her daily routine and then one afternoon, on her way to pick Jackie up, she thought she saw her husband sitting with a red-haired woman in a small café. Kaya was on the bus, so she could not simply get off, as she was already running late. She decided she must have been mistaken, but that evening after she had bathed her daughter and fed her, she made a beef stroganoff and opened a bottle of red Chianti. She had a shower and put on the grey dress she had been wearing when she had first met David.

David came home on time and was surprised to see his wife had switched off the lights and lit candles all over their small living room.

She nibbled at his ear over dinner and soon they were on the couch making passionate love. When they finally got to bed she asked him casually what he had done that day. He told her about his appointments, and how he was looking at different actors, to decide on whom he would choose for a film he was directing. Kaya was relieved he did not say actresses and she told him she thought she had seen him.

"I was definitely at the office, my dear," he told her. "You can even ask my secretary."

He snuggled down close to her, but Kaya remained staring at the ceiling for quite a long time. As she turned to look at her husband's sleeping profile, she could see how handsome he looked. Feelings of insecurity tugged at her. She only got to sleep around four, and when she awoke the following morning, he had left a note to say he had left her sleeping because she looked so beautiful, and had taken Jackie to Mrs. Perry. That afternoon, Kaya went to see her mother-in-law.

Doreen had always supported her daughter-in-law, and now she sat sipping her tea and listening to her. Kaya was munching on a cucumber sandwich and yet she had not stopped talking about David. Doreen was sure something was up! Kaya kept on telling her how much she loved David, and how grateful she was that she had such a wonderful mother-in-law. Doreen made a mental note to call her son the following day. Doreen took Kaya shopping that afternoon and bought clothes for Jackie. When she suggested buying some for Paul, Kaya was ashamed to admit she did not know his size.

"Don't worry," she laughed. "His other grandmother is doing it all!"

Doreen remained silent. It was not her place to ask her daughter-in-law about her child. He must nearly be seven and how could he possibly remember his mother? What a tragedy! Doreen wished things had been easier for Kaya; she knew she would definitely have to speak to her son about her concerns.

The following day she called David and told him she would expect him for tea. David had not seen his mother for over two weeks. He casually let himself in to the flat and kissed her on the top of her head. She wasted no time.

"Are you having an affair?"

David had not even sat down.

"God, mother, you are worse than a wife! What on earth gave you that idea?"

"Your wife did," she replied firmly "indirectly. I am telling you David that if you are, and I do not want details, you must end it immediately! You have always had a roaming eye but you have a daughter and a step-son, though god only knows what is to become of him. I will not let you ruin my granddaughter's life!"

David immediately denied it, but Doreen knew her son. He looked guilty and she quickly got up in order to make more tea. They spoke about his father who had died seven years before, and when David left, Doreen sat down wearily. If Kaya found out, she knew it would devastate her. She prayed the affair would end quickly, before anyone was harmed.

Three months later, Doreen opened the door to her distraught daughter-in-law. Kaya sat on the couch sobbing. She told Doreen that David had asked for a divorce, because he had fallen in love with a red-haired nurse! Kaya explained how she had thought she had seen David one day when she was on the bus. She told Doreen she had followed him a few days later, and seen him with a long-legged red-head. She explained further, how she had refused to believe her husband was having an affair, and that she had made sure she always had his dinner ready with wine and candlelight. She told her mother-in-law how David had started coming home later and later, and stopped spending time with Jackie, and that although she had ignored it, she had never imagined he would come home to pack his things.

"He has moved out!" she told her mother-in-law between sobs. "I have had to put Jackie in week-care with Mrs. Perry, and I am working again full time at Yolande."

"Why did you not come to see me sooner?" Doreen admonished her daughter-in-law. "I would have spoken to him."

"He doesn't love me any more!" Kaya wailed.

That evening, Kaya told Doreen she was going to move back into the boarding house. Doreen gave her a check for a thousand pounds to help, promising to take Jackie over the weekend. She tried calling

David the next day and the next. In the end she stopped calling and waited patiently for him to call her. She would wait for almost a year!

In the meantime Kaya had moved out and back into the boarding house. Yolande was paying her now for extra time, so she made sure she worked as much as possible. She saw Jackie on weekends and lived on cornflakes and milk for over three months, so when she met Edward, a young South African portrait artist at the boarding house, it took Kaya exactly ten days to decide she would marry him. She was sure he would save her from the perils of betrayal that had hounded her for so long. It was a rash decision, but one she could not escape from!

Edward had fallen in love with Kaya the moment he had seen her playing in the park one afternoon with her daughter. He had waited and followed her to Mrs. Perry. When he saw her turn into the boarding house later, he had smiled. Wooing her would be easier than he had imagined, as he had just that afternoon rented a room there.

What exactly drew Edward to Kaya, he could not say. His own life had been quite miserable! His Irish grandfather Henry James had been his idol when he was young. Edward had loved sitting on his father's knee, listening to stories about his grandfather, who was born in Dublin in 1861. His grandfather, who had died at the age of seventy-four, had gone to the Cape Province when he was in his youth, where he had worked as a civil servant. He was twenty-six when his son Andrew was born.

Edward loved his father, who often sang songs to him and spoke about County Down, which he had never had a chance to visit. Edward had never understood what had made his father Andrew, who worked underground in the gold mines, commit suicide! One minute he was in the bathroom shaving and the next minute Edward had run into the bedroom to find his forty-year-old father stretched across the bed that was soaked with blood. His mother Johanna Elizabeth had screamed for him to get out of the room, but he could never forget the gaping wound across his father's throat that spurted blood, or the razor still clutched in his hand! Edward was three years old when it happened.

By the time Edward was six, he was playing truant whenever he could, and at the age of eight, he began to draw on tiny pieces of paper he stole from school. They had never had money because his step-father always drank, and he did not like the fact his mother had given birth to four girls after him. His three sisters from his own father were too busy with their own lives to pay any attention to him. In the end, he almost killed his step-father one day, when he saw him hit his mother! He never understood why his mother Johanna did nothing to protect them!

Johanna let her husband beat Edward that day and Edward, who had just turned sixteen tried to defend himself! His anger had got to him and he had thrown the bread knife at his step-father, cutting his cheek! His mother had started screaming and his step-father had lurched drunkenly, before crashing to the floor. Edward had run then and not looked back! He had gone to Cape Town where he forged his step-father's signature and lied about his age. He then enlisted in the army that had taken him through Egypt and on to Europe. At the end of the war he was living in Piedmont with a plump Italian woman called Rosetta and painting the ceilings of churches. He had a good teacher, an Italian called Paulo, who refined his drawing techniques and had taken him with him, wherever there were churches to be restored. Lying on his back and painting the Virgin Mary and Child had cleansed his soul! He had left Italy for England, because he wanted to go back to the land of his birth! Ireland was a forgotten root that would eventually emerge in a very bizarre way.

He was waiting on the steps the following day when Kaya came home. He looked into her brown eyes and something happened. He took her out for fish and chips and told her he wanted to marry her. She smiled and looked down at the greasy paper, shaking her head. They met every day and on the tenth day he bought her a bouquet of flowers. He did not tell her he had won a game of poker, and used some of the money to buy her a small engagement ring. When he asked her again to marry him, as he had every single day since he had met her, she agreed. He gave her the ring, promising to take care of her until the day he died! She told him about Paul in Serbia, and he assured her she had to bring her son and mother back. He promised to be a father to both her children, and a good husband!

Kaya liked Edward. He had scooped Jackie up in his arms on the third day after she had met him, and held her up high. Jackie had laughed and Kaya had felt a tug at her heart. When she looked at him the following evening, she saw the pain, similar to her pain, in his eyes. However, they held passion and love; love she was in desperate need of! It was easy to fall in love!

Edward was tall and good-looking. His dark hair accentuated his blue eyes and they seemed to hypnotize her. She did not take any notice of the tattoos on his arms, or the rough way he used a fork and knife. She was convinced she could teach him the finer aspects of life, as long as he loved her and supported her children. She sent a telegram to Maria, telling her she was moving to South Africa, that she wanted her mother to sell her small house and come with Paul to England.

Maria was stunned when she received the news, but also excited. A new life meant she could at last leave Loznitsa and her past. She did not have many friends and missed her daughter. She immediately told Paul he would at last see his mother, and that they had a lot to do! She put the house on the market and began to pack her things. She knew it would not take long for her to sell, and the only part of leaving that saddened her were the few friends she would leave behind, whom she had met at Bible study meetings. When, two weeks later, she was offered a good price for the house, she was happy!

Kaya spent every day with Edward. She resigned from her job and argued with Yolande over money she was owed. Yolande, who was Paul's godmother, thought she was mad to follow a stranger to a new country. Even Doreen begged her to reconsider. David had not paid much attention to either her or Jackie! He hadn't paid any maintenance since he had left, so she was grateful when Edward told her he had a job waiting for him and a house in Johannesburg, and that she had nothing to worry about. The day her divorce was finalized, Kaya went out and bought a beautiful suit. She used some of the money her mother-in-law had given her when David had left, and which she had painstakingly saved. Her mother would bring money with her, and at last Kaya could live a new life – a life she fully deserved.

When Maria arrived with her suitcases and Paul who had grown,

Kaya clasped her son to her, but he soon pulled away and hid his head in his grandmother's skirt. He seemed so frail and constantly burst into tears. Kaya could not understand it. What was wrong with him?

She could not relate to the fact he only spoke Serbian, and was overwhelmed to find a family waiting for him. Instead she turned on Maria, blaming her for overprotecting Paul. Arguments were frequent and they culminated in a terrible confrontation when Maria told Kaya she had given most of the money from the sale of her house to the church. Kaya could not believe Maria had betrayed her. Tensions ran high and when Doreen met Maria she told Kaya she would regret taking her mother in! Kaya simply slumped back in her chair, aware that no matter how hard she was trying to put things into order, she had no control over anything.

Edward tried to calm her and promised everything would be different when they arrived in South Africa. He went to arrange for their passage and at the same time booked the registry office. On the day Kaya married Edward, she looked beautiful in a beige suit. Jackie was dressed in blue satin with a big bow at the back and Paul wore a blue suit. Maria looked neat in her dark blue hat with a veil covering her face, and Edward handsome as ever, in his beige suit.

They went out for lunch after the ceremony, and Kaya prayed things would at last work out. When, finally, they had packed their belongings and said their goodbyes, she mentally shut a door on the past. When they went on board the *Umgeni* that would carry them from Liverpool to Cape Town, Kaya looked very much like the young woman who had once taken walks along the banks of the River Drina, arm in arm with Dragan. For a moment, as she leaned over the rails and looked at the water, she thought about them all! She saw their faces so clearly – Dragan's, Masha's, Hans', Pino's, Ziegfried's and David's. The men she had loved and betrayed; those who had betrayed her. She let them sink into the ocean and turned to look at her family.

Jackie was chasing Paul around on deck and Maria was trying to hold her back. Her new husband was reading his newspaper, glancing every now and then at Maria. Eventually he put down his newspaper and caught Jackie. He pulled her close to him, and sat her on his knee.

She smiled, jumped off Edward's knee and ran to her mother! She was laughing and Kaya grabbed her hands, twirling her around. Edward came across. He was wearing brown corduroy trousers and a beige pullover. He looked so handsome and carefree. He put an arm around her shoulders and they both watched the sun set.

Everyone relaxed over the following weeks as the ship sailed on, carrying people from all walks of life to a new destination, or back home. Kaya spent her days warming herself on deck. They played cards in the late afternoons, and at night she gave herself to her husband with a new-found passion. When the ship finally docked in Cape Town, she emerged looking radiant. Her husband was as brown as a berry and looked even more handsome. Maria had relaxed and she looked like a perfect lady. Jackie's blonde hair had been carefully plaited and she was wearing a red quilt skirt with a white shirt. Her short white socks peeped out of her new black leather shoes and Paul looked smart in a blue pair of trousers, white loafers and blue and white checked shirt.

Everything was perfect, as perfect as Kaya could have imagined in her mind's eye. She was relieved both Jackie and Paul had accepted Edward was their father. They were young, and would forget all about the past, once they began their new life in Johannesburg. As she looked back at the ship they had sailed on, Kaya took a vow! She would stay with Edward until the day she died, no matter what happened! She would never tell anyone about her past and she would bury all her memories in the sea that had carried them to the shores of a new country. She closed her eyes for a moment and thought of Dragan, but then the memory faded. When she opened her eyes, she was a new person. Reality, lost to the wind, showed a different picture!

Paul who was now eight years old and could no longer speak English, suddenly found he had a pretty sister who was five, and a mother and father whom he knew nothing whatsoever about. He clung to his grandmother who also spoke no English and tried to make sense of a new and different experience. Jackie had suddenly been thrust into a family as well! She had lost Mrs Perry and missed her tall grandmother. She remembered another man playing with her, and she felt something hurt inside of her! Maria looked at her daughter Kaya and thought about the German officer, who had taken her to Germany! She did not like Edward and was not very sure she should have left her home in Serbia. Edward looked into the distance. He wondered what his wife would do when he told her he didn't have a house or a job! He really loved her and knew he would find one soon, but he worried about finding a home for his new family. He did not mind the fact he had a new family; he had already decided he would use his artistic talent to forge their birth certificates! No one would ever know he was not their father! Time would wash away the memories held, and Edward would give Kaya all he could! For a moment, he thought about his mother and wondered what she would do when she saw him.

Time passed, as the family who had little in common apart from what destiny had given them, traveled by train through the country-side that was so foreign to Kaya. She was shocked when she saw Africans huddled at their bus stop, and signs that discriminated between African and White. Kaya swallowed her growing anguish.

Exactly one year after her arrival in South Africa, Kaya began to wish she had never left London. She was horrified to find out her artist husband came from a very poor family, who had no social class at all. His seven sisters, half of whom were step-sisters, hardly spoke to him. They had had their first serious argument when he told her there was no house or job. She had shouted at him, telling him he would find both, and that he would support her as he had promised! The tragedies of the past, although having weakened her in many ways, gave her a new-found strength. She refused to accept that her husband might have betrayed her, forcing him to gain courage as well. Edward got a job in advertising. He found them a small house in Yeoville, after their arrival in Johannesburg, and told Kaya he would never allow her to work. Her place was in the home, cooking and looking after her children! Maria soon joined a local parish and spent her time going to Bible classes and baking. Jackie and Paul were enrolled in a local school and settled down, but Kaya was not happy. She knew she stood out as a foreigner and wanted so badly to prove her own worth, she changed her name to Katia, claimed to be British and whenever someone commented on her accent, blamed it on the fact she spoke seven languages. When Edward began to stay out late at night, gambling and drinking, she tried to raise her two children, both of whom were strangers to her – one more than the other! She tried to acclimatize to a new way of life, and to living with her mother again in the small house they rented. She attempted desperately to persuade her husband to let her get a job as a translator, but was doomed to her place in the home. Thoughts began to threaten her very existence. They pursued destiny in a country where she had not stood out as a foreigner; where she had got used to afternoon walks in Hyde Park and Kensington and nostalgia crept in, tempting her to put an end to yet another marriage and move back to England.

Katia found herself trapped, when she fell pregnant soon after she started thinking about returning to England! She resented this pregnancy that slowly dashed all hopes of returning to England, sealing her fate, for she knew in the heart of her being, she could now never leave Edward! She remembered having taken a vow to stay with him, and for a moment, wondered why she was unhappy with him. She had to admit she had always been unhappy! The thought made her shudder! Why was life so cruel? What had she done, to deserve the pain? Her shoulders drooped!

She tried hard during her pregnancy to keep the peace, and talk to Edward about his family. It was difficult for Edward to talk about his father and his tragic end. He had gone to see his sisters Jocelyn, May and Millie as soon as they had arrived in Johannesburg. They told him his mother had died, and he recalled how she had cursed him, when he had last seen her. Unable to mourn her death because he was so angry with her, he told them they were welcome to visit whenever they wanted to, but they were busy with their lives. When Katia told Edward she was pregnant, he was very happy. He wanted a child he could call his own, hoping it would be a boy. He tried hard to curb his weakness for alcohol and gambling, but had to admit it was the highlight of his week, when he met his friends at the Red Dragon!

When his wife went into labor, he rushed her to a hospital in Hillbrow and did everything he could to make her feel comfortable.

It had been a difficult pregnancy, because the baby she was carrying was big, so the doctor decided to perform a caesarian section. When he told Edward he had a beautiful four-pound daughter, Edward felt disappointed. When he saw her though, he was entranced, because he saw the innocence that he had lost, reflected back at him!

CHAPTER FOUR

The universe gives, the universe takes! The soul hankers after union with Love. Struggling to maintain balance, the spirit, carrying memories, breaks free to hurtle through time and space. Soul poised before union, gently gathers spirit into arms. Together, they travel in time to realize fulfillment.

The Calling

The soul-spirit of the baby growing in Katia's womb moved gently above mother and baby, connected in a very special way to the higher and lower levels of life. It curiously took in the subtle differences in vibration that made knowledge opaque, the more it entered the lower vibrations. As the time for birth drew near, it communicated far more frequently with its new body than the higher realm and when it was time, it lost consciousness as it entered darkness. The baby squirmed and opened her eyes. Something had changed. A new emotion now came, that made the body tense up and although connected still to warmth, it began to descend into a different space. Suddenly, harsh light and rough hands introduced uncertainty and with it a new sensation, a tingling of all the senses that grew in magnitude and the baby let out a cry.

Soul-spirit lulled by sound took form, settling into consciousness and the baby awoke to a new world of sensations that were extremely uncomfortable. A woman's voice was heard and then silence. The baby found something warm and began sucking. She was comforted, as she drifted away from the sounds again. As time went by the sounds changed. Sometimes they were pleasant and soothing, others were harsh and painful! The baby's body always tensed when the pain came and she learnt to avoid it as much as she could. There were times when she seemed to be at a great height looking down at her form, and she would curiously watch the body below her and other times when she looked out to see millions of dots moving around at great speeds, until they settled, and became familiar faces. She felt very safe when she was held close and rocked gently, but did not like it when she was placed on her stomach and the rocking stopped! Eager to explore the new world, she learnt quickly about her own capabilities, and eventually was able to look steadily out at the world and begin to judge situations according to their merit. She learnt to distinguish between the rough hands of her father and the smooth hands of her mother. Then there were two faces that peered at her every now and then, picking her up gingerly and making her frightened. There were leaves that danced above her and a gently breeze that made her skin tingle and sounds that came from inside of her, that expressed her feelings. Her laughter was like the sound of a running stream and her cries loud and robust. Eventually the world around her began to take form, and this was when she fell from a great height and into a different darkness that hurt every bone in her body.

The baby was seven months old and Jackie had taken her out onto the porch of their new house in Observatory. It was a warm, sunny day and Jackie and Paul had been told, yet again, to watch the baby. Jackie was tired of watching the baby, who did not seem able to do very much. Jackie was now seven years old and Paul ten. They started playing catch when the baby finally went to sleep. As Paul started chasing Jackie she ran around the pram, slipped, and caught hold of the handle. The wall around the porch of their new home had not yet been built, and the pram moved towards the edge with a speed neither Jackie nor Paul could calculate! It rocked for a moment back and forth, then tipped over, spewing out its contents into the rockery below! For a moment they were stunned and then they heard the shrill wail. Paul jumped down into the garden below and picked up his baby sister who was turning blue, as she struggled to breathe. Her mouth was full of soft brown earth and it clung to her nostrils. Paul worked as quickly as he could. He brushed the earth away with his fingers and gave her a big thump on her back. The earth that had formed a ball with saliva flew out of the baby's mouth and she gulped in a fresh breath, but carried on wailing. Paul tried to rock her, as he handed her to his sister and climbed back onto the porch. They ran in to find their mother in the kitchen, busy baking a tart.

"Look what happened to the baby!" Paul's voice was feeble.

His mother turned around and began to scream at him. She took the baby from him and he escaped into his room. When his father came home that afternoon, both he and his sister got a smack and then his parents began to argue. It was always the same. They argued frequently, and he hated it when his father always ended the arguments with a tall glass of alcohol that made his breath smell. He could hear his mother's raised voice.

"It's your fault that she fell. I told you to build the wall!"

"Why did you let them play out there? It's your job to look after them!"

Paul blocked his ears with his fingers and screwed up his eyes. Jackie played with her doll, able at will to shut out the noise! She carefully combed her doll's hair and began to take off her clothes. She cleaned her with a soft, damp cloth and then dressed her again. When she had finished, the noise subsided and she went to the window to look out at the new garden she was looking forward to exploring. Over the next few months, Jackie and Paul were not allowed into the garden because the workmen were building a swimming pool. Katia told them to spend their time reading, and went to the local library to choose books for them! Katia insisted they read all the important classics. Over the years she had bought a lot of books and was pleased there was an enormous bookcase leading down to the study.

Her new home was beautiful. There were three bedrooms, two reception rooms, a study, garden room and two bathrooms. The kitchen was huge and they had bought a sturdy wooden table where Jackie and Paul did their homework. Katia had spent hours at the market, finding copper pots to hang on the wooden beams and fabrics that brought out the colors in the wood. Edward, who now earned an ample wage, had painted murals on the walls, of an African village and a balcony overlooking the sea, and they were even able to afford a maid. Everything on the outside was perfect, but there were many other problems that tired Katia.

She had given birth and tried to be as much of a caregiver as she could. Dedicating herself to the chores involved in daily living, she found herself arguing with her husband and mother frequently. Edward did not like Maria and he often complained about her to Katia. Maria had become a Jehovah Witness and was always preaching about Judgment Day. Most of the time she went around the neighborhood, knocking on doors and trying to push pamphlets into reluctant people's hands. Then there was the problem of Edward's drinking and gambling! It scared Katia to know her husband was addicted to the two vices she knew could lead to their ruin. Katia felt as though she continuously had to try to keep the balance, and she was also suffering from post-partum depression. Nobody seemed to really care how she felt, and this began to weaken her, but she tried to keep her head above water.

The baby was easy, but soon after her first birthday, she began to black out frequently, for no apparent reason. She was taken for tests but doctors could not find anything wrong with her. Everyone doted on the baby, now become toddler.

When her daughter turned two, Katia moved her out of their bedroom and into Jackie's room. Edward built an extra room where the cellar was, and this became Paul's bedroom. There was a very long dresser that had a green and pink curtain that fell to the floor, in the room Jackie shared with her sister. They kept books and toys behind the curtain, and both loved playing behind it. The two girls often went to the top of the garden to play with bride and bridesmaid dolls they had been given as a Christmas present. Jackie's sister also liked playing under the table in the kitchen, but Edward always insisted it was not good for her! Very soon Jackie and Paul stopped playing with her, as they also grew up, so she got used to playing on her own, and then discovered how to fly out of her body at night. She often woke up crying, and inevitably her father would be beside her bed. He would tell her stories about the Amerindians, caressing her and tucking her in, when sleep came. Jackie never woke up.

Jackie's sister had just turned four, when Katia finally contacted her father and they began corresponding. A constant stream of letters also arrived from Risto and one day an envelope came from Dragan. Katia had written to him and Dragan had written back to her from his heart. He told her he had spent time in Marseilles, after the Americans liberated him in 1944, and how he had settled in Zvornik in 1952. He told her his mother had never liked the woman he married, someone he did not divorce because of the two children that kept him going. The letter was one of many, in which he told her how happy his mother was when she learned that Kaya had written to him; how, at seventy-one, she was frail with a weak heart, having also had a number of minor strokes, and how ruthless the game of destiny was, that had forced them apart. He told her his best time was waiting for sleep to come, when his thoughts would go back in time to 1939, because emotions, having carved themselves into memories could never be replaced! He recalled all the minute details of the time they had spent together and although Katia felt guilty reading about the love he still apparently felt for her, it gave her strength. She allowed the memories to come forth then, only to become even more depressed. She realized how different her relationship with Edward was, and how much she missed the gentle poetic nature that had given her so much joy when she was young. Katia knew she had never loved anyone the way she had loved Dragan, but afraid to think of going back to Serbia, even though Dragan assured her she could, she became more and more depressed. In her depression, she began to flashback to moments in the past that brought a heavy guilt into her heart. She recalled how she had once left her youngest daughter sitting in her highchair crying for more than four hours, because she had locked herself in her room. She had been feeding her daughter when she had seen a mouse! She was terrified of them and had dropped the dish with scrambled egg and stayed in her room, despite hearing the cries from the kitchen! The thoughts only made her fall deeper into the darkness where eventually the only solution she could find was to get used to taking the heavy black revolver Edward kept under his pillow into the garden. She would carry it in her apron and then sit on the bench amongst the freesias, crying and wondering if she would ever find the strength to use it. Whenever the thoughts came too quickly and made pictures in her mind, she would hit her head over and over again with her hand, until it would begin to hurt her. Then sleep would come after the tears; she would dream about the river in Serbia, the blue violets Dragan had loved picking for her, and the fear of returning to Loznitsa, because he knew nothing about Hans.

Katia's children did not like it when their mother hid in the garden or hit her head and then locked herself in her bedroom. They did not like it when their parents argued or when their mother threw things at their father. It happened too frequently – shattered glass smashed in the kitchen, sticky jam smeared on the wall! Katia's youngest daughter hated it when her grandmother Maria chased her and Jackie around the swimming pool, with a wet flannel that stung her legs. She worshipped her father who always made her feel warm and tingly, but there was something about him that also scared her. Whenever he was angry, it seemed he became a different person and he would then ignore her, sometimes for days on end.

She was very sad when her angelic friend left her and she often hid in the garden herself, crying and looking up at the sky. She had identified so completely with the man called Jesus everyone spoke about at school, that she pleaded with Him to let her go home. She had been lucky to have started school when she was only four, as she had taught herself how to read, but had never felt like a child. She was six when she decided she had come from another planet, and had been exiled to live with a group of people she did not even like. Her sister often ignored her and Paul was always busy reading books and getting into trouble because of bad report cards. Her grandmother Maria was always shrieking about God and his wrath, which made her feel alone and helpless. Her God was loving and kind; He read stories to her and was proud of her; He loved her in a way no one had loved her, and made her feel safe and yet, He had also punished her by leaving her with her family. Katia's youngest daughter soon began to feel a heavy sadness that made her feel very lonely.

It was soon after her ninth birthday she finally found freedom. It was late and she was flying in her sleep. Suddenly, her body shuddered and she awoke, sitting up abruptly. She could see her sister asleep on the bed next to the window. Her parents were arguing again, and she could hear them so clearly, she slid off her bed and went towards her sister's bed. She tried to shake her sister awake but Jackie was in such deep sleep, she did not stir. She let herself out of the bedroom and padded down the passage towards her parents' bedroom.

She opened the door and walked in. Her mother had pinned her father against the built-in wardrobe and was slapping his face!

Suddenly, her father pushed her mother away, went over to the bed, pulled out a gun and handed it to her mother.

"Go ahead," he yelled at her. "Shoot me!"

Katia's daughter stood perfectly still, watching her mother point the gun at her father! Her hand was shaking, and then her husband snatched the gun from her and hit her so hard, she flew across the room and smashed into the dresser! The sound must have woken Paul, whose bedroom was under his parents' because she heard him running up the stairs. She quickly went over to her mother, and helped her up. Time had stopped and a very adult-like person had taken over, who gently pulled her mother up and took her to the armchair. From the corner of her eye she saw her brother fly into the room and start fighting with her father! The fear came slowly, as she watched them. She was afraid her father would hurt Paul, and held her breath. Her mother was crying and mumbling something, so she bent down to hear what she was saying.

"He is awful. I can't take it anymore!"

Katia's daughter felt the space between her mother and her widen; it became vast and endless. From far off she noticed her father was no longer in the room, and that her brother was walking towards her. She could hear her father swearing, and then the sound of the front door slamming, and the squeal of tires in the driveway. Her ears began to ring as she began to sway back and forth, ready to black out, just as she had so frequently, when she was young!

This was when I emerged… …quite in control of the situation! I gripped the back of the armchair to stop my body from swaying and ordered my brother to make a pot of tea! I told Mother everything would be fine, to put her slippers on and come to the kitchen! I ignored my grandmother who was standing in the passage making the sign of the cross, and helped Mother sit down at the kitchen table. She sat drinking warm tea, and eventually we went back to bed.

For the next three days, I buried myself in the book I was reading, and tried to cheer Mother up. Grandmother Maria made soups,

pancakes and soft corn bread. We ate often and a lot, gaining strength
we had lost and desperately needed, and on the third day, became quite
silent because Father had still not come home. Mother was distraught!
She asked Paul to call the local hospital because she was sure he had
had a car accident. She began crying and wringing her hands, and
eventually started pacing up and down her bedroom. This was when
she started talking about the war and the Nazis and the time she had
translated for the Russians! I was completely amazed by her stories.
I saw a woman of incredible strength and admired her for it. Deep
within, the stirrings of family tradition and duty came to life. Jackie,
Paul and I sat on her bed listening to her, and this was how we did not
realize our father had returned. Suddenly he was there, apologizing,
telling us all his car had broken down on a long, deserted road; that
he was starving and hadn't eaten for three days. He held out his hands,
full of grease to support his tale! I was conscious then, of a small inner
voice that silently spoke out.

"He is lying of course! If he had been fixing his car, the grease
would not be so smoothly spread! It would have jagged spaces. He
poured the grease into his hands and smeared them!"

At first I was surprised, but then got used to my inner voice, not
realizing this was the part of me that had gone into hiding, because of
the turmoil in my home. It helped me look beyond the material and
into the immaterial! However, it also made me aware of a subtle
difference in the way I saw the world. I no longer worshipped my
father, but rather pitied him. I was tired of my mother and my grandmother, and yet started observing them until I knew exactly when to
turn a growing argument into a heated discussion, by asking strange
questions. I realized my questions made Mother uncomfortable and
although she liked talking about her past, she also became guarded
whenever she replied. I tried to talk to my siblings but the space
between us kept widening, and this was when I decided I had to grow
up very quickly if I ever wanted to reach them!

That year was a turning point in my life! I started menstruating,
even though I was only nine, and this made me feel I was no longer a
child but a woman. I started reading novels and began to dream
about my white knight, who I wanted desperately to re-connect with.

At school I began preparing for my First Holy Communion, only to realize I had never been baptized! The awkwardness of the situation affected me deeply, because I would have my baptism in a cloud of secrecy! Only my parents and the parish secretary, who was to be my godmother, were there to witness it! A week later I took my vows to become a soldier of Christ, and this reunited me with the universe I had loved so deeply as a child. I received a gold cross I placed with reverence around my neck, and a book about the Saints, which I read avidly. I started going to mass every Sunday from then on and found comfort there. At last I could immerse myself in the world I had once belonged to, and this was the world I could now escape to, every time my parents argued with each other.

I was so immersed in this world I paid little attention to what was happening around me! I started living in a dream world that was magnified when I lay in the garden studying nature or looking up at the stars at night. I looked for the light in those around me and nurtured my Soul whenever I found it reflecting back at me. This world was amplified by the books I read and dreams at night that took me out of the mundane and into an extraordinary world, where I found freedom. This was why when I turned twelve I did not even realize my sister Jackie and my brother Paul had moved out of the house!

I often ignored the tension in the house and so was brutally brought down into reality one morning, whilst eating breakfast. Grandmother Maria had made a soft porridge and I was twirling my spoon around the melting butter. Mother as usual was arguing with her, but I wasn't listening to her. Father was somewhere in the background making toast when suddenly Mother banged the kitchen table so hard, my bowl of porridge jumped up and crashed back onto the table. I looked at Mother whose eyes were glaring at me, and heard her voice as if it was magnified in my ears. She seemed to be talking to me, and I tried to focus on her words.

"You want the truth, well I will tell you the truth!" she shrieked.

For a moment I wondered when I had asked her to tell me the truth, but did not have any time to dwell on the thought for long, because she carried on yelling.

"Your sister and brother are not your real sister and brother! They are your step-siblings. Now, go to school!"

Mother slumped in her chair and I got up, wiping my mouth with my napkin. I went to my room and picked up my satchel. On my way to the bus stop, I came to a conclusion. Either Mother was mad or else she was close to madness! At school I crawled under my desk and told my best friend Anne that Mother was going mad and that she had told me some ridiculous story about my siblings. This was when I realized I hadn't seen them for over a week, and it made me feel awful. The guilt I felt when I realised I hadn't wondered where they were was so strong – strong enough to underline the fact that my siblings would never become step-siblings! I would always look on them as my brother and sister, because that is who they were. This is how I knew them and even though I felt the guilt, honour was more important to me than anything else.

My dream world had crashed around me and, conscious I could not survive without it, I still did not know Grandmother Maria had told my siblings my father was their step-father. Driven by the voice of God, as she said, she had told them the truth. A number of things happened that year, changing my perception of life. Jackie and Paul came back home but nobody discussed where they had been, and neither did Mother talk about her outburst. I overheard Grandmother Maria and her arguing one day, and this is how I learned my siblings had been told the truth about their births. I felt very sorry for them, and only many years later, realized they came back because Mother told them they owed the man who had raised them as his own! My breast started hurting me and I found a small lump that was removed in January. In April, I was preparing for a school debate when I started having excruciating pains in my side and went to hospital to have my appendix removed, because my fallopian tube had wrapped itself around my appendix! When I came out of the anesthetic, it was as if a well inside of me opened, and I could not stop crying. When my parents were ushered in to my room, I immediately stopped crying and behaved normally and the moment they left started crying again. A mountain of emotion kept rising up inside of me and I tried desperately to contain it. When the time came for me to be discharged, I refused to go home! Part of me felt safe in hospital with the doctors and nurses, and I did not want to leave this safety. When Matron decided I had to see a psychologist, I was relieved and Mother was livid.

It was not easy for me to talk about my feelings. I had buried a lot of memories deep into my subconscious, but I started talking to Doctor Jacobs about the gun Mother had pointed at Father. Information began to stream forth and just as quickly stopped, when the psychologist asked to see Mother.

Over the years Mother had managed to find ways to deal with the pressure in her life and one of these ways, was to deny everything happening around her! I don't know what Doctor Jacobs told her, but when she came out of his office, her eyes glinted dangerously. She politely told me we were going home and then ignored me completely. A flickering flame of hope that someone would help me was completely snuffed, as I followed Mother down the corridor and out of the hospital. In the car she told Father I was simply suffering from post-operative depression, and that the doctor had told her I was fine. It was later that afternoon, when she brought me chicken soup, that she shut my bedroom door, put the soup down on the dresser, and came to sit on my bed. She grabbed hold of my arm, and her long red nails bit into it. Her voice was soft but her words tore into me.

"Do you know what the doctor told me? He told me you are a liar and a manipulator! He saw right through your stupid lies about me and your father and you will never lie again! Do you understand me?"

She got up and went to the dresser.

"I have made you a wonderful chicken soup! After lunch, you can take a short walk in the garden and then we will have tea."

The pain in my side was throbbing and I looked down awkwardly at the tray. Mother carried on talking.

"We spoiled you as a child, and this is the thanks you give us! You don't appreciate anything! Your father works hard and you go to the best private school! What more do you want from us? What more do you want from me?"

For a moment Mother swayed on her feet, clutching her chest. She then slumped onto the bed.

"Oh my God, I'm having a heart attack!"

Fear exploded in my mind, as I felt a rush of shame run through me.

"I'm sorry, I'm sorry!" I cried out, holding onto her. How could I have been so selfish? Why couldn't I hold on to the pain Mother was in? This was when I began to absorb Mother's pain, as though it were mine.

I started calling out for Father who came into the room. He took Mother to hospital where she stayed overnight for tests, and when she came home the following day, Father sat us all down at the kitchen table.

"Your mother has *Angina Pectoris* and she is not to be upset by any of you!"

He glared at Jackie, Paul, Maria and me as he spoke. I looked at my grandmother. She looked disdainfully at my father and then got up. As she walked away, mumbling in Serbian, I realized the only person she loved was my brother Paul, and once again, I questioned what I was doing in this family I believed I had nothing in common with.

Over the next few weeks, the atmosphere at home was very strained, and it reached a climax in June when Jackie went to hospital! I had no idea what was wrong with her, and was not allowed to visit her in hospital, because Mother told me I was too young. Soon after Jackie came home, she went on vacation with Mother and Father, and I stayed at home with Paul and my grandmother. Paul and Jackie were both studying law by then, and it was almost impossible for me to reach either of them. So I remained in my world of novels and when my parents and Jackie returned, I often wondered why Mother apparently loved Jackie more than any of us.

It had always been obvious to me Mother loved Jackie a lot, because they never argued. Although I should have been jealous of this, I wasn't. On the contrary, it made me strive to be like Jackie.

Jackie was beautiful! She had fair hair that hung to her waist and beautiful green eyes. Her figure was perfect and she had always excelled at school. She got on well with Father and they often joked with each other. Paul was also close to Jackie, however, sometimes he seemed quite distant. It saddened me to know I knew nothing about either of them, and that the only memories I had of us growing up as children, were card games played on Sunday afternoons and pool parties, where I was always the youngest. What no one realized was that by not confiding in me, they forced me to judge them according to what I did know, which was very little.

Feeling lost, in September of that year I found myself escaping into the dreams of my past, and into a space that could hold me for a little while, because time had speeded up and I was losing balance. I knew that unless I turned to the Church for comfort I would not survive the pressure of living in such an abusive situation.

Sean O'Connor was in his early thirties when I first saw him, standing on the steps of St Francis' church. He had jet black hair that curled over the back of his collar and the deepest blue eyes I had ever seen. Something about the way he stood and moved reminded me of the knight in my dreams. Two days later he was introduced to us at a morning assembly, as the new parish priest, and the following day I bumped into him as I rounded the corner in a hurry, with a pile of books I was taking to Sister John Mary. He held my arm to steady me and smiled. I could feel his hand burning through my white shirt and I quickly mumbled an apology. That afternoon, I sat on my bed looking out of the window.

Something unseen began to stir in my heart and I felt a glow taking the edge off everything I had been through up to that point in time. It was as though I could begin again, so the following week I made my way to the rectory office. My godmother Sybil had moved to Durban, but every Christmas she sent me a beautiful silver stocking filled with Blue Grass bath salts and lotions. I missed her because she was so normal, and now wished she was there to support me. I knocked on the rectory door and waited. I was wearing my navy school uniform and had tied my hair in a ponytail that morning. As I heard him come towards the door, I almost fled but remained standing there! Then he opened the door! He was wearing a light blue shirt, open at his neck, and his missing clerical collar helped me look brightly up into his incredible eyes.

"I am really sorry to disturb you," I said quietly, "but I wondered if I could make an appointment to see you?"

I did not expect him to smile softly and step back, ushering me into the small passage I supposed led to his bedroom upstairs. I don't know what I expected as we went into his office, and he motioned for me to sit down. Flurried, I explained I had come to borrow his Bible, and that I did not want to disturb him.

"You are not disturbing me," he said and proceeded to ask who I was. I briefly told him about Mother and Father and my siblings and when I had finished, he asked me if I wanted to join the youth choir he was planning to set up. I began to perspire as I told him how I always attended mass, and how I would love to become a member of the choir. He seemed to have forgotten about my request, but then got up and began to look for his Bible on the desk. He moved his guitar and a sheaf of papers and then mumbled something about it being upstairs.

When he left the room, I let out a sigh. I hadn't realized I had been holding my breath and felt awkward. When he came back into the office, I was already standing, ready to leave. I explained I was going to miss the bus, thanked him for the Bible and hurried out, promising to return it by the end of the week.

I put the Bible in my school satchel and ran to catch the bus. As soon as I got home, I went to my bedroom and took out the black, leather-bound Bible. As I opened it, a sheet of folded paper fell out and I picked it up. He had copied out part of Corinthians 13 and as I read the words, they seemed to bore into my soul. I was sure this was a sign – a sign from the universe, because he had underlined what I knew in my heart to be true – *only Faith, Hope and Love abide; but the greatest of these is Love*; I had lost this love, in a life so full of shadows, fear and suffering!

It took me a further two weeks to pluck up the courage to knock on his door again and by this time, we had already met four times: once when I returned his Bible and he offered me a cup of tea and a biscuit, twice at choir practice and once at school, when he came to my classroom to talk about God. He was not surprised to see me, and we went into his office. He casually leaned against his desk and smiled. I sat down and looked at the floor.

"I am so sorry to disturb you, but I really need to speak to you. I don't know how to say this and I don't know what to do!"

He moved away from the desk and drew a chair close to mine. I looked up at him and for a moment held his eyes, then looked away again.

"I need to know if it is a sin," I said softly, "to love a priest, because I love you?"

There was a moment of silence and then he replied gently.

"No, it isn't a sin to love a priest, but I can never give you what you want!"

From far off I heard his words, and it was as though they echoed in my mind.

"*What you want, what you want!*"

I knew what I wanted. I wanted to feel love, something akin to the brilliance I had felt when I had drunk from the golden chalice that had introduced me to it! I was desperate to feel this love; to hold it, touch it and become it. It welled up inside of me and seemed to grow all around me. The golden chalice and the abbey filled my mind and I knew that if I did not hold onto this love, I would be carried away like a broken stick to be smashed on the rocks of time, by an angry river called Life. This love was different from the love I had met on Earth. It had nothing whatsoever to do with it, and the inner child I had buried deep down inside of me had begun to scream silently!

My inner child had watched things happen from a distance, until she realized she was losing herself and that a different person was emerging, one who could no longer listen to her. She knew life was a teacher, and held my heart in her hand.

Every Sunday I left home early and walked to church. Sean and I sat talking for an hour before we went to choir practice and, on occasion, I visited him for an hour or two after school. I lied to Mother, telling her I was practising with the choir whenever I was late coming home, and I lived for the times spent with Sean. Sean often played his guitar singing '*The First Time Ever I saw your Face*' and '*He ain't heavy, he's my brother.*' He told me about his sister, who was a nun in Ireland and about his ordination. I loved him with my entire heart and soul, slowly freeing myself of the weight I had carried for so long. A year went by, finding me engrossed in the role of Liv Ullman in *The Abdication* and the beautiful *Love Story*, aware I was feeling something akin to what they had! I tried on more than one occasion to hold his gaze and eventually he let me, pointing out it would never work! This pleased me deep inside my soul. He became my life and when Jackie was rushed to hospital and nearly lost her life, he comforted me.

Jackie was brought home from university one morning, because she was not well. By the afternoon, she was in so much pain she was screaming; she was operated on a few hours later and given three pints of blood. Nobody slept that night or the next, and when she was let out of intensive care, only then did we all relax. Mother was very upset and the only way I found out what had happened to Jackie was when I opened the hospital bill that was sent a week after she had been discharged.

I enjoyed opening bills and handing them over to Mother, but this bill was not welcome, because I immediately asked Mother what an ectopic pregnancy was. Mother brusquely told me it was a mistake and that the diagnosis was peritonitis. I did not believe her, and later that day I read about it in Mother's old medical books, on the steps leading down to Paul's room. The fact my sister had been to bed with someone fascinated me! She had always been so perfect and I was shocked she had fallen pregnant. I wondered who the father was, because she had been dating, but not seriously. But then again, I hadn't been paying attention to her! I was surprised no one seemed angry with Jackie, so tried to pay more attention to what was happening at home, but it was impossible. A few months later, Jackie started driving lessons and the day she got her license, she announced she was marrying her driving instructor. Mother was furious!

"You will never marry that peasant, who has no money! You are under twenty-one and I will never condone the marriage!"

One week later, I was plunged into a past nightmare, when awakened by raised voices. Jackie had decided to move out and Mother was arguing with her! Doors slammed and then my sister came into our bedroom and switched on the light. Hauling clothes out of the cupboard, she began to stuff them into a suitcase. Father came in and started yelling at her. She told him he had no right to tell her what to do, because he was not her father. Father paled and then his hand shot out and he slapped Jackie across the face. She told him in a steely voice not to lay a hand on her, because she would go straight to the police. Jackie finished packing and left the house that night. As she left, Mother shrieked:

"As far as I am concerned you are dead for me! Don't ever come back to this house again!"

I felt sorry for Jackie. I knew what it was like to fall in love and did not understand Mother's inability to ever accept anyone as being good enough for her children. She often criticized our friends and always said the same thing: none of them came from good enough backgrounds! After Jackie left, a strange silence fell over the house. I shook every time I thought about Mother's words and prayed as much as I could. Then one morning, Mother announced we were to go on holiday to Europe that summer. Going to Europe was something both exciting and incredible. no one I knew had been overseas, and I felt proud I was going. It was February and five months seemed a long time to wait. That Sunday, I excitedly went to see Sean to tell him my news, but when he opened the door, he looked worried. He told me to wait in his office and went to the kitchen. He came in a few minutes later, with two cups of tea and his hands were shaking. The tea sloshed into the saucer, soaking the biscuit. He went back to the kitchen and came back with napkins and started mopping up the tea. When I asked him what was wrong, he tried to be as gentle as he could, when he told me the news.

"I'm leaving the parish! I have been transferred to another parish and I leave on Wednesday!"

I stared at him and then the tears came. I sobbed and longed for him to take me in his arms and hold me, but he awkwardly sat in his chair looking at the floor. Conscious time was going by and we had choir practice, I tried to calm down. All through mass, I watched him and when he gave me Communion, my hand burned from his touch! I looked up at the cross hanging down and asked why I was being punished? I did not understand why Sean had to leave, not even when the headmistress called me in, to tell me I had to forget my infatuation and concentrate on my studies. Eventually even Mother found out, and told me I should be ashamed I was trying to tempt a Catholic priest! No one understood how deeply I had grown to love Sean, and that he had become the angelic friend I had lost in the space between worlds, when I was a child. When Sean left he gave me his telephone number and even though we spoke often, I fell into deep depression, wondering whether Mother's threats of suicide were an option.

I no longer cared about going to Europe and that year barely passed my exams. When summer finally came and we drove to the airport to catch our plane, all I could think about was the growing pain in my heart.

CHAPTER FIVE

In our strife to heal our wounds, we think those around us will eventually fill the spaces that ravage our heart. Inevitably, it is we who must become the healers of our own madness, for in more ways than one, we all walk across the bridge of sanity and into an insane world when we take our first breath.

Release

Our flight was long and tiring and when we finally arrived in London, all I wanted to do was sleep. We checked into our hotel and I fell into a very deep sleep. When I finally woke the following morning, I looked out of my window at the grey sky and decided it reflected my soul. That morning after breakfast, as I sat listlessly in the reception area, I suddenly saw a group of children who caught my attention. They were challenged children, most of them with Down's syndrome. I had never seen people like that before, but deep in the recesses of my being I recognized a light I had once been introduced to, that was shining back at me. It had been a very long time since I had seen the light, and immediately turned to Paul and told him I wanted to work with children like that. Paul was reading the newspaper and looked at me sharply!

"Are you sure," he asked gently.

"Yes, I am!"

"Well if you are, I will arrange for you to visit a home for them and find out if you can work there during the holidays!"

I smiled at Paul and thanked him. Somehow the knowledge I could do something worthwhile cheered me up, but I still felt very melancholic. It seemed as though I was on automatic pilot. I did what was expected of me; smiled when I had to and listened to Mother talking about her life in London, but nothing really touched me. We went for a long walk in Hyde Park and had tea with a tall woman called Doreen who kept on whispering during the time we were there. I thought it strange Mother kept on whispering back to her, but what was not strange about my family? We went on to visit a woman called Yolande, who excitedly hugged my brother Paul but then again, no one told me who these people were. We walked down Oxford Street and went to Madame Tussauds and the Tower of London. I tried to pay attention to Mother's voice as she diligently explained things to us, but almost immediately forgot what she had said. We stayed for five days in London and then flew to Rome, where Father and Mother chatted away in Italian.

Both Paul and I fell asleep on the tour bus and Mother was upset we were not paying attention to the sites. I remembered everything about Vesuvius because there was a young boy in our group called Sal, who held my hand until Mother saw us and chillingly told me to change seats. Sal's mother on the contrary, was a robust Italian woman who kept smiling at me, and at the end of the afternoon, she asked Mother to let us sit together. Mother was forced to comply with her request, but I could see she was angry with me. Sal told me about his life in Chicago and at the end of the day we exchanged addresses and promised to write to each other.

Back at the hotel, Mother told me Sal's father was probably a Sicilian gangster, and that she had not liked the way he looked at me. It was hopeless trying to point out to Mother how she made everything out to be so dramatic. I tried not to pull a face at her when she turned her back, but it was impossible not to. The next morning we went walking along the Via Venetia and I bought a pair of rope sandals and a blue scarf for my sister. I wondered when I would see her again, if ever, but I wanted to get her something from Europe. That afternoon when we flew to Athens, I played cards with Paul and looked out of the window at the clear blue sky. This was the sky I had befriended and when we landed in Athens, I began to look forward to our tour.

Athens was a dirty city and yet there was something quite magical about it and I enjoyed walking around the ancient sites. I felt the stories of gods and goddesses reflected my dreamy nature and watching the sun set from the Parthenon, I began to feel whole again. There was a silence in Greece I could not explain, calling out from the depths and hauntingly reminding me of my dreams and visions. We went to Evia for two days and the water was so clear I was fascinated, and yet at the same time afraid to venture out into the deeper water, where I could no longer see the bottom. When it was time to leave Greece, I had absorbed something I buried deep in the recesses of my heart. On our way back to South Africa, we stopped off in London again, and that evening, I noticed a young man watching me at dinner. It was nice to have someone hold my gaze and softly smile when I left the table. We met later on in the evening in the corridor, and I do not know what made me whisper 'I love you' to him.

He was startled and yet held out his arms. I walked into them and he held me close. It was the first time a man had held me in his arms, and I liked the smell of his aftershave. He suggested we go to his room, but then asked me to tell him how old I was. I could not lie and when he realized I was only thirteen, he immediately stepped back. We spoke for a while in the corridor and then he kissed me on the cheek and said goodnight. In the morning, I found a blue envelope under my door. He told me he was a drummer and that he played in a band. At the end of the letter that spoke about his life in Chester, he had written:

When a man almost approaching twenty-eight begins to feel sixteen, someone, somewhere has intervened; which brings to my mind the words of Grace Kelly speaking about Clark Gable: "Now I can see the stars, moon and sun clearly, and this you have given to me in those few moments we spent together."

Wounded by love and unable to fully comprehend what I was doing, I went back to South Africa and thought about Jim. Something about the way he had written the letter touched my heart. He had understood the depth at which I perceived the world and given me courage; what I did not realize then, was that he had understood and respected the child who was struggling very hard to make herself heard. I was a child, and yet had grown to womanhood, almost overnight. Balancing between perceptions of life that came to me through love stories, I avidly read Guy de Maupassant and wrote poetry that welled up from my innermost being, and pondered on the reality I saw etched in Mother's eyes.

I carried on speaking to Sean, but missed him a lot. Sean had brought the Divine world to life because he was sacred. I desired so deeply to connect with the sacredness of depth that I was often blinded by the harsh reality of my growing and changing self. I felt home had evaded me, and as I became more and more conscious of the pain held in each and every person's psyche, I became more clairvoyant. Mother's pain ran deep, stretching across aeons and it became more apparent at the loss of Jackie and so, in October of that year, Jackie was forgiven and allowed home without her husband.

I had never spoken to Jackie about her feelings and was unsure about them. She seemed to be satisfied with her new life, and yet I was sure it had been a form of escape, as mine would be. It was not easy to live with Mother because she demanded so much from us all. There were times when she asked us who would look after her when she grew older, and Paul and Jackie always assured her they would. I never answered her, because I could not imagine living with her as she had chosen to live with Maria. Mother hankered after a life that was peaceful and surrounded with love, and at the time, I could not see how much we all wanted the same. Destiny had woven a tight net around us all, and it slowly blinded us.

That Christmas, Jackie came home with her husband Simon, and we all tried to make him feel welcome, but there was a vast space between us all. Mother was unhappy with him, so she did what her own mother had done – she found someone else for her daughter!

We often went shopping as a family on Saturday mornings to town. Johannesburg was a beautiful city, tidy and balanced with a grid of neatly angled streets. We would go for walks around the town, and often sat drinking hot chocolate, window shopping and buying tasty Italian cheeses and freshly baked rolls. Both Mother and Father recalled the beauty and love they had for Italy, so we often went to Italian coffee shops and restaurants, and Mother began to talk about Europe which she greatly missed. It was February when Mother and I sat at the small Italian coffee shop, drinking thick chocolate. There were a group of men sitting in the corner, chatting and drinking beer.

One of them kept on looking at us and eventually it was apparent they were all talking about us. Mother was flustered and suggested we leave. We had been waiting for Father who was at the barber shop, so I pointed out he would not know where to find us! Mother settled back in her chair and then the tall, rugged man who had been staring openly at her, was suddenly there, asking if he could treat us to lunch. I was completely taken aback when Mother asked him to sit down and began chatting to him. She discovered he was a Swiss reporter who worked for Reuters Press, and single, within a very short time. He was flirting with her and it was obvious Mother was worried about Father coming in, because she kept looking at the door. Suddenly she asked him if he would like to come to dinner the following evening, because as she said, "I have a beautiful daughter I would like to introduce you to!"

My mouth gaped open as I stared at Mother. Carl laughed and got up, shook her hand and asked for our phone number. Mother carefully took out Father's business card from her bag, gave it to him and smiled shyly. As Carl walked back to his table, I jumped up and told Mother we had to leave. She seemed confused again and then called for the bill. We went outside and she gaily waved at Carl as we were leaving. I was stunned, unable at the time to understand her motives.

"How could you do that?" I asked her angrily. "Jackie is married."

I had dared to speak to Mother badly and she was shocked by my outburst. For a moment there was a dangerous glint in her eye as she took hold of my arm.

"Your sister does not love Simon. He is rubbish from the lowest dregs of society!"

I felt my throat constrict and suddenly saw Father walking down the street towards us, but he had become a stranger to me, just as Mother was becoming. All the way home, Mother told Father about the handsome Swiss man who had come over to our table, because he thought I was older and wanted to complement her on my beauty. Laughing, she told Father how she had invited him to dinner the following day, because she was convinced he was perfect for Jackie.

The lie had come easy and that evening Mother called Jackie and asked her to come for dinner without Simon. She spent the following day cooking and made sure the table was laid with her best crystal and silver knives and forks. Carl arrived punctually with a bouquet of flowers and sat down with ease. Jackie had still not arrived and when she did, she did not at all seem surprised to meet Carl.

Over dinner it was apparent everyone was comfortable. Grandmother Maria spoke about Serbia, Father discussed bits about the war and Jackie began to glow. As we were having dessert, Carl turned to Mother and asked if he could take Jackie out for coffee.

Mother had asked Jackie to stay with us that evening, because she did not like her driving late at night, and Jackie had brought her small vanity case with her. She smiled at Carl and got up to get ready. That evening, my sister did not come home! She arrived at nine in the morning, flushed and ecstatic with news about the wonderful evening she had spent with Carl, talking. Jackie kept on telling us all how they had sat at a bar talking until the sun rose and then realized how hungry they were. They had gone for breakfast at a small café, owned by some Greeks from Cyprus and she announced she was leaving Simon because Carl had asked her to marry him. I stared at my sister and something snapped inside of me! I could no longer understand what love was and how easy it could be to terminate one marriage and decide on another, in less than twenty-four hours. I felt a deep sense of loss, separating me from everyone in my family, as I contemplated on the void slowly enveloping me, as it had when I was a child. Fear surged through my veins and settled within my heart.

Jackie asked Paul to accompany her to her flat to get her things, and this was the beginning of a very difficult time for us all. Carl began visiting daily, even though Jackie had become very indecisive about leaving Simon. He started flirting with me and 'teasing' me by touching my foot under the table with his. He began to corner me in the corridor and when I told Mother, she accused me of trying to steal him from Jackie. Jackie came home for a week only to move back in with Simon and then came home again. She left for a third time and I came home from school that day to find Carl pacing back and forth in our living room, yelling at the top of his voice.

"I cannot believe she has done this to you! You have done everything for her! I won't stand for it! We are going to get her! I wouldn't take her back for all the tea in China, but I will do this for you!"

I was so taken aback at his words, I felt sick. His words were so blatantly manipulative and Mother seemed to be under his spell. She turned to me, suddenly noticing I was there, and said, "Come, let's go and get your sister!"

I left my satchel at the door and followed them out to Carl's car. All the way to Jackie's flat in Hillbrow, he repeated over and over again: he was not going to fetch Jackie for himself; he was doing it to help Mother. When we arrived at the flat, Carl told us to stay in the car and went to find Jackie. Thirty minutes later he had still not come back, so Mother told me to go and see what was happening.

I had only been once to Jackie's flat, the previous week when I had gone to help her pack, and she had started crying and told me she still loved Simon. I hadn't known what to say to her. I had looked around the flat I thought was pretty, and in the end, simply told her to stay.

I stepped awkwardly into the lift and pressed the button for the third floor. As the lift stopped and I stepped outside, it was just in time to see Carl head butt Simon. Blood was streaming from Simon's nose and from Carl's forehead. Jackie stood between them, mopping up Carl's forehead and then holding onto her husband crying out,

"You broke his nose!"

Carl grabbed hold of Jackie and literally dragged her to the lift. Simon had gone back into the flat, holding his nose. All the way back to the car, Carl told Jackie he did not want her back, and that he was only doing this because she had upset Mother so much! Jackie tried to get out of the car that he pushed her into, and Carl ordered me to get in and not let her out! This stranger who had come into our lives had taken over to such an extent that Mother had nothing to say. That evening, Paul went with Jackie to pack her belongings and eight months later my sister married Carl in the garden of our home. Apparently, Simon had not wanted children and using this as a reason for their divorce, it had been dealt with quickly and swiftly.

I looked at Jackie on the day she got married. She was wearing a beige top and a long brown skirt. She had cut her hair in a bob and did not look like the Jackie I had known. I felt very sad! Carl and Jackie went on honeymoon and when they returned, they moved into a house in Bramley. A few months later, they announced they were moving to a beautiful home in Cape Town that overlooked the harbor.

I had lost every opportunity to get to know my sister, and the shock of the events that had led up to this marriage weighed heavy on my soul. I wanted to get away from this family as quickly as I could! My dreams of love had been shattered when Mother had introduced Jackie to Carl. Even though I could see she was happy, I could no longer define happiness.

I do not know whether the shock was so great that it influenced my own perception of life, or whether or not our lives had all been pre-determined before any of us were alive; what I do know, was that the following summer, when Mother announced we were returning to Europe for our summer vacation, I was to meet my future husband. I was fourteen years old and had lost a lot of my innocence, but not the intuitive aspect of my being that seemed to know something I did not.

Mother, nostalgic for the atmosphere of Loznitsa, decided she wanted to buy a house in Greece. At first, I wondered why she had not decided to buy something in Italy, especially since both she and Father spoke Italian fluently and none of us spoke Greek. Italy, though, still held memories for Mother, so we flew to Athens on the 16th of July. Mother had not yet decided where she wanted to settle and we went on a day cruise around the Aegean. We visited the islands of Poros, Aegina, Hydra and Spetses and I was lost in their beauty. There was an incredible atmosphere in the air that spoke of the ancient world and it suited me, because I began to hope I could find myself again in its beauty. When we returned that evening to Athens, we went out to Plaka for dinner.

The narrow streets and the smell of roasting chestnuts, souvlaki and corn and the Parthenon, pristine in its beauty as it sat on the Acropolis like a jewel, was something that touched us all. Mother was not sure what to do. She wanted to be close to Athens, because the idea of living on an island that was far from the mainland scared her. We were sitting at a small tavern overlooking the square, eating, when she suddenly turned to look behind her. A policeman was standing near the Orthodox Church in the square and Mother jumped up and went over to him. They started talking and when she returned to our table laughing, it was as though she was years younger. Her face had lost its taut look and the wind had ruffled her hair.

"I have decided," she said. "That policeman helped me to decide! We are going tomorrow to Epidavros."

This wonderful charisma of spontaneity Mother had was something I admired. When she wanted to do something, she did it! There was no thought behind her actions as she spontaneously took decisions, acted on them and came up confident things were for the best. I felt a lump form in my throat! I wanted her to always be like that and to see happiness in her eyes. I felt ashamed I was so judgmental of her and Father, so I touched her arm gently. Mother turned to look at my hand resting on her arm and hugged me. I laid my head against her and tears filled my eyes. It was as though we had been on such different rollercoaster rides through time that we had missed each other so completely. In the brief moment of union, I knew I admired Mother and loved her deeply.

That evening as we walked back to our hotel, she insisted I buy a beautiful long beige cheese-cloth dress with the Meandrous design on the sleeves and bottom. She told me how beautiful I looked in it and as we left the shop, she laughed when an old lady spat at me.

"She's is warding off the evil spirits," she said gently.

The following morning, we took a taxi to Epidavros. The drive took us through the Corinth Canal and we stopped for lunch on our way. The sea was an azure blue and it was impossible not to feel the magic that came from such beauty! Mother's face had softened, as she explored the scenery with eyes half closed. It was wonderful to feel the grandeur of the universe reflected in the calm blue sea and the pine forests dotting the landscape. Eager to explore, we booked into a small hotel near the sea when we arrived in Epidavros, and went to visit the theatre. What we saw and felt was so complete, it was not surprising the following day that Mother and Father visited the only public notary on the island, Dimitris Livanos. As neither Paul nor I were interested in looking at properties, we stayed at the hotel. Over a delicious *psarosoupa* and fried red mullet with *horta* later that day, Mother told us how she had found a delightful piece of land that overlooked the bay.

"We can build a beautiful villa," she said excitedly to Father, who was drinking some of the local *Retsina*. Father had, over the years, begun to drink less and less because Mother always stopped him whenever he got to the fourth glass. He had mellowed and enjoyed fishing or playing chess with Paul. They had stopped arguing so much and we had all relaxed since. Now that Mother had finally found her heart, buried in the quaint atmosphere of Epidavros, we could begin to enjoy life.

It was a Wednesday and we had gone into town to buy some fresh bread and honey, when I noticed a tall, handsome young man striding down the street. He was wearing a yellow polo shirt with white shorts, and something about the way he walked, made me turn and watch him. Just before I lost sight of him, as he walked up some stairs, my inner voice spoke loudly and clearly.

"*That is who I am going to marry!*"

I was distracted by Mother's voice calling out from the fruit and vegetable stall she had stopped at, and this inner knowing faded as quickly as it had come, so I did not think about the young man again. The following day, when my parents returned from yet another appointment with Dimitris, they told Paul and me about his son who was studying law.

"You will have a lot in common," she said to Paul. "He is translating for us and speaks fluent French and English. You really ought to come with us next week when we go there again, and meet him."

She turned to me with a strange expression in her eyes.

"Dimitris made a joke today – something about a dowry and how it would be funny if you married his son and the property returned to him. Of course I laughed. They have this custom here you know, where the bride's family pays a dowry to her husband."

"I told him about '*lobola*', and how the Africans pay for their brides with cattle," Father said gruffly, "but he didn't seem to understand!" He smiled.

I looked at Mother, wondering what the notary's son looked like. I decided he couldn't be as handsome as the man I had seen walking down the street, and the idea of a dowry seemed ridiculous! I smiled and paid little attention to what Mother said next, wrapped up in the feelings that came from within.

That evening, Paul and I joined our new group of friends on the beach. Annette and Annika were from Sweden, and I was entranced by their free sexuality and the fact their parents were so liberal; there were Dimitris and Alexander, two students from Athens, who were communists and fiercely spoke up against the Junta. Then there was Roulis! Roulis was an American Greek from Chicago, who gathered firewood and built a fire on the beach. We drank coke and roasted fish that Dimitris and Alexander had caught that afternoon. Annette had brought her tape recorder and we were all soon dancing to the strains of 'Dancing Queen'.

I was wearing my beige cheesecloth dress and had plaited some of my long, brown hair on either side. I wore a thin blue ribbon around my head and lying back on the sand, I looked up at the stars. The sky was filled with them and I began to dream. I was so entranced I did not notice someone had joined our group and when I finally sat up, I felt my body tingle. The man I had seen striding down the street in town was sitting next to Roulis, an apparition from the past and the future, delicately caught in the net that began to weave its way into my heart. He was laughing at something Roulis had said and then noticed me, looking at him. He bent his head and smiled at me. I flushed and quickly looked away. Annette jumped up and began to pull Roulis up.

"Let's have a swim," she said excitedly, kicking off her shoes. I watched the group as they began splashing at each other. Only Paul and Alexander were left and then I heard Alexander talking to Paul about my Greek god.

"Why don't you ask Philip? He's studying law in Thessalonika with us."

I had missed part of the conversation, as I watched Philip splashing in the water and then swimming fearlessly into the darkness. My heart missed a beat in fear, but then I watched him slowly move forward towards the beach. When everyone finally came back, soaked through, Roulis introduced us to Philip. Philip started talking about the differences in law to Paul, and I got up to go and sit next to Roulis.

"Please tell him to ask me to dance!" The words were out of my mouth before I had a chance to think about them. Roulis smiled.

When everyone had dried off, Dimitris brought a cassette out of his bag and we listened to the haunting music of Love Theme from Phaedra by Mikis Theodorakis. Alexander explained no one was allowed to listen to his music since the Junta had taken over the government in Greece, and warned his brother to keep it low. Philip was talking to Roulis again and suddenly looked at me, inclined his head and then asked me to dance. We stood in the sand and he put his arms around me. My heart began to beat and I lost all sense of time. We danced for the rest of the evening, until Paul tapped me on the shoulder and said we ought to go back to the hotel. It was nearly midnight. The fire had burned low and Roulis and Dimitris put it out, collecting the ashes. Philip was holding onto my hand and then he moved towards me and kissed me on the forehead.

"It was really good to meet you," he said in a flirtatious way.

I smiled at him, wondering how I was going to ever tell him I was only fourteen. He was nineteen and looked so mature and as we walked towards the road, the inevitable question came. I told him how old I was, and could see he was taken aback. He mumbled something about thinking I was seventeen! We walked in silence back to the hotel and finally said goodbye to Philip, who walked off into the darkness. Paul went to his room, but, unable to end the evening so abruptly, I invited the group to my room. We sat listening to music, talking and eventually Roulis said he was going to raid the kitchen in order to find something to drink. More than an hour had gone by since Philip had left and I wished he was there with us.

"Why don't we walk into town and get something there to drink and then we can find Philip?"

"Find Philip....?" Roulis said incredulously. "Philip must be at home in bed! Do you realize what time it is?"

"Well I am not tired," I said. "Oh come on, please?"

Alexander's rebel nature took over.

"Do you know where he lives?" He turned to Roulis.

"I have no idea," he replied. "I think somewhere in town!"

"We can ask a taxi driver," I suggested. "Won't they know?"

Roulis laughed out loud, whilst putting his shoes on. "Even if we find out where he lives, what are we going to do? Knock on his door at two in the morning? You do realize it will take us thirty minutes to walk into town!"

Everyone started talking at once and then we were outside, walking down the quiet road. The smell of night flowers coupled with the sound of the sea lapping on the shore brought memories of promises to me. Sacredness and connectivity allowed a union of sorts to take place in my mind and heart, as I was quite unable to contemplate the effects of my sudden decisions. The moon hung low over the horizon, and we all began to sing softly. Finally, we reached town and Roulis asked one of the taxi drivers where Philip Livanos lived. I paid no attention to the name and began to skip when Roulis pointed up a narrow passage.

"You can't knock on someone's door at two in the morning!" Roulis said.

"Watch me!" I replied.

"My god, she's more insane than you are!" Alexander told his brother.

My group of friends positioned themselves around, hiding behind huge pots of Jasmine bushes and a tree, as I rang the bell. I waited, listening for a sound behind the closed door. When no one came, I sat on the top step with my finger on the bell!

"You are mad!" Roulis hissed from behind the tree. "What will you do if his father answers the door?"

I had no time to reply because the door suddenly opened and Philip peered out, rubbing his eyes. We waited for him to get dressed and then walked back to the hotel. Philip and I sat on the balcony and he told me how his father had gone to Lesbos for the weekend, and his mother had shut all the doors because his niece, who had arrived from Uruguay, walked in her sleep. The gods and goddesses were shining on me that day and I smiled, wrapped in the aspects of soul union and destined love.

The following day, Philip came to the beach to swim and we were playing in the water when suddenly we heard a shriek.

"Philip, it's wonderful to see you!"

Mother was coming towards us and I was totally confused. Philip went to say hello to her and as I got out of the water, Mother turned to me.

"Darling," she said. "This is Dimitris' son I told you about!"

I stood there gaping at her. I looked at Philip and then back at Mother. I could not believe I hadn't made the connection, and later on that afternoon, I casually mentioned we had all met at the beach, and that I had no idea who he was. Philip stopped coming to the beach from then on, and I breathed a sigh of relief his father hadn't opened the door. We decided it was safer to meet late at night, and so started going for long walks on the beach, every night after my parents and Paul had gone to sleep. When it was time to go back to South Africa, I gave Philip a school friend's address, and asked him to write to me. This aspect of secretiveness simply added a notion of greater mystery to my life, as I knew our lives were thickly intertwined. Something greater held out arms and, unhesitatingly, I walked into them ready for love.

CHAPTER SIX

Destiny plays strange games in the unseen. The Fates gather in the hall of Knowledge to read from the Book of Life, in which everyone has a chapter. Gently they re-arrange paths to carry us to union. When they have finished, the Book begins to glow, and if we are aware, it begins to glow in our hearts.

Escape

When I returned home, I started getting ready for my final year at school. I was the youngest person in my class and yet no one could tell. I had matured but was not ready to face final exams. I tried to concentrate on work at school, but then asked Mother if I could do my final year by correspondence.

I had started working the previous Christmas at Woodside Sanctuary, a home for challenged children. Paul, true to his word, had found me a position to help in the day care center. I wanted desperately to carry on working there and promised Mother I would study. I had never really been happy at school. Apart from Anne, I hadn't made many real friends, and those I did always left a space in my heart. Anne was leaving that year for another school, and the only other friend I had was Tessa, a young Chinese girl, who I knew would remain friends with me, even if I left. After nights of persuading Mother this was the best thing I could do, she finally agreed, so I began working at Woodside and studying in the afternoon for my final exams. The psychiatric nurse who worked in the day care center really liked me. She asked Matron to show me around the small clinic, as they both felt I had a talent and vocation.

I found my calling twinkling in the eyes of Heidi who locked me in the storeroom one day and stood on her head outside chuckling. There was Mona, a young child who looked like a doll but every now and then screamed shrilly. There was Frank, who had seizures every afternoon at the exact time his father had beaten him with an electric cable. It seemed I understood these children perfectly, and love streaming from my heart towards them gave me courage to continue communicating with them in some unseen realm.

I walked through the hospital absorbing everything I saw, the day Matron invited me to follow her, conscious of my young age and curious to see how I would react to the worst cases. We had been on our rounds for over an hour when suddenly, I stopped at a cot. Rita had encephalitis. Her face had a different form. As I stared into her heart and soul, I touched her gently and her deformed mouth opened in a giggle. My work was laid out for me in that moment of anguish and despair, for I had brought a smile to the face of a child suffering with a massive head and tubes draining on each side. I saw myself reflected in Rita's eyes. Beyond form was Spirit and beyond Spirit, Love; Divine Love I had once known. I was unable to see form, but only the perfection of Soul and this touched me deeply!

I finished school that year and wrote daily to Philip. Mother had found two of his letters under my pillow two months after we had got back from Greece, and had been greatly disappointed in me. She told me I was deceitful and that I should have told her Philip wanted to write to me. From that day onwards, every time I received a letter from him, I had to read it out to the family. I became an expert at leaving out those parts where Philip told me how much he loved me, but resented the fact I had no privacy, which only helped in widening the gap between Mother and me.

The following year, I went to college to complete a Diploma in Public Relations and a course in modeling, which I started doing in my spare time. When I saw Philip that summer he was shocked and told me he did not like the idea of me modeling, and that I should do something else. I told him I was thinking of becoming a psychiatric nurse, but that did not satisfy him either, because he said only poor girls nursed in Greece. Nursing was considered to be a vocation in South Africa, but I listened to him and decided to go to university to study social work instead, bent on his acceptance of me.

That year, I lost myself through a number of events. After the summer, back at home, I met a young German boy called Helmut Von

Reitlich, at a party. He was very attractive with blond hair and blue
eyes. He was in the army and we went out for a meal one evening
with friends. We started dating and he gave me a beautiful crystal
dolphin as a present. He was the perfect beau, always coming with a
red rose for me, and one day he saw a picture of Philip I carried in
my purse. Helmut was very upset when I told him about Philip and
he accused me of betraying him. That night we broke up.

I then started dating an Italian called Paulo. I did not tell Philip I
was dating because I was convinced he was too. It didn't last long
and then I was accepted at university. I was pleased and looked
forward to becoming a social worker. I had only been at university
for three weeks, when a group of us went into town to sell the
university magazine. It was raining and that evening they were
choosing the semi-finalists for the rag queen. I had hoped I might be
chosen, following in my sister's footsteps.

Jackie had been a prefect at school and a finalist when she had
gone to university, so this was something I really wanted to achieve.
I was also upset I had stopped modeling and was conscious of my
body and looks. At the end of the afternoon, my hair was wet and
had frizzed so I was eager to go home, change and do my hair. I asked
if anyone could give me a lift. Someone suggested I borrow their car
and for a split second I actually considered it, simply knowing deep
down inside I would be able to drive. Without warning, I had a flash
of an overturned car, as I shuddered.

"I can't drive. Please, you have to take me!" I told Peter, who had
suggested it.

We drove out of town and suddenly I saw it, a black car that came
out of nowhere and hit us. The Mini Cooper we were traveling in
swung around and I hit my head against the windscreen. I was rushed
to hospital where I had numerous tests, but no one realized I had
fractured my skull. I was discharged from hospital and did not go
back to university, because I decided to apply to do nursing. I felt I
would be a perfect nurse and not even Philip could stop me! I was so
happy to have at last decided to do something I loved, so that evening
I called Sean, needy and on the lookout for some support.

Sean and I had kept in touch and I had told him all about Philip, but had always felt he was part of the Soul I hankered after. He told me he was proud of me wanting to become a nurse, and then said quietly.

"By the way, I am coming back to Johannesburg."

I couldn't believe it! I was so happy I would at last see him again. He told me which parish he was being sent to, and I vowed I would pass my driver's license and go to see him. On my eighteenth birthday, I got my license and Paul bought me a shiny, new red Corolla. Paul had graduated with honors and was working at a law firm in town; I deeply appreciated his gift.

Paul had become like a father to me. He had offered to pay for my university and when I left, had promised to buy me a car. Although we were not that close, I felt he loved me more than anyone else did. He had always supported me, buying me poetry books and nurturing my desire to help others. I was careful with my new car, and drove out to the new parish where Sean had been transferred, ready to show him how much I had grown and matured over the years. As I parked the car, my heart began beating so fast I had to sit in the car for a while to calm down.

He opened the door, a blue pullover thrown casually over his shoulders and led me into his office. He pulled the door shut, turned and took me into his arms. I had wanted this closeness for so long, to rest there in his arms, but suddenly his mouth was on mine and his tongue darting into it, shredding the aspects of sacred love apart. From deep inside I heard my inner voice.

'How can you do this? He belongs to the church! French kissing is a mortal sin!'

I let him kiss me, conscious of the growing feelings of guilt that began to wrack at my heart. We sat down and he held my hand. In a quiet voice he said clearly.

"We can have a relationship, now you are eighteen, but you must know you will be one of many."

I stared at Sean. The rush of an ocean filled my ears as I remembered something he had once written in the parish news I had kept in a box, with a picture of him and his ordination card. He had written about a sparrow trapped in a room, battering and bruising its wings, in an endeavor to escape, when all the while there was an open window in the room.

I wanted to fly out of that window and find my freedom in Sean's arms. However, I could not find freedom in the arms of someone betraying his God and mine, and someone I felt sure would betray me. I did not know if there were other women in his life, or whether he was suggesting we have our relationship in the midst of a thriving parish that would need his devotion. I never stopped to ask, as I left in a hurry, and although I never stopped loving him, I found my heart had broken.

Three months later, I moved out of home to go and stay at the nurse's residence. I had torn Sean's picture and ordination card up and buried it in the garden, with my inner child, whose heart had broken too many times. When I told Mother I was only leaving because I needed to become a nurse, she was pleased one of her children had taken after her and was interested in medicine. Neither of us realized I seemed to be re-living her life, and walking in her shoes.

I met Victor whose father had had a heart attack a few weeks later and we began dating. The fact he was separated from his wife and had a young son did not bother me. That summer when we went to Greece, I told Philip I had been dating Victor, and that I would become a nurse. We broke up!

I had asked Philip if he would come to South Africa to do his masters and he had promised he would. Although we spent time together swimming and taking walks, we were never alone. Father had found him in my room one night and Mother called me a slut. She told me how he would never respect me, now I had slept with him. It had happened one afternoon, when we had taken Roulis's boat out to sea. We had gone to a deserted beach and there under a Platania, I had tasted something that left me with an empty heart. I stared up at the leaves covering most of the sky waiting for Philip to stop, because it hurt me there was no gentleness in his actions. Philip had tried to satisfy me in the best way he could and I had felt nothing at all.

I had told Philip about Victor, because I wanted to be honest with him. I had on occasion spoken to him about Sean, but could not explain matters I hardly understood. It was perhaps a cry for attention, a cry for promise, but instead Philip told me I had betrayed him and that he wanted nothing more to do with me. The fact he had told me about his girlfriends did not matter. That year when we parted with tears, he gave me a small golden cross I wore around my neck even though, when I returned home, I burnt all his letters, including the one he had written to me with a postscript in his blood, that said he would love me forever. Blotting out each and every memory of love, I threw myself into the depths of Hades, accepting fate had abandoned me to the fire; I had little chance of finding solace in the disastrous life I believed I was living.

I tried to confide in Mother, but our worlds had separated and she was only relieved, as she had begun to worry I would decide to live in Greece. She was not happy when I started dating Victor again, bent on defiance, and told me she did not approve. To keep the peace, I told her I would break off my relationship with him but did not, and one weekend I went home having made arrangements to play tennis with Victor. When she asked who I was playing tennis with and I told her, Mother could stand it no longer. With force, she began to hit me repeatedly on my head, yelling at me and telling me I was a liar, and inconsiderate of the fact Victor had not divorced his wife. I managed to pull away from her, unconscious of the fear and anger that bubbled up inside of her, reminding her of her past. I grabbed my bag, ran out into my car and roared out of the driveway. As I looked back at the house, I could see her on the porch, gesticulating wildly. In place of her face, I saw a skull. As I drove up the street, thinking again about Sean and how I should never have left him, I blacked out and crashed into a car parked at the side of the road. I lost consciousness to wake up in hospital.

The doctor was surprised when he realized I had a fractured skull and that it was an old fracture. He asked what had happened to my head and I told him I had bumped it just before leaving the house, too embarrassed to tell him Mother had hit me with such force. I had a lumbar puncture and because I could feel nothing on my right side I stayed in hospital for three weeks. Paul, Mother and Father came to see me and Mother did not say anything about our argument. Instead, she told me I should give up nursing for a while and that she had arranged for me to visit my sister in Cape Town for a few months, in order to recuperate.

Mother had called Jackie and told her about Victor. She instructed my sister to watch me carefully and not let me contact him at all, but I was unaware of this. Arriving in Cape Town, I was reminded of the difficult time I had been through with Carl, but I had missed my sister.

Jackie lived in a beautiful, Victorian house. The ceilings were high and the main bedroom had bay windows looking out onto Villiers Street. At the top were beautiful stained glass windows and in the front of the house an enormous garden surrounded by a white picket fence. On the first day Jackie took me around the city. We had sole with boiled potatoes and cold white wine for dinner and then watched the sunset. That night I tried to be pleasant to Carl.

I went to sleep and dreamt I was standing in the broken ruins of a temple and when I awoke to the smell of eggs and bacon frying in the kitchen, I felt fear knot in my throat. I didn't like the dream and found solace in drinking a pot of sweetened, milky tea with toast that was heavily smeared with butter. Jackie announced we were going to spend the day at Sandi Beach.

We took a picnic with us and a group of Jackie's friends joined us. Sandi Beach was a nudist beach, and I felt extremely awkward, so I kept my bikini on. Carl laughed at me! One of Jackie's friends was a young girl called Georgetta. Georgetta sat beside me on the beach and asked who my father was. I was stunned as I realized Mother's secrets had at last been revealed. Georgetta told me Jackie's father was a British writer and film producer, that Mother was Serbian and could not return to Serbia because she had fallen in love with an SS officer. Bits of information I had heard over the years, slowly fell like pieces into a giant puzzle, reminding me of people we had met in England, like Yolande and Doreen and suddenly, I felt a sense of relief but also one of impending danger and fear, for I knew Mother had guarded her secrets well. I could not understand either how a stranger was confiding in me about my sister's personal life with Carl, showing concern for the way they had chosen to live. Unable to cope with these events and needing a shoulder to cry on, I wrote a letter to Victor and asked my sister to post it the following day. Jackie steamed open the letter and read it. She cornered me in the bathroom, demanding to know why I had written to Victor saying I was unhappy. I looked at Jackie. She was so beautiful and so lost at the same time. I told her about the friend who had confided in me, and that she had more to worry about because of what I had learned – how she had betrayed Mother – and that my writing to Victor was the least of her problems. Jackie slapped me across the face, and I demanded to go home.

The following day Jackie drove me to the airport and when I arrived in Johannesburg I told Mother what had happened, not realizing how I was betraying Jackie as well. Mother was sitting in my bedroom and she got up and walked to the door. She turned to look at me, unable to face the events that had suddenly brought her into the reality of how we were living life, and said in a steely voice,

"I never thought that you could be so vindictive! You are lying to me. I do not believe you! You are making it up just to hurt me! You are such a disappointment!"

Mother walked out of the room and I lay on my bed sobbing. I cried on and off for three days and when I stopped crying, decided I had to find a job and escape from the home where I had been raised, as quickly as possible, if I was to remain sane. A week later I found a job as a dental assistant, and looked forward to the day I could move out as far as possible away from my family who, I believed, had betrayed me too many times.

Peter Zibaras was an excellent dentist. He taught me all I needed to know about dental hygiene and I enjoyed working for him. We worked in a tall highrise building full of dentists and doctors and I began to have an affair with a neurosurgeon who worked on the second floor. Two months later I was sleeping with Lawrence, a dentist who loved hooking me up to laughing gas before we made love. I was used and abused; I waded in the dark murky remnants of that which lay around me and in me.

The astral plane was dark, filled with lost boys who belonged to the world of Peter Pan and my childhood dreams where shadows reigned, pulling me closer and closer into the abyss. I began then to contemplate deeply on the fires of Hades, seeing in them the dark and despairing loss of self, the ease with which one blames another for loss of self, and the feeling of futility and degradation that comes with it. It seemed perfectly natural to follow in the steps of shadows and become consumed by them. Although I had a good job and an employer who respected my work, I allowed myself to be abused, as I drifted through shadows that were only trying to reflect back at me, what I believed myself to be. This was the wheel of suffering the Buddhists spoke about, the wheel that turned in hopelessness, watching and waiting for consciousness to rise out of the ashes like a Phoenix.

I had started taking the pill, as the terrible cramps I suffered whenever I got my period were so powerful, I sometimes used such boiling water to soothe them that I burned my stomach. Having been given a hormone treatment at twelve to mature my uterus, my hormones were imbalanced, so the pill brought relief for my pains, but further complications. As fate would have it, the day Mother was admitted to hospital with heart problems and her angina pectoris yet again, I was admitted into hospital with a deep vein thrombosis. How close we were struggling for freedom and how inextricably tied we were, to whatever destiny had given to us, as a solution for whatever metanoia we felt for the lost past – aeons of struggling to break free!

Something was hurting me deep in the recesses of my psyche, and in order to alleviate the pain I could feel burning in my heart, I wrote a letter to Philip telling him I was not well. Philip replied with a letter full of concern and admiration for my spontaneous nature and this is how we rekindled our romance.

I returned to Epidavros that year, full of the promise that I could forget my inner pain and sordid past, to finally come together, because I was sure Philip would love me physically, mentally, emotionally and spiritually. This is what I thought would set me free.

I had always flirted openly and often Philip had complained about it. That year, I kept my eyes lowered and so, whilst walking down the street I met two shoes, a pair of trousers, a shirt and a blue pullover slung over shoulders and a face – the pullover reminded me of Sean, and Philip's deep eyes reflected my desire to break away from the past. We met and he kissed me; that summer I told him I would move to Greece and begged for forgiveness, not sharing with him my sordid past, ashamed and unable to explain how and why I had befriended the darkness to such an extent that I was losing my soul. I did not fully comprehend the price one pays to look into the darkness and become part of it, or the dangers that lurked there, wanting to feed off my soul.

That September, I asked Mother to let me go back to Greece, the Greece I had left only two months before, to go back to a job I was no longer interested in. At first Mother resisted. She told me I could not go away on holiday alone; then she recalled her own life and marveled at how similar our lives had become, losing sight of the greater objectives, in trying to pay back whatever I had unconsciously deemed to be part of my inheritance. She had left Europe and I was returning; she had lost so much, and I would be gaining something through love, or following footsteps in the sand I had decided to trace, and make mine. Mother finally gave me permission to go to Greece and meet with Philip, taken up by the sparkle in my eye and promise of love, reminding her of Dragan and stolen moments that robbed her of her future, and plunged her into despair.

Philip was in the navy doing his military service. He was stationed in Athens and when I knocked on his door he was still in his uniform, having lunch. I hadn't told him I was coming; as I had once rung his bell in the early hours of the morning, I arrived at his doorstep, totally immersed in the promise of love and completely thoughtless about repercussions. Philip opened the door, looked at me in total shock and then I was in his arms. I had turned his life completely upside down and Philip had no idea how he was going to tell his parents I had arrived. We sat in the kitchen and I told him I could not live without him! Once again I had been spontaneous, and Philip seemed pleased to see me. We went out with a group of his friends and he told everyone how we had met, and how again I had arrived at his door unannounced. It seemed as though he admired me and that my daring inspired something in his heart.

We spent two glorious weeks going to Kolonaki for coffee, to clubs along the sea front and walks in Kaisariani. When the time came for me to return home, we started discussing my move to Greece. That night I called my parents.

"I am going to get married," I told Mother in an excited voice. "I am staying in Greece!"

Mother could not cope with situations that threatened her well-being. She put Father on the line, who told me that unless I returned of my own free will, he would have the embassy escort me home. When I tried to reason with him, he put the phone down.

I left all my clothes in Philip's small orange cupboard in defiance and flew home. I told Father, who was waiting for me at the airport that I was going to return to Greece, no matter what anyone thought. My relationship with Father had always been strained. There was never any physical contact between us and I was only aware of the fact he played the role of mediator in the family. He would listen to Mother and then repeat whatever she said. Whenever she changed her mind about anything, he would promptly change his. Father always protected Mother fiercely and would not let anyone upset her. His face was grim and on the way home, I was silent.

My heart had soared, touched by the freedom of a different life in Athens. I was determined I would leave, no matter whether I had the approval of my parents or not. A new found strength surged through my being. Mother was cool and distant when we arrived. She spoke quietly, a vacant look in her eyes, repeating over and over that she would not condone my move to Greece. I immediately called a friend of mine whom I had met at university, and asked her to find me a job. If I was to move to Greece, I knew I had to earn money.

Spatsi was a German researcher from South West Africa. She arranged for me to help with a research project she was involved in, and I started going to the university the following day. I called Philip every day from university and, finally, broke Mother by threatening to sell my jewelry to move to Greece; I assured her Philip's father would welcome me with open arms! On the 4th November 1978, I had packed two suitcases and stood waiting to board the plane that would take me to a new life in Athens.

How little I understood about reality! How unconcerned I was about leaving behind a sprawling mansion with a guest house, and swimming pool. How little I thought about saying goodbye to family and friends, knowing deep within my heart I was answering the call of my destiny, faintly recalling the certainty I had felt when I had first laid eyes on Philip.

Philip and I settled into our new life but something was not right. I was trying to fit in with friends who often did not speak English and into a new culture where I needed support. Philip was twenty-three and doing his military service. His mother Vaia was not happy with the fact I had come to live with her son! She hadn't sent Philip abroad to study because she did not want him marrying a foreigner and suddenly she realized her greatest fear had become a reality.

Vaia had come from a relatively poor family in the Pelopenese. She had studied to become a midwife and after she had married the handsome lawyer from Lesbos, had moved to Epidavros. Dimitris became public notary and enjoyed going out with his friends to the local coffee shop every evening. He was handsome and often flirted with his secretary who adored him, but he tried to be a good father and husband. He had been strict with his son when he was young, at times losing his temper and beating him with a thick stick, but he had also been raised with the rod.

Vaia adored Philip! Her daughters were seven and ten when she gave birth to him and she spoilt him, because he was her only son. Katerina, her eldest daughter, had gone to Athens to study law when she was twenty and five years later she had come home with a sea captain, whom she had fallen in love with. Vaia did not approve of Petros. She did not want her daughter marrying a 'sailor' and so she disinherited her. Katerina returned to Athens, worked hard and eventually built a small apartment on the top floor of the family home in Athens. Three years later she married Petros in a quiet wedding.

When Athena graduated, she decided to train as a beautician in Athens and her mother began to look for a suitable husband for her daughter. Some friends told her about a young man called Andreas who was reasonably well off, who lived in Uruguay. They arranged the marriage and when Athena finished her beauty course she went to Uruguay and got married.

Ten years later, Athena returned to Greece with two young daughters and her husband whom she had grown to care about but whom she had never truly been in love with. Although Philip told me about his sisters, I did not see how similar all our lives were. I simply tried to fit in, which was something quite difficult to do! I disregarded the growing feelings of fear that invaded my being, promising myself it would all turn out perfectly, because love would conquer all.

Unfortunately I felt quite insecure in Athens. The Greece I loved suddenly appeared quite hostile. Philip's home was small and dark and his mother resented me using her things. She had shown clearly that I was not welcome and I could not reach her. I could not even go to our beautiful home in Epidavros, which had three bedrooms and overlooked a beautiful pine forest and the sea. Although the apartment was only used for one month every year, my parents had rented it indefinitely, but did not give me the keys, as Father did not trust me with them! It did not take long for my leg to swell up again. I called Zoe, the daughter of Mother's landlady in Epidavros, who immediately called her best man, a vein specialist.

Dr Kandarakis insisted I had to be hospitalized but it was too difficult, and far too absurd to think Philip's parents would suddenly foot the bill for a private clinic, and I did not want to tell my parents what had happened, so I asked Athena if she could recommend some-one else. Athena was pregnant again and having problems with phlebitis, so she asked her doctor to come and see me. He told me to stay in bed and bandage my legs if I got up. Three days later the pain moved to my side and then, I began to have chest pains. We called Dr Kandarakis again and I was rushed to hospital with a suspected embolism.

As I lay on the hospital bed, struggling to breathe, I suddenly found myself in a space where there was no time but Spirit weighed down by its purpose; Spirit carrying a heavy past, Spirit that led me to the borders between life and death and Spirit that reminded me of a tragic past.

I find myself on a road. Passing me by are men, women and children all dressed in grey rags, their faces etched with deep suffering! They trudge along, moving into oblivion and I instantly recognize they are on a path leading nowhere. I feel their pain and suffering as if it were my own. Behind them is home – a beautiful green hill where the sound of music calls to me, gently caressing my mind. I soar in flight, down a tunnel, towards the green hill when suddenly something stops me, pulling me back!

A nurse standing beside my bed told Philip I was dying, but Philip was shaking me, ordering me to breathe. Philip had called his parents and his father had come immediately to the hospital, arriving just as I was being admitted. He was sitting at the foot of my bed crying, as Philip urged me to breathe. I felt I was being pulled in two directions when suddenly, with a jolt, my eyes fluttered open. The doctor insisted I had to be operated on and Philip informed my parents, who called Jackie.

Jackie had got a job as a medical representative in Cape Town. She called a well-renowned surgeon who spoke to doctors in Athens. He demanded they do further tests and yet time was running out. I had already been given a pre-med and in a state of euphoria I signed for the operation, even though I was under age. An hour later, I was in the operating theatre and an umbrella clip was placed in my vena cava, partially closing it. I recovered slowly and steadily, dismayed by the events and deeply perturbed by my vision. That Christmas, after a month in hospital, struggling with the language and the aloneness that was slowly threatening me, I went back to the small, dark flat I had tried to get used to.

Philip's parents' apartment was below street level. The furniture was a heavy dark wood with gold and black upholstery. Our home in Johannesburg was a sprawling mansion with beautiful gardens, something I had not fully appreciated when I was surrounded by such luxury. I found myself wilting in the small space, pining after the wide open spaces of Africa and the freedom of something that became more and more ineffable. As I watched Philip decorate a small Christmas tree, tears began running down my face. Paul had written a letter I had received that morning, telling me about life at home.

The garden had always been a refuge for me and its beauty inspired me. Mother had planted beautiful flowers and trees and it was her pride and joy. Mother was an excellent cook and on Sundays we often sat in the garden, having philosophical discussions and eating; lazing around the pool or sitting in the garden room, playing cards. There was a gentle flow of unseen love that connected all of us, but had never been enough to keep the peace. Although my heart hurt due to our gloomy past, I had spent some of the most idyllic moments a child could have spent, in the company of my family.

Paul had written about a Hawaiian party Mother had thrown. They had all worked so hard, stringing daisies as welcome necklaces and scooping out pineapples to use as dishes for the food. Father had laid palm branches over the awnings and Paul said how much they had missed me.

Pressure began to explode from within and I started crying. The truth was I missed them all, and my life in Johannesburg; an inner feeling of extreme loneliness began to envelop me. Philip tried to console me but I could not stop crying. In the end he called my doctor who told him to give me two Mogadons, and a twenty milligram Valium three times a day. I had never taken medication and it had an adverse effect on me.

That night, shadows took form and my black knight stood beside me, challenging! I felt as though I was being suffocated by the dark and as the shadows began to threaten me I was caught up in their darkness. The next morning when I awoke, I found a small razor blade beside the bed and cut my wrists.

I was yet again rushed to hospital where the resident psychiatrist, gave me more pills. I found myself torn between a past I could remember as a flow of love and Mother throwing glassware and it shattering against the wall. Philip tried to console me and when the psychiatrist suggested transferring me to the mental hospital for electric shock treatment, Philip suddenly awoke to this garish new situation threatening our very existence. He told me to stop taking the extra pills I was given, and I collected them in a glass case in the drawer beside my bed.

Philip called Zoe who came over with her husband Constantine. Constantine was an artist, who at the time was reading a book by Mircea Eliade about soul loss. He explained to Philip that loss of soul in the Shamanic tradition was a diminishment of essential spiritual energy and that if the soul left the patient, death was the result.

Mircea Eliade had written, 'disease is attributable to the soul's having strayed away or having been stolen, and treatment in principle reduced to finding it, capturing it, and obliging it to resume its place in the patient's body'. Constantine, convinced I had lost soul, told Philip he was going to consult a priest friend of his, because he was sure something was happening to me, quite beyond my control.

My wrists had been bandaged and I was lying on the bed heavily sedated.

Spirit slowly rises out of the heavy body, which stops breathing and Spirit begins floating up above the body. Spirit has no emotion whatsoever, apart from a mild curiosity as it watches doctors rush around the body on the bed. Time has ceased and Spirit is conscious only of spirit. It has no personal being but belongs to something greater than itself. Doctors have attached an iron lung to no avail and desperate, at last, the kiss of life is given to the body. Spirit floats downwards losing the space it has become part of. A sharp and painful tug is felt by the body, which then connects with reality, and consciousness returns, to shatter every illusion ever had about death.

Constantine had not slept the previous evening. He had tried praying for me and at six thirty was at the small chapel where Father Georgios lived. Father Georgios was pleased to see Constantine. He listened carefully to Constantine's thoughts and then lit a candle. Swaying back and forth in his blue vestments, holding a rosary, he began to pray. After a while, he opened his eyes and said to Constantine in an urgent voice.

"Call the hospital at once and tell the nurse to go to your friend's room. Something evil is trying to kill her. Quickly!" he broke off, handing the phone to Constantine.

Constantine dialed, his hands shaking. He asked the head nurse to please go and check on me, saying he would call back in a few minutes. When he called back, there was no reply and Constantine was worried. Father Georgios gave him a cross, holy water and a small icon and told him to go to my side. He promised he would carry on praying.

When Constantine arrived at the hospital, he stopped at the nurse's quarters. The head nurse was there.

"Thank goodness you called me," she said flustered. We nearly lost her! She had stopped breathing. You can go and see her!"

Constantine tiptoed into my room. He put the cross on my bed and the icon on the bedside table. My body began to shake. I was aware of his presence and yet locked in a battle, where shadows loomed towards me, not allowing even a cross or icon to help me. Philip arrived in time to see me writhing on the bed and pushing the cross away from me. Constantine left Philip at my side and ran to call Father Georgios who told him. "Someone is sending very negative thought forms to your friend Philip. They are using this young woman to weaken him, and trying to kill her. When she goes back home, I want you to bring her to me so I can bless her! Her path is unique and very difficult!"

That evening, clutching a small bear, I found my angelic friend somewhere in the recesses of my mind. I placed myself back in the space where I had met him, and imagined he was holding light around me. I worked hard to maintain the image in my mind and the following morning, found I could sit up in bed and drink some tea. When Philip and his parents arrived, I seemed to be detached from them and when Mother and Father walked into my room, I was not happy at all to see them. It was as though I had detached from the world completely.

Mother looked piqued and hovered at the end of my bed asking me why I was punishing her.

"We came on the first plane after Philip called us. Why are you doing this to me?"

Father immediately pointed out how I had upset Mother and how ungrateful I was.

"You wanted to come to Greece and we let you! You made your bed, you lie in it!"

I tried to smile at them and as I turned to look out of the window, I told my parents I wanted to go home. At first they both told me it was impossible because they had just arrived, but I insisted I wanted to go home. I hardly looked at Philip or his parents and the following day, when I was discharged from hospital, Constantine took me to see Father Georgios. Father Georgios clasped me to him and then took me into the small chapel. He moved around me slowly and blessed me, chanting in a low voice. When he had finished he spoke to Constantine in Greek and Constantine told me he would be coming to the house to say a mass. I asked Constantine to thank the priest and we left.

Two days later, Katerina and Athena were in the small living room where Philip had placed the small Christmas tree. They laid a white tablecloth on the dining room table and white candles. They had bought '*prosfora*' a loaf of bread that had been blessed and we waited for the priest to arrive. Philip had gone to fetch him and his parents were in their bedroom getting dressed. When Philip arrived, Father Georgios sat down beside me and held my hand. He began to speak to me in broken English and told me not to worry. Just then Dimitris called Philip to his room and began shouting at him. He told Philip he wanted the priest to leave.

"But he hasn't even done the blessing yet!"

"I don't care! Get him out of the house! Get him out of the house!"

I had never heard Philip's father shout at anyone before. I did not understand what he was saying and when the priest got up, making the sign of the cross, I was surprised. He put his hand into his pocket and drew out a small, plain wooden cross. He pressed it into my hand and said gently.

"My child I must go now! They do not want me in the house! As long as the Devil is here, I can do nothing. Pray as much as you can! I feel sorry for you because you must fight this Devil!"

With that, he left. I asked Philip what was going on and two hours later, Dimitris could not tell us why he had reacted so violently to the presence of Father Georgios. Two days later, I waved gaily at Philip's parents as I left for the airport, conscious only of a need to connect fully to the spiritual. Paul had arranged for my ticket and even when I left Philip standing at passport control, I was happy. I knew exactly where I would go the moment I arrived in Johannesburg.

The flight was long and tiring and when Paul came to fetch me I was exhausted, but the simple idea of going to my old bedroom and the garden I had missed so much, gave me strength. I tried that night to tell Paul what had been happening but it was not easy, because I did not even understand it myself. I did not believe in the evil aspects of nature, and yet had I not been warned in my sleep state as a child, that a dark knight wanted something I held in heart? Had I not been given an elixir to protect me? At the time, I could not make the connections, as I stared at the cuts on my wrists that were quite shallow and had started healing. The following morning, I asked Paul if I could borrow his car because he had sold mine and went to the only place that could give me comfort, Sean's office.

When Sean opened the door he was surprised. I sat in his office and told him about my ordeal. Sean shifted in his chair and then spoke.

"You only seem to come to me when things are not working out in your life!"

His words were cool and I was stunned. He was, after all, a priest and it was his job to listen to me, or so I thought! He had been a spiritual mentor, someone who had carried the traits of the Unseen Universe, I was compelled to follow and honor in my heart. Sean however, was not the priest I had fallen in love with. He had become a man and although I could not see this, he could. From far off, the Universe smiled. I had begun walking a path only I could follow. I had to learn to master the force of darkness that threatened my well-being alone, because this was part of walking the path. I did not see or understand it! I left Sean's office and went sadly home. I went to the hairdresser and cut my long, brown hair short and the following day, told Paul that I had made a mistake by coming home and that I was ready to return to Athens.

CHAPTER SEVEN

We seek life and, in turn, life reminds us of death. The two come hand in hand to teach us of the seeming impermanence of this life. Perhaps we are simply wanderers who find shelter for a short period of time in order to learn something more about the Self that longs to set us free after birth. The two faces of life are enigmas we refuse to accept and yet the one cannot exist without the other.

Death

On my return to Greece, my parents insisted I find somewhere else to stay, so I moved in with Zoe and Constantine. They had a nice apartment in Kiffisia and although my room was small, I felt safe. I found a job at an advertising agency and on weekends went out with Philip. Our relationship had been through its difficulties and I tried not to recall what Philip had once said to me after my operation. He was sitting next to me in hospital when he suddenly turned to me, and said, "You want me to be a mother, father, sister, brother, friend and lover all in one. I can't do that!"

I had not fully realized the magnitude of his words, because I was unable to analyze them. I did not realize I wanted the union I had experienced as a child; someone who could be everything to me in partnership. It seemed as though I had no choice but to prepare for my wedding, with the man I knew I had to marry. Philip was not happy I was living in Kiffissia and so, one afternoon in February we went into town and ordered wedding rings. Philip chose a very thin ring because he did not like wearing rings, and neither was he committed to this marriage. As though we were both being swept by an unseen force, we went to Pendeli the following week with a bottle of champagne and exchanged rings. We went home, called my parents and told them the news. Of course, Mother immediately agreed I could move back in with Philip and that evening, when Philip's parents arrived, we told them we had got engaged. Vaia's mouth set in a firm grimace as she kissed me lightly on the cheek. Dimitris was happy because he had always liked me, so I did not think about Vaia's reaction. Over the years Vaia had grown bitter. She wore a pained expression of sacrifice on her face and had decided if her husband was handsome and debonair, he could enjoy himself out of the home. She wore no make-up, dressed conservatively and slaved away in the kitchen. Her purpose was to serve her husband and only son. Inadvertently, she expected me to do the same and so did Philip, although at the time, I was unaware of this. My parents were excited about my wedding, and began to make plans. Of course they would not abandon me to the small dark flat Philip wanted us to live in! Mother promised she would buy me everything I needed to make a new home, so I began to look for apartments.

That year, I asked Paul to ask Matron at Woodside Sanctuary for a reference letter and applied for a teaching job at a local British school. I enrolled at the University of La Verne, an American University in Kiffisia and began doing my bachelor's in Psychology. I was overjoyed when I got a job in the kindergarten and although I knew little of the dedication needed in this type of job, I felt I was born to teach. I quickly acclimatized and, with a new sense of self-worth, found a wonderful apartment in Psychico that had two bedrooms and a perfect view of Athens.

The apartment was on a hill and the space around it beautiful. When I took Philip to see it, he told me he thought it ridiculous to rent when we already had a home. I told him I would pay the rent, as I could not imagine starting married life in the apartment that had been a shadow in my past, so when the container arrived with beautiful African carved furniture, I was ecstatic. Mother had sent us brochures to choose furniture from, and had bought the rest. An entire household had been sent to me and I loved everything she had sent us. Mother had excellent taste, and I deeply appreciated the sacrifices she had made to choose everything that matched so perfectly.

I had decided to wear an ankle length, beige lace wedding dress, Mother had found a seamstress to make to measure, and Philip went out and bought a beige suit. Grandmother Maria had painstakingly crocheted tiny beige baskets for each guest, filled with sugar coated almonds; bonbonnières were usually made out of tulle. It was customary to give them out at weddings but I wanted mine to be different. Paul had placed a tiger's eye in each and our names and wedding date on a small beige card. I could not have wished for a more perfect wedding! A fellow student from university, Helen, had offered her garden for our champagne breakfast and on the morning of my wedding, as I sat looking at myself in the mirror, I saw a beautiful girl looking back at me. The hairdresser had caught my shoulder length hair with two pearl combs on either side and had placed pearls throughout my hair. My make-up and nails were perfect and at nine thirty on the 20th of June, I walked up the steps of St Dimitris Church on the arm of my father, who wore a dark blue suit. Mother looked radiant in a purple dress and Paul in a light blue suit. Jackie had not been able to come to the wedding and I missed her presence, but accepted she was busy.

As Father handed me over to the man who would become my husband, Philip looked at me and said, "Oh, my God, what on earth have you done with your hair? It looks awful!"

My eyes flashed as I retaliated. "You can be a bastard at times!" I replied sharply.

As we walked into the church, my headmistress, wearing a blue hat remarked, "Oh come on you two! The least you can do is try to look happy. After all, it is your wedding day!"

I had on more than one occasion gone to school with tears in my eyes over the previous weeks. Philip had not wanted marriage and he started complaining about everything. He expected the house to be spotless and well-cooked meals on the table when he came home. He had not wanted me to get a job and had made it clear I was to do everything perfectly, if I insisted on going out to work. I had never cleaned a house before!

We had been lucky when Rose had started working for us, when I was little. She had always taken care of my clothes and cleaned, so I had never thought about cleaning. I tried the best I could and did not appreciate Philip coming home and inspecting everything to see if I had left any dust anywhere. He often compared my cooking to

Vaia's, pointing out she had never put a roast chicken in the oven with giblets inside. I pointed out chickens in Johannesburg didn't have the neck, kidneys and heart stuck in a paper bag in the chest cavity. We laughed about it later, but it appeared that Philip only wanted to find fault rather than commend my endeavors, and I needed reassurance. We had on occasion argued about our best man, a Dutch client of Philip's who had five daughters from a previous marriage, who enjoyed wrapping their arms around Philip when they were topless.

As I looked around the church I took in a deep breath. I would smile because I knew that once we were married, everything would change. Philip would grow to love me even more than he did and we would always be happy. I would never argue with him, and when we had children, I would do everything I could, to make them and my husband happy. These were the gallant thoughts I harbored in my mind and heart, convinced life would be a bed of roses, rather than a heap of dried and gnarled stems, thorns peering out ready to ensnare.

I had told Philip, when I was seventeen, about the time I had woken up to find my parents grappling with each other and a gun pointed at each other; I had also told him about a bowl of porridge that had jumped up and crashed back on a table and words that had hurt me and yet healed my relationship with my siblings. I had asked Philip for the only one thing I had hankered after most of my life: I asked him to love me without reserve and told him he would have everything from me, if only he could love me fully and unconditionally. Perhaps I had asked him for too much, for I had failed to see then, that unless one has fully understood their inner worth, there can never be such dedication and honor in a relationship.

When I took wine from the golden chalice the priest handed me, it meant the world to me, for the cup held the memory of Love, and yet, was I fully conscious at that moment of marriage? As we went around the altar and rice and rose petals landed softly on us, I smiled. Then some of Philip's friends began to throw almonds and the priest had to ask them to stop. The rest of the service became a blur and then we were in the dark blue Mercedes that took us to Ekali, and Helen's beautiful rolling lawns. We cut our traditional wedding cake that was a beige heart Paul had almost not got through customs, and then we were home, in our new apartment packing to leave on honeymoon. Our wedding had come and gone and I knew I had lost the endeavor to imprint and share its sacredness with the man I expected to become whole with.

Our best man, Dirk, had arranged for us to travel with him and his young wife through Europe, and I was disappointed because I had so wanted a honeymoon where we would be alone. I felt my husband was only happy when he was surrounded by his friends, and that he did not want to lose himself in me! I tried to bridge the gap by reminding myself I should be grateful. We spent two days alone in Norway before going again with Dirk to Holland where we spent two weeks with him and his wife.

My ideals of love began slowly to fade. Union is not something that happens easily. It is a commitment made between two people to reach the stars, stay in that consciousness and to know fully, something ultimate. Love has many forms and levels. I wanted to experience the ultimate within physicality and did not believe it was impossible. Philip did not know what union was, and I could not blame him, because he had no idea what it meant to touch the light, and be burned by it. Sadly, what I knew to be the true essence of marriage was beyond us both.

When we returned from our honeymoon, I became fully involved in my teaching job, studying and preparing meals for my new husband, but something vital was missing. We hardly communicated with each other and if we did it was usually to argue about something. We mostly went out with Philip's friends and never mine because Philip did not like any of them. I struggled with the language, almost falling asleep at a number of outings, because I was so bored. We got a cat and I knew something was terribly wrong with my marriage, when I began to feel jealous of Tinkerbell, who seemed to bring out more tenderness in Philip than I could. I tried to persuade Philip to come with me to a marriage guidance counselor, but his logic and my need for psychological support could not match. Philip had grown distant, and a part of me remained an observer, wondering why love was such a difficult emotion to hold and keep. Was I totally in denial or had I become so enveloped in the shadow of my path that I had to suffer in order to break free?

I fell pregnant only to miscarry and soon fell pregnant again! This time, the pregnancy was ectopic and I recalled what had happened to Jackie. Luckily we caught it in time; however, I was devastated. Women become extremely vulnerable when they fall pregnant and even more so when they miscarry. However, it is not always easy for men to give them support and Philip was unable to move beyond our separateness in order to carry me across the bridge. Building his career he was busy and unable to take me to hospital. I went alone and when I came out of the anaesthetic and went home, it was with the help of a taxi driver that I walked up the stairs to our apartment. Over the next few months I drifted in and out of deep depression, wanting to ask over and over again where basic kindness and support had gone; in despair, for the inner knowing that I could not find and hold onto what I so desperately knew to exist. My leg began to swell, as I stifled emotions that threatened to erupt. I was placed in hospital for observation and heard the same story – it was all in my mind.

The psyche plays a very important role in health! Life was not flowing within me and therefore it was not surprising I kept on getting a deep vein thrombosis. However, my hormones were also out of balance, surging forth, dipping and soaring. Sadly, no one doctor tried to delve deeper into my psychosomatic problems and, in true Asclepian fashion, attempt to heal body, mind and spirit. Instead, I was made to feel as though it was my fault and that I was responsible for it all; I had created the disharmony in my body and was not yet fully conscious of my role as creator of my own despair – however no one attempted to bridge this gap.

It seemed as though we were hanging by some unseen thread that wafted us in and out of our drama. We had been married for less than a year when the phone suddenly rang, jolting us out of our misery and into another, which was much harder to bear. Philip and I had gone for the weekend to Epidavros to visit Vaia and Dimitris. It was October and we had been out, drinking ouzo under a setting sun and nibbling at local delicacies. I struggled to contain these happier moments rather than dwell on the widening gap between us. When we got home, and the phone rang, I was sitting in the dining room talking to Dimitris. When Philip answered the phone, I realized he was talking to Mother, who was weeping when he handed the phone to me. She told me what had happened.

When Jackie had been operated on at the age of eighteen, a malignant tumor had been removed from her right ovary! The doctor who operated had assured Mother all traces of cancer had been removed, and there was no need for Jackie to ever know cancer had touched her. The following year, when Jackie's fallopian tube on the left side had burst, Mother had been terrified, but had followed the doctor's advice and not spoken to Jackie. Jackie had been trying to fall pregnant, but it was impossible, so she had had a number of operations to try and remedy the situation to no avail. That summer, Jackie began to have pains and when she went to the doctor, he told her she had a cyst on her left ovary. Furthermore, he assured her it might disappear. Jackie called Mother, told her the news and simultaneously said that she wanted to meet her biological father, which seemed to be more important. Mother was devastated and also angered. She blamed Carl for persuading Jackie to meet her biological father, who was a wealthy film producer.

Money, as ever, had always hidden behind the scenes; it had crept up and destroyed so many hopes and it was yet again to rear its head up. Jackie and Carl had gone to England immediately to meet with David in London, who was overjoyed to see the daughter he had not seen growing up. He had taken Jackie out shopping, proud of her, and lavished presents on her, to make up for the many years he had not been there to support her.

They had no doubt discussed a lot and when Jackie returned to Cape Town, she went to the doctor. The cyst growing on her ovary had reached the size of a melon. She was operated on, given a hysterectomy and no treatment. Mother asked me to promise not to tell Jackie I knew about the cancer, but she wanted us to come that Christmas, because she was worried it might be the last we would all have together.

I was shocked, upset and angered at life. I was sad and this sadness went into the depths of my being. I promised Mother we would come home for Christmas and that I would not tell Jackie what I knew about her health.

That Christmas, Philip and I flew to Johannesburg. I felt as though I had been flung onto a rocky platform. No matter how hard I was trying to keep my balance, I seemed to be drifting through an almost make-believe world, where I could not speak out and where I began to almost disbelieve what I had been told! That Christmas, I worried about my weight whilst my sister worried about death! Jackie was limping heavily and she had an open wound on her face. However, she assured me it was because she had hurt her ankle, and had an allergic reaction to a new foundation she was using. Unable to connect to reality, I was nervous and tried not to look at her and even less at her husband. We were going out for New Year's Eve, and I was standing in front of the mirror complaining about my green dress that bulged at the sides.

"Oh for God's sake," Jackie said abruptly, "there are far more important things in life than putting on weight!"

My sister's words still ring in my ears! I wish I had had the courage to drop the defense, to turn around, hug Jackie and talk about the cancer. I would have opened up a dialogue between Jackie and Mother. A greater dialogue would have been opened up between us all, and a family would have come together; however I chose to remain silent. This was the first time I clearly understood free will; and yet, stunned and shocked by the news, afraid and yet grateful Mother had confided in me, confused and torn between wanting to speak having given my word, I remained silent. Ultimately, it took a long time to realize it had been Jackie's decision – one Mother had thought, rightly so, necessary to share with me, but one I was bound to respect. I had been protected by Mother, prepared by her to accept the unacceptable, and yet I could not see the truth then.

On the 10th of January, I kissed my sister goodbye and left with Philip to return to our new home, unable to reconcile myself with my heart. I never reconciled myself with my spirit-soul either. Instead, I harbored feelings of regret, waiting and watching how life in its attempt to free those who have been caught in its net, trapped them even further. It was at the end of January, while Paul had a court case pending, when Jackie called Mother to tell her she had lung cancer and was going to begin chemotherapy. Mother was devastated and decided to fly to Cape Town to be with Jackie. She did not ask Father to take her, neither did she take the decision to fly alone; rather she asked Paul to take her, who told her he had to go to court and could not leave immediately.

A week later, as the snow blanketed Athens and schools were closed, Philip and I made a snowman outside. When we had finished, we admired our work and went inside.

That morning at six-thirty, I had sat up in bed suddenly, and hit Philip three times on his chest. He had woken up in shock, to realize I was still asleep. As we were busy taking off our gloves and scarves, the phone rang.

"You get it," Philip said, going into the bathroom.

I carried on taking my jacket off.

"No, you get it!" I called out.

The phone carried on ringing and in exasperation, when Philip did not appear, I picked it up. It was the airline company calling to inform me we had two tickets for Johannesburg the following day, because my beloved sister had died at 6.30 in the morning! I immediately called home, to be informed by Grandmother Maria everyone had left for Cape Town. There was no reply from Jackie's house and Philip suggested he take me to his mother, whilst he went to the office to make arrangements.

Vaia had come to Athens for the weekend, and when we rang the bell and went in to the house, she was coming out of the kitchen, drying her hands on a tea towel. Philip told her quietly why we were there. Vaia turned to me and said nonchalantly, "What can we do? That's life!"

In the same breath, she turned to her son. "Surely you aren't going back there?"

Philip's teeth clenched as he replied, "It's her sister!"

From far off, I saw the sunlight dancing on the marble step. What was I doing in this house? Why had I married into a family where everyone was so cold? What was this inability to connect? I turned around and said in a dull voice, "I will be going home now! I do not want to stay here."

I closed my ears to Philip's reply and walked outside. My boots crunched on the snow and I got into the car. On the way home, I remained silent and it was only when I was back in our flat, alone and shaking that I called on a colleague, Wendy, who immediately came over and helped me pack. The following morning, we set off for South Africa. My heart had frozen and yet nothing could prepare me for what awaited me in Johannesburg.

Jackie's body had already been flown to lay in St Francis church. Mother was devastated and clung to me when I arrived and a few minutes later, unable to control the feelings of guilt that threatened to explode, she was shouting at Paul.

"It is your fault I never saw her before she died; you and your stupid court case!"

Paul escaped into the bathroom and I stared at her. Mother had once been to see a medium who had told her she was a victim – a paraplegic in a wheel chair, surrounded by persecutors. She had wanted to run away from her failed marriage and the man who lacked class and was stupid, as she often told him, and yet she was trapped, like a fish caught in a net. The victim role had subtly shifted into one of persecutor and as the clock chimed on the wall, I easily shifted into the role Mother had chosen. I secretly judged her actions, wondering whether Jackie would still be alive if Mother had told her the truth about what had happened when she was eighteen. Judgment clouded my ability to feel and connect. Paul swallowed his anguish, arranged for the funeral and bought a double grave to bury our sister in. Walls began to close in and I turned to the only strength I knew – Father O'Connor. Sean came over and tried to give comfort. He spoke to Mother and Father, feeling awkward and yet dutiful at the same time. When he left I felt the cold beginning to seep in and the following day, as I stepped into the room adjoining the church, where the coffin lay, I stared at the body – the body of my sister Jackie. My hand shook as I placed a small, rag doll Grandmother had crocheted for Jackie and her prefect badge, into the coffin. My hand hovered and I touched her forehead briefly, only to turn sobbing into Philip's shoulder, repeating over and over again:

"This is not my sister!"

I knew there was an empty body lying in the coffin! I could not relate to what my sister looked like. What was the use of the body, when the soul had flown? I needed to touch the soul! That afternoon as people came and left, drinking coffee, brandy and eating silently, Jackie's sister-in-law asked why her biological father had not come for the funeral. Mother snapped back he had no business being there and when everyone left, including Carl, she went to bed, her shoulders drooping. The next morning when she awoke she told us Jackie had visited her in a dream during the night and told her she herself would die in two years! I was wracked with questions. Why had the doctor been so flippant when Jackie was eighteen? Why had he been so determined Jackie not be told about her cancer? What could have been done differently and how could life have been preserved? I listened to Mother, trying to understand what was happening. In my opinion, Mother felt guilty, and the only way she could cope with this guilt was by telling us she could no longer carry on living. I was so taken up by my judgments, I blocked all my emotions. Over the next few weeks, when Philip returned to Athens and I remained to support my parents and brother, a different Self emerged, unkind and full of reproach. A double marble stone had been erected over Jackie's grave and we all went to visit the grave daily. I could not watch Mother caress a cold stone and weep because I wondered who would be laid to rest beside Jackie, and therefore chose not to stand at the grave but rather under a tree a little way back, full of resentment. This was how I behaved because deep inside of me, I was petrified. Who would be next and why had Paul bought a double grave? I could not understand why Paul would buy a double grave and neither did he attempt to explain. It was all too much, as I knew my grandmother could not be buried there. It sent chills down my spine!

Mother felt I was betraying Jackie by not being present at the grave. It was impossible to share with anyone how I could not pay homage to the physical. I felt Jackie's presence in my heart. I preferred to stand looking on from a distance, recalling her as I had known her.

The following week, Paul and I flew to Cape Town to collect my sister's belongings. Carl sat in a chair weeping. He had lost the only woman he had ever loved, I presumed. In his despair, he went through her things, choosing the best and most expensive for his sister. When he refused to give me any of Jackie's jewelry, I had had enough. I got up and told Paul I was leaving, and when I watched my brother insist on taking an antique heirloom that had belonged to Maria, and Carl arguing over it, I felt despair in my heart that I had felt so many times. I found myself staring into the faces of men, women and children who had appeared to me, when I had nearly lost my life. Was this world so shallow, that its essence was weighed in gold? Was there such a thing as love that existed in the hearts of men and women who decreed life was worth only the gold and diamonds one could hold onto, for lack of anything deeper?

I felt sad and angry – two emotions that made me give up the fight and walk away, wondering who would wear my sister's charm bracelet and her rings. I despaired at the masks worn, and the harsh words that came and went with the breeze. I returned to Athens, plummeting into an even deeper despair and sense of loss, wondering if my sister would have still been alive had Mother only told her about the cancer when Jackie had tried to fall pregnant or when she had discovered the second cyst. I longed for my husband to take me in his arms, to heal my heart and hold my soul, revering my inner pain and anguish, but he could not. I began to flounder and wonder what the true meaning of life was, and how I could touch it. I tried desperately to live!

One afternoon, Philip called me to tell me his sister Athena was moving to Epidavros and that she was going to let her apartment.

"I think it is perfect for us," he said gaily. "We will not have to pay a high rent and then we can start building our own apartment over Katerina's."

I told him I didn't want to move back to the family property and that I wanted us to build somewhere else, but he thought I was being selfish. We moved in a few weeks later and my hopes of a bright future began slowly to wane. After a particularly violent argument, five months later, with nothing more than disaster in my heart, I called Paul once again and asked him to arrange for my flight home.

I flew to Johannesburg and found a job in a personnel agency; I went out with old friends determined not to give in to my husband's pleas for me to return. I needed to break free and find my place back in a culture I belonged to – to give up the attempt to fit into a society that may have had rich roots, but to my mind were further away than I could ever imagine!

One evening, as I fell asleep in my old bedroom, I found myself walking along the sea shore on an island in the Aegean.

The sun is setting and an old fisherman pulls up his nets. I stop to look at his catch, only to see that all he has caught is a dead fish entangled in the net. I look at the fish and know it is me!

I was entangled in the web of destiny, and when I awoke to find Mother standing next to my bed with the phone in her hand, I did not need to be persuaded. I told Philip I would return to Athens. The symbolic fish represented my lost spirituality and the sacrifice entailed surrender!

CHAPTER EIGHT

Death brings us life, in all its intricacies. We attempt to make amends and sometimes, after Death, we experience birth; birth of Hope and birth of a new tomorrow. When we choose birth, we especially need to take responsibility for the life to come.

Birth

On the flight that took me to Athens, I looked out of the tiny window at the sky. If I closed my eyes, I could see the fisherman and his nets as clearly as I could the sky. Was there such a thing as destiny?

Philip was waiting at the airport for me with a bunch of flowers. He gathered me into his arms, kissed me and told me I looked nice! I had deliberately chosen my outfit to make a statement of independence! From my thick, beige tights, green suede hot pant suit to the beige headband, I looked as though I was on a photo shoot. Philip preferred me to be conservative, but had promised to make an effort; he apologized for his harsh behavior and was sincere. That night we made passionate love and the following day set off for our only holiday away alone. We drove up to Meteora and the tiny monasteries, peaked and glistening like jewels in the crisp morning, inspired us. We ate at tiny taverns, huddled in a corner, spending quieter moments holding hands and kissing. At the end of the week, I felt reluctant to go home and also very uncomfortable. I had a niggling pain in my side and tried not to pay attention to it. When I started spotting, I immediately went to see my gynecologist.

Spiro examined me and told me I may have fallen pregnant, but that it was too early to say. I could not believe I had fallen pregnant on the day I arrived in Athens, so a week later I went to have a blood test. I was ecstatic when it came out positive, but equally worried I might again have an ectopic pregnancy. Spiro told me it was definitely not, but ordered bed rest. I had resigned from my teaching job when I had left Philip and as I lay in bed, my thoughts turned to the events that had led to my leaving him.

It had been at the time of the elections and Philip had been assigned to travel to Crete as a legal representative. He was excited and came home to find me lying on our bed reading. I had packed our suitcases and was waiting for him. When Philip walked into the kitchen, which was spotless, he asked me why I had not cooked and I immediately jumped up because I had completely forgotten about food. We began to argue and Philip became physical because I was slamming cupboard doors, as I began to prepare lunch. I refused to go with him then, and called Paul, who came to my rescue as always.

When I had settled, I had arranged for shipping agents to pack everything and ship my furniture and belongings back to South Africa. Philip had stalled them, knowing that once the furniture was packed up, there would be no going back.

I thought about my dream and the dead fish, and how it had completely affected my decision to return. I lay my hand on my stomach and prayed the tiny baby within me would be fine, and that I would not miscarry.

Philip went to work every day leaving me food beside the bed, and I lay reading and watching television. Three months went by and I went to see Spiro who told me I could finally get up. When we left the doctor, Philip and I went home. As I still had to be careful, I made toast, kissed my husband goodbye and went to lie down. I called a friend of mine and as we sat chatting, I felt the rush of something warm run down my leg, and started crying. Wendy arrived in less than ten minutes and called Spiro. My waters had broken and half of the placenta had detached from the wall! I was rushed to hospital where Spiro told me there was no chance of me having this child.

I sat in bed refusing to let go of the life within me, and that evening the sac filled again with liquid. Spiro called it a miracle and I spent three weeks in hospital until I was finally discharged. Back home, as I was on strict bed rest and only allowed up once a week to have a shower, it was imperative someone look after me. Mother told me to find a maid and that they would pay for her. I found a tall

African girl called Princess. She sat with me, whenever the chores
were finished, telling me about her home. She had grown up in
Botswana and then moved to Nelspruit in South Africa. She told me
about the terrible conditions there and how Nelson Mandela, who
had fought for their rights, had been imprisoned. She told me about
Steve Biko and police brutality and how she had been lucky to get a
job with a Greek family who had brought her to Athens. She had
worked for them for five years and when they told her they had no
need for her any longer, they had taken her to the airport, ready to
send her home. She had hidden in the toilet after they left and then
decided to live illegally in Athens, rather than go back home. I heard
about an Africa I had never really touched, and this saddened me.

I felt sorry for her and when she sat talking about the farm in
Nelspruit where she had lived in a hut, painted with colorful designs,
I closed my eyes and allowed her descriptions to make pictures in my
mind's eye. They took me back into the sands of Africa and the
'Tokolosh' Rose had often spoken about; they took me to America,
where I saw the Amerindians, and into Africa where regal, tall
warriors fought for freedom. I began reading as much as I could about
these lands, which only strengthened my belief that humanity was
cruel. It was painful to think about the Spanish who had murdered and
pillaged the Aztecs; painful to think about the British, who had boldly
ruled the lives of so many Indians and this is how I began to identify
with people like Nelson Mandela and Mahatma Ghandi.

The fact that Philip was always at work until the early hours of
the morning during this entire time no longer hurt me. A part of me
was dying and another was coming to life. I was filled with the joys
of motherhood and nurtured this closeness I felt. I learnt as much as
I could and dared not think about my sister or my marriage.

Although Philip tried to be there for me, the gap was ever widening, as he became fully involved in his career. I had pleaded with him
on more than one occasion to spend more time with me, oblivious of
his need to build his life and the money needed for our future. There
was no future, for I lived in the past and although money had always
been an issue when I was growing up, it had no particular importance
to me. I often reminded Philip I could be happy in a single room,

only to feel surrounded by love, but could still not feel this love I longed for. Although my love for my baby was everything to me, I believed the gift of life growing within me was a gift to Philip, so tried to include him in the many plans I had for a natural birth. I studied the Lamaze Method and whilst talking to him about the birth I thought I was creating a bond between us. When I entered my eighth month and was finally allowed to get up, Princess left us. Alone again, I began to take long walks and then Anne came to visit.

It was lovely seeing Anne again. We went back into the memories of our life at school and I hankered after the girl who had fallen so completely in love with Sean. Sean had finally left the priesthood and moved back to Ireland. We still wrote to each other, letters that were nostalgic and held a certain amount of pain on my side. I had written to him about the Thornbirds which I had read three times, but he replied he thought the women a trifle unreal. When Anne left, I was sad, but there was not much time to dwell on the past, because Vaia arrived to take care of me.

I had never liked my mother-in-law because she had never made me feel welcome. However, as we went for long walks, I warmed to her and she proudly made plans for her grandson. I had known from the moment I found out I was pregnant, I would have a son. When Spiro finally confirmed it, I was not surprised. I knew I had a very special bond with my son.

Vaia left to go back to Epidavros and I prepared my son's room. My parents had once again come to my rescue, by sending all the furniture and baby clothes, which arrived in a container. Mother and Father had finally put the past behind them and grown to love and support each other. They often came to their home in Epidavros and had stayed with me for a week just before Anne had arrived. I realized during that week, Mother was almost helpless without Father. She had become completely dependent on him to support and help her. She had not forgotten her dream and every now and then would talk about her impending death. I told her she would create it herself and she would sigh heavily and turn to Father.

As I washed and ironed tiny garments and admired the beautiful furniture she had bought, I was torn between the love I felt for Mother and the apparent dislike I had for her personal being. There was an unseen bond that held us together and this was part of the world I knew; I was also, though, conscious I could not seem to reach her.

I was sitting on the beautiful wooden rocking chair I had placed near the window of my son's bedroom, when I felt the contractions come. It was a week before I was due and I quickly began timing them. I tried calling Philip, but he was in court so I called Wendy, who arrived soon after. She called for an ambulance and together we went to the Mitera Hospital on the outskirts of Halandri. She hugged me as I was wheeled into the delivery room and promised to visit the following day. Spiro left a message for Philip and I waited for my husband to come from work. What seemed hours later he arrived, dressed in scrubs, with a newspaper in hand. He sat beside me, told me he had informed everyone and opened his newspaper. As I struggled to recall my breathing exercises, I felt a constricting inner pain that told me I had lost the battle with my husband. I was upset and my body began to tense up. Spiro finally broke my waters but he told me that, due to the complications I had been through, and the fact the baby was not coming down, I would have to have a caesarian section. I was devastated but knew my son's life was of paramount importance. I closed my eyes as I was wheeled into the operating theatre, feeling a sense of failure. When I came to, I looked at my beautiful baby. The tears came as I watched the nurse bathe him. I wondered whether Philip would have been able to overcome his apparent fear of his feminine side had he been able to witness the birth of his son and bathe him? I cried as I looked down at my son's fine features. I held him gently to my breast and vowed he would be a happy and healthy child.

I recovered quickly and enjoyed every moment I had with my newborn son. Vaia and Dimitris brought flowers and went out to celebrate with my parents. When we finally left the hospital and went home, I was ecstatic. I had read everything I could about newborn babies. I had studied Child Development at university so did not share Vaia's apparent worry that I did not have enough breast milk. Mother fully supported her concerns. They told me I was being selfish because I kept on insisting I had enough milk. Mother pointed out it was quite ridiculous and when she came with bottles and formula, I felt defeat wash over me. When Philip began to come in late at night and wake his son, so he could play with him, I began to feel I was losing a battle I had not even realized I was fighting.

Days became months and although I bonded with my son, trying to hold onto him as hard as I could, I found him drifting away from me. I read him stories and held him close to me but could not help feeling we were drifting apart, because I seemed to have little control over his life.

So when we christened Dimitris, to carry my father-in-law's name, I was ready to have another child – another child who would save my marriage and bring Philip back to me. I carefully began taking my temperature every morning and waking Philip whenever I was fertile. The fact I was trying desperately to fill a growing void in my heart did not enter my mind. When I fell pregnant almost immediately, I was determined not to have complications. I told my two-year-old son he would soon have a brother and that we would become a happy family!

I had gone back to teaching at a British school, pleased they had a crèche where Dimitris was happy playing with other babies. My decision to go back to work was because I was desperate to earn my own money. Many of the arguments I had with Philip were money-oriented. He felt I squandered money on buying imported products and not local products. I thought it ridiculous because things like ketchup and mustard could not be compared. I resented the fact he always criticized me every time we went shopping, and it became vital I become independent.

I was busy preparing for a parent-teacher meeting when I started having pains. I could not believe I was three months pregnant and again being threatened with miscarriage. I went home, hugging Dimitris to me and put him to bed. I called Spiro and told him I was spotting.

"I'm sorry my dear," he said as gently as he could. "I know you wanted this pregnancy to go by without complications, but you are going to have to go to bed and I will come and see you tomorrow."

I began to panic. Philip was still at work and I did not know what I was going to do with Dimitris. I called Zoe, who immediately arranged for a young Greek girl to come the following morning but I knew it was not a solution. Fotini could only stay until five thirty and Philip was never home before ten.

That evening when Philip came home, he found me in bed. I told him what had happened and he suggested asking Vaia to come for a while. I froze, unable to face the idea my mother-in-law would take over so the following morning, after Philip left, I called Paul. I was crying and begged him to help me.

Paul told me he would do his best to find someone to take care of me and I waited for Spiro to arrive. Spiro examined me and then told me he would send a nurse daily to give me injections in my stomach. It was imperative I stay in bed, but when Fotini left that afternoon I had to get up. I began praying nothing terrible would happen, as I bathed Dimitris and put him to bed. I lay down and began sobbing. The phone rang and I picked it up, to find Mother on the other end.

"Darling, don't worry about anything," she said gaily. "Your brother has found a wonderful nurse called Agnes. We are just getting her papers in order. By the end of the week she will be with you."

I began crying even more when I put the phone down. Guilt wracked at me as I thought about the previous Christmas when we had all gone down to Durban. We had had a wonderful holiday. Philip and I had taken Dimitris down to the beach every day and we had gone out on New Year's Eve to a wonderful Brazilian restaurant. We had danced until the early hours of the morning and then watched the sunrise. I had fallen into the bliss that comes from rare moments when happiness stretches out and blankets the world with a rosy hue. Philip had returned to Athens and I had flown home with my parents and Paul, because Mother had found a lump in her breast.

I was convinced Mother had made herself ill to reassure herself Jackie had forgiven her for her silence. I had tried to be a loving daughter when Mother had her breast removed, but I had often escaped from her bedside to play with Dimitris or lie in the sun. I was conscious Mother had needed to be the center of attention and I had denied her. I knew she would use the fact she had cancer to make me not bring up her past, as I so often did, and I resented it. I had asked her so many times to tell me the truth about her past and who Paul's father had been, and about Jackie's father, but she had remained silent, only telling me bits and pieces that never made sense. I felt she had locked me out, so I would do the same to her. It did not help either, that she doted on Philip, and always supported him even though she knew about our arguments.

I had felt frustration boiling up inside of me and then guilt. However, I had not made the effort needed to make Mother feel loved and as I realized she had always supported me financially, I began to feel even worse. This guilt almost choked me as I thought about Agnes, who arrived at the end of the week and brought blessings to my home.

She took on the perfect role of a housekeeper and teacher to Dimitris. She rocked him, played with him and told him stories about Africa. She miraculously cleansed the energy around our home and even Philip became more tender and loving towards me. I spent five months in bed having injections daily and began to feel a weight had been lifted.

When I was finally able to get up, I felt refreshed and renewed. Agnes was sad to leave but told me that if I needed her after the birth, she would fly back. I looked forward to the summer and when Spiro told me he wanted me to stay in Athens, I felt relieved. Philip however, was not happy.

"I find it ridiculous we cannot go to Epidavros; it is only two hours away! There is nothing wrong with you and Dirk will be coming this summer to Hydra. He has invited us to go there for a week. It's only three hours away by boat and I want to go!"

"Well go then," I replied dully.

"No, I am not going alone! You are coming with me and so is Dimitris. Don't worry so much about your health. We will have a wonderful time!"

I thought about Dirk's daughters who all had beautiful figures and the way they loved draping themselves over my husband. I tried not to look at my body, still carrying the weight from my first pregnancy. We left for Hydra and I had to admit I was feeling good. It was a Saturday, and Dirk and Philip went fishing. I stayed with his wife Pearl and we chatted about how unhappy we both were in our marriages. When they returned they had a big basket of fish that was, of course, my duty to clean. I stood over the sink. The smell made me feel sick and after a while I was tired of swatting wild bees drawn to the stench of rotting entrails. My leg began to hurt and it slowly swelled.

I could not believe I had got another thrombosis. We traveled back to Athens the following morning and I called Spiro. Spiro was livid when I told him what I had been doing. He confronted Philip angrily as he admitted me into hospital. Philip looked at him disdainfully and went to work. Philip came twice in two weeks to visit me. He told me he was busy and that Dimitris was with Vaia and his father. He added that I was in good hands, and could not expect him to come and visit me, when he had to earn money to pay for hospital bills. It was clear he was angry, so I stayed alone in hospital and could not believe it, when he came to take me home, that he complained I had been using the phone so much. The bill was not that high as I had only made local calls, but I looked at my husband and wished I was a man and not a woman, so I could have stood up to him.

I started having contractions eighteen days later, and because it was one month early, I sobbed as I tried to find Philip. Philip as usual was unavailable, so I walked down to the main road, clutching my stomach. I waited in the midday heat until a taxi stopped with a gentle man in it. I asked him where he was going and the gentle man said it did not matter – it was obvious I was giving birth and so they took me to hospital. I was given a drip, in the hope I would not give birth, but three hours later I had another caesarean.

When I looked down at my son's tiny body in the incubator, with tubes in his head, deep in my subconscious I recalled Rita, the girl who had mirrored a part of my soul at Woodside Sanctuary. My connection to him was very deep. We decided to call him Andrew after my great grandfather and this tiny baby became my savior. I breast-fed him for nine months and felt completely enthralled with his beautiful smile and his tiny clutching hands. I buried myself in love that began to stream from my heart and although my husband paid little attention to me, it hurt me but did not destroy me.

What was tragic was another thrombosis that sent me to hospital for a month and wrenched my son from my breast, when he was nine months old. I found myself drifting in and out of the darkness that I knew was deep despair, and it no longer mattered that my husband came to see me only once, during that month. I was used to it by then.

I believe firmly we can play a leading role in caring for other's well-being. However, I had chosen a man who was financially well-grounded and yet unable to provide any emotional support whatsoever. Beyond this barren landscape, I recalled the many curses that had left their mark and often thought about the famous saying 'the sins of the fathers are borne by the children.' I made a vow I would find a way to make sure my sons did not carry the weight I believed I carried. Perhaps this was wrong, to try to carry a load that could possibly heal them as it would me, but at the time I knew deep down inside of my soul that my vision of men, women and children filled with suffering could also have been the generations of blood line that were doomed, and that something had to free their souls. I was ready to carry this burden.

Mother, in her many tales of the past, had once told me that Grandmother's ancestors, who came from a prominent aristocratic family tree, had included two brothers, one of whom was to take the throne. He was murdered by his brother, who then drank his blood to seal the transfer of power. Whether or not this was a dark figment of Mother and Grandmother's imagination, I will never know. What I did know was that darkness, created in mind, was manifesting through desire. I began to wonder whether the shadow of darkness in our family was so dark and large that I was an easy prey to the ill-wishes of others, or whether this was the ultimate work of karma weaving its web.

My husband was, as far as I was concerned, covered with a thick, invisible veil. Although he claimed to love me, he was unable to see he was trapped in the darkness and had seemingly lost his soul. Unable to carry on hurting and being hurt, I knew it was only a matter of time before we parted. He perceived something that was reflected back to him, but was unable to reach out across the growing rift between us, to hold my hand and comfort us both. He could not see the soul that had always taken precedence in my life, or that I was slowly wilting in our world. He was totally oblivious to the fact we mirrored each other often, and that he needed to work on those reflections.

Although our marriage was difficult and I often blamed him, I tried to understand him. When this was almost impossible, I left him, to walk on down my path, carrying with me the guilt of breaking up my family, close to heart. That I was guilty, I knew. Lacking strength to stand alone, I broke my vows with him by having two brief affairs during our marriage that gave me breath and yet robbed me of my beliefs. I once tried to explain my actions to him as those of a starving man who steals a loaf of bread, because he is so hungry. It was a feeble excuse and yet it was born through the gaping hole I had in my chest and the need to dream.

However, at the time and under the circumstances, my perception was that I needed proof of my worth as a woman and that I deserved to be loved. My affairs may have been wrapped up in the glow of desire but they were not real love. They were simply physical needs for some kind of caring and were obviously totally self-destructive in that they brought so much guilt. Moreover, I saw myself ready to grab at anyone who came along to satiate my hunger and thirst, thinking it would heal a very deep wound inside of me. Of course, this was an illusion, but I had already a fixed idea in my mind that, as I did not feel whole, someone else could make me whole. In some way though, they seemed to also be part of my path; as though they came when I needed them the most, because I was in so much inner turmoil.

There was a doctor who was doing his residency in Epidavros. He was a close friend of my father-in-law, and when I opened the door to him in my mother-in-law's house, I was very depressed. Since Andrew's birth, I had tried unsuccessfully to get close to my husband. I was devastated by my sojourn in hospital, shocked when I was told by a family friend of my mother-in-law's curse at my wedding – that I never have children – and pressurized by Philip's desire to open a travel agency in Epidavros. That summer, I rented out apartments that hardly reached the standard of my descriptions. My sons were with my parents the afternoon the doctor was invited for lunch. I was at least ten kilos overweight and dressed in a salmon drawstring dress that made me look even fatter. Opening the door, I stared up into two beautiful eyes that seemed to pierce my soul for a fraction of a second. It did not help that this tall, handsome doctor held onto my hand for a fraction longer than he ought to, as I introduced myself. When, towards the end of lunch, I asked Philip if we could go swimming together, I had no idea where my question would lead. He politely refused, saying he wanted to have a siesta and the doctor's voice rang out across the table.

"I'll come with you."

My observing self took in the startled looks that went around the table, but I was fed up. I wanted to go swimming and wanted company, so I got up from the table and said gaily.

"Great, I will get my things."

That afternoon, I sat on the beach oblivious of time and spoke about my life. We shared details of our personal being and even though he was also married, it was as if we had stepped over and into a garden that had nothing whatsoever to do with our lives. When I got home, I quickly showered and pretended nothing at all had happened out of the ordinary and went to work at the agency. When we met again, two days later, it was inevitable we both drop our wedding rings in the glass of wine we were sharing, in my mother-in-law's dining room. My in-laws had gone to Athens with Philip, and I had done the unforgivable; I had invited the doctor for dinner, even though my sister in-law lived in the downstairs apartment. The following evening I dodged the shadows of night to meet with him and realized how painful tenderness can truly be. I wrote a poem about it and left my poetry book beside the bed.

The following day, there was a glow about me as I sat in the office. I was gazing dreamily out of the window, when a friend of mine, Trish, came in. She had just arrived for her summer vacations and took one look at me and smiled.

"Are you having an affair?" she asked me, her eyes twinkling, "because you are glowing!"

My hands fluttered as I stared at her. Was it so obvious and if it was, would other people notice? When Philip returned three days later he found my poetry book beside the bed. He hadn't noticed the glow but he knew something had happened when he read my poem about the cruel world of reality, and forbidden love. That night, he suggested we go out for a meal alone and when he asked me if I had been unfaithful to him, I told him I had. The fact I could not lie cost us all. Philip jumped up and almost dragged me home. He immediately told his parents and his father called the doctor's wife, who was in Cyprus at the time. My mother-in-law delighted at the fact she could now look fully into my eyes, and call me a whore!

At the time I never realized how similar Mother's and my life had become. Entwined in the shadow of darkness, someone had spat at my mother calling her a whore, and Vaia had done the same thing! I became the mother of Philip's children and no longer his wife and this was how he introduced me to his friends from then on. I had never felt I was a wife but that did not seem to matter. The glass had cracked and it would break completely.

Although I tried to talk to Philip on countless occasions, it was impossible. The doctor was never mentioned again as we struggled to get on with our lives and when we returned to Athens, my heart was heavy. It was so heavy I visually buried it under a tree on the little beach where I had first made love with my Greek god when I was seventeen. Perhaps it was this that drove me months later to confide in yet another doctor, who I met at a children's party, about my problems. He told me I had to take a decision to leave my husband if I did not want to become an alcoholic, a drug addict or go mad. The fact I had never taken drugs and did not like alcohol did not matter. Somewhere in my heart, I knew he was right!

Perhaps it was my loneliness, and his desire to reach out, that brought us together as it did, one afternoon when he was on duty at the military hospital he worked at. A week later, the darkness reared its head up as I sat with my dear friend Susan, telling her about my affair with him.

Susan, who was British and married to a Greek man, had two children called Nicholas and Caroline. They often played with my sons, even though they were older. The children were in the garden playing as I told her how unhappy I was. As the afternoon wore on,

I repeatedly checked on the children who were having fun. Suddenly, though, Susan and I sensed a dark presence in the house. Susan did not particularly believe in the paranormal, but there was a stench that seemed to emanate from the wall in the kitchen. We got up to investigate and both began to feel ill, unable to work out why there was such a bad smell in the kitchen.

Trying to logically work out what smelt so bad, we were both stunned by an awful wail that suddenly came from the garden. Rushing outside, I found Andrew standing with his forehead gaping open and blood spurting out of it. Susan ran gathering the children and I held my son, putting pressure on the wound. I was in such a state I went to hospital barefoot and three hours later, twelve stitches in place, Susan left with her children and Dimitris. I called Philip who was in Epidavros and begged him to come to Athens. His reply was short and curt. He was sure I could manage. Desperate, I called the doctor, who immediately came over. He stayed with me that evening as I sat beside my son, who was only two and a half. A week later, he called me to arrange to remove the stitches and Philip, who had tapped our telephone, wondering at my newfound strength, was listening in to the conversation from the downstairs apartment and heard him speak tenderly to me.

I realized my marriage was over and that I needed to move on. This was not an easy decision due to the fact I had two very young children, however; I was trapped by circumstances, and wondered if I had the right to raise my children in a home where Dimitris often ran between us, begging us to stop arguing. We were breaking both his and his brother's spirit, and I prayed they would forgive me for leaving their father. A month later, with the strains of 'Blueberry Hill' playing in the background, I told Philip I wanted a divorce. There was no going back! Philip was not happy I wanted a divorce. He tried to be nice but we drifted through the ebb and flow of arguing and then trying to make up.

One evening, when I had put my children to bed and paced back and forth on the balcony like a caged tiger, I drank a bottle of gin and invited the neighbor in, when I saw her and her sister peering up at me from the street. Nancy and I had never officially met. We greeted each other daily and, once, we had shared bits of information when we had met at the bakery. She had been sitting with her sister on the balcony, watching me.

It was her sister who suggested they come over with a six-pack.

"That woman looks as though she is about to commit suicide!"

Nancy's sister had looked into my heart. There was no way I could carry on living with Philip. Our wedding had gone as had all memories of peace. I could not survive in these difficult circumstances, so I found an apartment and tried to set myself free from the constraints of the past. I slept with my children until I forced myself to let go of them. A big toy panda bear then became my companion until he was placed back in my sons' bedroom and I learnt to sleep alone. Friends supported me, lovers came and left. In the spaces that ravished my heart, I began to seriously look for my Self. I hated a part of myself and often recalled having sat under the apple tree in the garden of my dreams in Johannesburg, promising to love my husband and to never quarrel as I had watched my parents quarrel. The guilt was there, locked in my unconscious with all the archetypes I had stored in me, and perhaps this is what I needed desperately to become free of. My eldest son would open a door to my heart!

We were sitting in our new living room, playing. Dimitris, who was now five, suddenly stopped playing with his Lego, looked seriously at me and told me he was older than I was. I was shocked and asked him what he meant. He got up, placing his hands by his sides and said clearly.

"I don't know how to say, but I was wrapped up like this and put in a box."

My son was clearly describing the process of mummification.

I immediately recognized this was something rare and clearly a memory of an ancient past. Conscious I could not lose this moment, I quickly went over to the bookcase and took four books out, to lay them on the table we were sitting at. My son who seemed to find it perfectly natural, walked to the table, ran his small hand across the books and then picked up a book on Egypt, for there was only one. He randomly opened it to a page where there was a picture of the great pyramid and details of the pharaoh Khufu. Inspired by what I had read about the East and the way the young child Dalai Lama was chosen, it was all perfectly natural for me.

"That's who I was," my young son said seriously.

Aware I could not let this precious moment go, I asked him if he knew why he had been born.

"Of course," he replied softly. "It is to teach you all about love – you, daddy, granny, grandpa, *yaya* and *papou!*"

Yaya and *papou* were his Greek grandparents and when I asked him to tell me more, eager to explore his inner realm, he told me he was tired and curled up on the zebra skin clutching his toy panda. My son had unwittingly opened the door I had banged on as a child, almost the same age as he was.

Altered states of unconsciousness had always been the true meaning of life to me and I stared at my small son, who had given me back the reason for my birth as well. He brought a sudden light into my life as I realized both my children were mirrors of the most precious aspects of my own spirit. They were extensions of my soul, given to me through life but always belonging to their own selves and this was a profound truth that took time to settle into my heart and mind. They had given birth to my struggle for independence; they had given birth to my continued search for my real self, and they gave me untold courage, for I pledged to carry the karmic curse, that had hung over us all to its finality, that it might never touch them. Later that night I prayed to take the weight from their shoulders and once again asked if I might carry it for them. As I looked up at the night sky, I recalled an angel and knight. I gave thanks for the brilliant moment of consciousness that re-affirmed my conviction in spirit and soul. Death had brought with it birth, as it always does. Both belonged to the same. I was ready to move forward.

CHAPTER NINE

In the infinite space of life, we have two reasons for being. One of those reasons is to pro-create and to raise our children to believe in the just ways of the world. The other is to free ourselves of the memories that come to teach us we are unique in our purpose; not so much to dwell on the past but to integrate it into our present.

Light

My son had urged me to recall my past. With determination I began to meditate frequently and as my body slowly filled with light and I looked through the door I had struggled so hard to open, pictures came streaming out of a place where I found past, present and future wrapped up in my experiences. A door had not only opened for me through my son, but through my own release. I began to walk up Jacob's ladder and have experiences of altered states of consciousness.

My first jolt into this new mode of being came through past life. It began with a landscape that was definitely Ireland in around the seventeenth century. I saw a young man of the gentry, sitting at an old mahogany desk, writing late into the night by candlelight. He was in love with a young girl who worked in the local tavern and his mother was totally against his desire to be with her. I felt his pain of longing and the increasing release from this pain, as I realized his mother was known to me.

After the birth of my sons, I had left the British school and got a job as an English and Drama teacher at a Greek private school. I immediately bonded with the head of department, who had lived in Africa. Perhaps it was our similar background that brought us together, for both of us had commented on a flow of understanding between us that went beyond words. I liked her a lot and we became friends as well as colleagues. I never forgot she was my boss and felt proud of my ability to keep boundaries in place. I had met new colleagues at the school, some of whom shared my beliefs in the deeper mystery of being. I realized the mother of the young man reminded me completely of my boss, and that the young woman who worked at the tavern was one of my colleagues. This sudden realization placed me into the emotions of the young man so completely, I knew I was him. Feeling betrayed by a mother's dislike of the girl I wanted to marry shocked me, but at no time did I see the similarity with my own life. Rather, I remained fully conscious of the different time and space and did not want to lose this feeling. When the image faded, I recalled all the emotions and when I went to school the following day, I was very surprised when my colleague Dora asked me to take a walk with her.

Dora told me that the evening before she had gone through a Regression Therapy and that she had recalled a past life with me. I was ecstatic and yet cautious because I could sense emotions were still tied to what I had seen. I told her I understood exactly what she was saying but that it was important for us to write down our experiences in sealed envelopes to be opened by another friend, as what we had experienced seemed so real.

When we read each other's experiences it all fell into place, to such a degree it felt as though time had stopped. The emotions I had experienced changed as though the energy we both felt so strongly was releasing our pain spontaneously and simultaneously. I wondered though, about my boss. We were getting on so well it didn't seem to fit the picture of what I had seen and felt in my vision. Three months later I would understand it completely.

My boss's husband was working on a project abroad. I do not know what he thought about my friendship with his wife, because I had never wondered about it. On his returns we often went out for a meal or coffee with their young daughter who adored me. One day, I called to speak to my boss and her husband answered the phone. He told me she was not there and asked me what I was doing. I told him I was watching a film because the children had gone to their father. He asked me if I was alone and then told me he was coming over to watch the film with me. I took no notice and told him to ask his wife to call me. An hour later the downstairs bell rang and I pushed the buzzer to open the door. However, fear began to rise inside of me, and when I heard the lift arrive on the fourth floor, I looked through the peep hole. I saw my boss's husband step out of the lift. I began to shake and even more so when, after banging on the door for a while, he put a key in the lock that of course did not fit, telling me to open the door. I ran into my bedroom, covered my head and began sobbing.

As I heard the sound of the lift going back down, I carefully went to the balcony to see with shock, my boss, her husband and daughter walking towards the car. I screamed at the top of my lungs for them to come straight up and opened the door in a rage. I contained myself for the time it took me to settle their daughter in front of the TV with a snack and faced my boss and her husband. Their story brought me the deepest feelings of betrayal that could be imagined.

Obviously tired of hearing my name and suspicious of the happy change in his wife, this man had told his wife he was going to prove to her I was not the sweet friend she thought I was. He told her to walk up four flights of stairs and be witness to the fact I would open the door to him. Of course he had told his wife he had suggested coming over to 'keep me company' and she had agreed to his plan. I was drained. Our friendship was put to a great test and I was forced to deal with my feelings, accept what she had done and let go of the betrayal because she would remain my boss for another two years. The past had certainly been put to rest even though it would be very difficult to relate to what appeared to me as a double betrayal, but I began to see the pattern of experience that gave birth to freedom and light. In this sense I forgave her and years later she would come back into my life and I would treat her beautiful daughter. This pattern of transpersonal connections was the beginning of a very full experience of altered states, visions and dreams.

My next experience, not long after, was with a young man I met who initiated a flood of memories to do with India. We were having a dance at school and I had gone with a male friend whom I had met on the flight back to South Africa for Christmas. My parents regularly sent us tickets to go home every Christmas and on a particularly bumpy flight, I had started chatting to Manolis, who became a good male friend. He readily agreed to accompany me to the dance, and then my colleague Catherine arrived with her husband and a young man who, she said, she had brought for me. I was enchanted with him. At the end of the evening, Manolis, smiling secretively, told me he had to go home. I thanked him graciously for coming with me, wondering what was going to happen next.

Fortunately it was the children's father's weekend, so when Cliff offered to take me home it was inevitable I invite him in. We sat until the sun rose in front of the fire place, talking, and when he left, he said to me, "I feel as though I have known you all my life."

We spoke every day and I was excited and hoped that at last I had found someone to love. A week later, we made love and as I fell into a deep sleep, I found myself walking along a narrow road in India. I could see children running to and fro and a woman, who slowly began to walk towards me. She was beautiful and her sari hung in soft folds around her and yet she was extremely sad. The next morning, when I awoke, I felt as though I was her and even though I tried desperately to shake off the sadness, it stayed with me. For another two weekends, Cliff and I went out and although I had a wonderful time with him, I kept on seeing the woman's pained expression in my mind. Abandoning all control, I started doing meditation regularly. I found myself clearly back on the road and found Cliff in my vision, walking next to the woman with the sad eyes. I realized they were twins and the next time I saw Cliff, I told him I thought we were twin flames.

Cliff had come with gifts. He had bought me a silver ring with a gold band across it and silver earrings. He told me the ring would be my rock and the earrings the rain and gently said goodbye to me. He never returned. Four weeks later, tired of trying to call him and never getting any response, I found out what had happened. Cliff had decided to go back to the wife he had divorced. It would take me another six months to work with the sadness India had brought and to let go of the desire for this relationship and love, because I had another dream that would prove to be a very deep message from the Universe, and one that would eventually free my heart, spirit and soul from any kind of pain I may have perceived to have experienced.

In my dream, Father was sitting at a table and behind him stood my ex-father-in-law, who had died two years before from a broken heart. I could not think that his sudden heart attack was just a biological repercussion of the usual physical symptoms. He had accepted my marriage to his son and I believe he did love me. He often told his wife to stop whenever she started blaming me for different things and showing her clear dislike of me. Although I had brought two sons into the family and she appreciated this a lot, I was the foreigner who had taken her son away from her. I knew my father-in-law was a broken man when we told him we were getting a divorce, and I somehow felt responsible for his death.

Seeing him in the dream choked me and I also worried about my own father's health, because I sat on one side of the table and they were both on the other.

Father is seated in front of me, and a wooden table separates us. Dimitris Livanos stands behind him. Father picks up a big wooden box and places it on the table between us. He asks me to open the box. As I open the latch of the beautifully carved box, he tells me I am a twin and that my twin brother was never born. For a moment in the dream, I recall the little boy who came to my wood between the worlds. Was he my brother in Spirit and was this the reason I always felt as though half of me was missing? I open the box and draw out two Chinese bowls. They are beautifully decorated and I stare at them, holding one in my right hand, the other in my left. I know automatically they are the cups of joy and sorrow. I put them down and lift up the layer of soft straw to take out a beautiful porcelain statue of a man and a woman, their arms entwined.

"When you have experienced the same amount of joy as you have sorrow and understood them both," Father says solemnly, *"you will find love."*

The depth of experience could not be understood when I awoke. It was only many years later, I attempted to analyze what it must have meant. The joy of learning about Divine Love is a completion, but only when it can be fully integrated into this life. Although I was grateful I had learned so much, I was still deeply unhappy; I had to accept fully and appreciate my life exactly as it was. I still lived in the 'what if' world that is so common. I had often looked back at life to judge the decisions that had been taken, and to wonder what would have happened had these decisions not been taken. However, life cannot be judged. Although often I had been reminded of my 'mistakes', with hindsight I truly wondered why they were thought of as mistakes. To make a mistake surely one has to be conscious of all possibilities at a particular time? I knew this was impossible and if it was – then that meant self-realization and cosmic realization had taken place. I started learning about acceptance even if it was a very difficult task but still had to understand the meaning of the dream in all its wholeness, as it brought spirit back to me and nudged at my heart. I needed the balance of masculinity and femininity and to recognize fully the experience of Earthly life, no matter how painful. I needed to integrate spirituality into reality and had a long road still ahead of me!

Confused, I went to see a wonderful soul called Bob Najemy at Harmonic Life, a small spiritual center in Halandri, and shared my experiences with him. I acquainted myself with the teachings of the guru Sai Baba, and walked around telling everyone I had to go to India to find my soul.

One evening I had a profound vision of Sai Baba.

He is tall and fills the space of the living room, as he puts his hand on my head.

"My child," he says to me. *"You do not have to come to India to find your soul. You can find it in your very own living room."*

The next day it was difficult for me to go to school. I met with a colleague, Margaret, in the staff room. She took one look at me and told me to rest and that she would take my class. All my perceptions were heightened and I did not want to share my vision, because it was too precious. I managed to get through the day, and that evening, we had a parent-teacher conference. I held my scarf over my face often, as my sense of smell was extremely heightened. As we finished the meeting, Margaret caught up with me and spoke softly.

"You know, all the while I was sitting and watching you this evening, you reminded me of an Indian girl".

A few moments later, Catherine caught us in the passage.

"How strange," she said. "I could have sworn you were an Indian woman walking down the corridor."

I had not shared my experience with anyone.

On my way home, I stopped at a small mini-market and bought vegetables. I went home and made a curry for myself. It was as though I had gone to India and returned, only to realize I had not found my soul, but would still have to work hard in order to recognize it existed.

My experiences were very clearly related to forgiveness and letting go. They certainly convinced me that we shared short moments with people on our path through life, in order to work with memories that seem to hold us in bondage. I could not explain things differently! How could I possibly ignore the visions, the dreams and the apparent thread that kept on appearing in my everyday life? My third eye had opened in such a way it gave me information about a number of scenarios that I began to heal. I opened myself even further to experience of altered consciousness, travelling back in time, to find different faces in the past I believed were buried deep within my psyche. I felt connected totally to the universe and experienced a spiritual joy I had not felt since I was a young child, knowing I had gone beyond the personal and into the transpersonal. My mind became a movie screen that began to play scenes from different times and spaces which I tried to integrate into my daily activities. I taught during the day and spent as much of my daytime with my sons who were growing. At night when they went to sleep, I let down the mask of the present, to claim the veil of the past. I found myself in Egypt; I found myself in Morocco, in India, in China and then in Africa. I met with an Amerindian tribe, who taught me diligently about healing, and how to look in remote places for hidden, blocked energy.

I respected my journeys and those people who inevitably drew memories from me, for I could see my relationships as they had always been; some needed healing, and others gave me strength to move on through the veils, to a deeper and deeper sense of psyche. I was happy as I started becoming a more true self and finding so many talents. An inner beauty began to be a constant sense of achievement and so the pain of my divorce became a little more bearable. As far as I was concerned, I was finding my home in the heart of my relationships and I did not stop to think I was finding it within as well.

The visions and dreams that were constant became part of me. I found inexplicable feelings of closeness nudge at my heart. I could be sitting having a cup of coffee and a picture would flash across my mind's internal eye. I could sense things that were hidden and felt responsible when I realized I was not separate but in unity with the universe. Everything I had fought so hard to keep: my memories, identity, understanding that I was somewhere up in the expanse of sky, totally and completely free, suddenly became my inner and outer reality.

However, I expected friends and lovers to be as fully involved as I was, yet I was still unable to see I had buried all my wounds, without dealing with them. I would find mean personas, sarcasm, willful jealousy, deep anger and unkindness around me. People were afraid of love, trying to win unseen battles, trying to make each other feel small, because they did not want to dive into the depths of their own psyche. As I had absorbed the beauty and grace, I began to absorb the pain from the outside world, a mirror of the pain within. The suffering on the faces of the men, women and children in my vision were no longer part of a lineage. They were me in different facets of existence when, it seemed, I had failed to fully comprehend my purpose in life. Time and time again, the purpose of loving unconditionally, given to me in a vision of Saint Nicholas, at Harmonic Life, reared its head up to remind me I had yet another chance to succeed where once I had failed, because I was awakening to a mystical existence in daily life. To find the mystic experience and to become it was the challenge I needed, to break free. I knew it was important for me to understand what I was experiencing and seeing but again, there lacked balance as I tried to live my daily life, with its different obstacles.

No matter how deep my spiritual experiences were, there was always the understanding of how difficult it was to bridge the gap between my actual and ideal selves. I knew I needed this balance, but growth could not be hurried. Growth is an internal process and it definitely has its own life.

Parts of my inner beauty had slowly been snuffed out by the pain brought by my divorce. I missed Jackie and blocked out memories of guilt. I longed to have a meal every now and then with my children and my ex-husband but it was not possible. Having left the family circle, there were new rules and laws that would cost, because Philip saw things differently. I had betrayed him and he was unable to respect the need of some togetherness, even though we were apart.

At the time I got divorced, I truly was unaware of consequences! To me, everything was part of a whole and everything I did was spurred on by my feelings, and never once did I look at logic; I was unable to, as I seemed to be moved by a force that led me – a force I always followed and perhaps it was this force, that took me swiftly and suddenly that April. I had a hemiplegic migraine attack that left me with all the symptoms of a stroke and was sent again to hospital for two weeks. Every night, during these two weeks when I had difficulty in speaking, I experienced.

A part of me sits up in bed to receive a figure dressed in a long white robe, with a long beard. He communicates with me but no matter how hard I try to recall what I learn, I cannot. Every evening he speaks to me and for seven days I learn. Only one word remains with me when I leave the hospital. It is the name Paul.

I wondered if the figure was St Paul and began to read his letters in the Bible. I thought about the events that led up to my hospitalization. I had started having double vision, whilst driving with Margaret to school. I went home and by the evening, when Jane, a dear friend of mine called me, my speech was slurred. Jane immediately called her partner who was a doctor, left her young daughter Rebecca alone to come to my apartment, and took me to hospital. I did not understand what had happened to me.

I recovered slowly and when the spring came I decided I needed to plan a holiday away on my own, and yet could not think of where to go. Every year had always included holidays in Epidavros, where I had met Philip, and it was inevitable my parents expected to see me and the children. My parents wafted back and forth living like millionaires. They would spend six months in Epidavros, going out for dinner every night, ordering lobster and prawns frequently.

Having settled into the understanding they would always be together, the many arguments had stopped. Grandmother Maria had died at the age of ninety-eight from Alzheimer's and Mother had looked after her until the end.

My grandmother had been remarkable. She had started studying Ancient Greek when she was in her eighties and although she still believed firmly we would not be saved unless we joined her church, she had mellowed. I missed something that was a part of my heritage, and I knew Mother missed her a lot.

My parents would take long walks to the town from their gorgeous three-bedroomed home overlooking the bay, hand in hand. Mother lay in the sun whilst Father went fishing. Books were avidly read, short trips planned and evenings were ripe with social events. Mother loved Greece and still held the dream in her heart to build a house on the piece of land they had bought so many years before. She still resented the fact Father had desperately needed to buy a farm, so money had been invested in the farm, rather than in the building of a house. The farm was a beautiful place called '*Nooitverlaat*' which means 'Never Leave' in Afrikaans. It was about two hours away from Johannesburg, in Middleburg and Father had become fully ensconced in becoming a weekend farmer. Different managers had been hired over the years and it brought in a substantial income. The farm was where I found peace, every Christmas when I returned with the children to South Africa, and yet the journey to the farm and back always scared me.

When school broke up, we packed up and went to Epidavros. The boys loved their grandparents a lot and spent time swimming and fishing. They were to stay a week with their grandparents, and then Philip would be taking them for a month. One day as I lay on the beach, a friend suggested I go to the island of Santorini. A week later I settled on the deck of the ship that was to carry me towards the mystical union of soul and heart.

The cliffs that greeted me the following morning were sheer and frightening but equally embracing, as I gazed in awe at the tiny white houses, like jewels at the top of the dark brown rocks that emerged from the deep blue sea. I saw a world of opposites, allowing me the freedom to find balance in the tiny paths that led to coffee shops, overlooking the volcano. Classical music touched my heart and I began to fly. Soaring up into the expanse of sky was easy, as was the gentle hovering, reaching out and touching places I was sure I had never touched before. It was inevitable I fall in love.

He was a young Italian on holiday, and the moment we met on a trip to the volcano, I began to glow. We met daily and so began a romance to the strains of music, friendship, love and laughter. We watched the sun set, sipping on cold wine and wrapping our dreams in our arms, for the short time we spent together. It was glorious because there was a sense of feeling that began to surge within me. I was young and free – able to bask in the sense of love which was all I needed. So it was inevitable when we were forced to part, he to return to Italy and I to Athens, that I throw caution to the wind. As I still had leave from my teaching job, I went to Italy where I allowed my inner beauty to unfold. We visited Positano and Capri; we sang out our song 'When the moon hits your eye', and feasted on pizza and wine. My dreams of life were slowly taking on a different hue and I tried not to focus on the fact he was ten years younger than I was. On the contrary, his youth and fresh innocence were so complete I was able to feel safe with him. I could see his feelings in his eyes and so began to discover a sensual aspect of self that had never emerged till then. I danced for him and allowed myself the luxury of discovering I could be a goddess because he adored me.

When I left Italy it was with a promise for new life. Antonio wrote to me and I wrote poetic letters back and we promised to meet again the following year. Antonio lived in Ercolano in Southern Italy, where he was studying medicine. He was warm, charming and had not considered the fact I was older than he was. My friend Margaret smiled at the change in me and gently encouraged my transformation. Perhaps, being in a state of altered consciousness, happy at last, I was highly intuitive because one day, when Margaret came into the staffroom, I asked her what was wrong with her. She looked surprised.

"Why, nothing is wrong", she replied sweetly.

Two months later she was diagnosed with cancer and I was the only person, apart from her family, who she saw, towards the end. I was devastated when she died! I mourned Margaret's death and the following year, when I met with Antonio again, something had changed. I was no longer under a magic spell – reality showed me a young student who could hardly give me the security I wanted. The time frame in which we had met was all wrong and so we parted in a strange atmosphere of betrayal because nothing whatsoever had changed for Antonio. I never thought about the similarities I shared with Mother. She had also left an Italian who loved her dearly and I would do exactly the same! The sense of loss was almost overwhelming, because I felt completely empty inside of me and was destroying the only aspect of life that had given me joy.

When summer came, I wanted to recapture time because I needed to think about life, the fact I had lost my friend Margaret and also the joy I had felt with Antonio. I returned to the island of Santorini, to walk amidst the devastation and beauty that reminded me so much of myself. I found a room overlooking the volcano and spent a glorious week in the sunshine, taking walks and exploring Oia. I avoided Fira, the busy and cosmopolitan capital, choosing the stillness of the lazy afternoons, sipping iced coffee and absorbing the energy that wrapped me up in a protective cocoon. The dark volcano stared back at me as I sat looking out to sea, feeling my body one with my soul. My sons were happy with their father, so I decided to extend my stay for another week and took the bus to Fira in order to change my ticket. My parents, who had spent six months in Epidavros, were due to leave the day before I went down to Fira. I called them to say I was sorry I wouldn't see them. I felt guilty that I had not seen much of them that year, but I found it tedious listening to the same stories over and over again. I found it boring eating at the same restaurants night after night and found I often felt suffocated whenever we were together. They promised to give my love to Paul and said their goodbyes. I bought a new boat ticket and caught the bus back to Oia.

As I looked down at the sheer drop below, the bus, that seemed to be hanging by a thread to the cliff, made me feel as though I was flying. I felt very calm and content; almost expansive. It was still relatively early in the morning when I got off the bus on the outskirts of Oia and made my way to a small coffee shop that was empty apart from the owner dressed in black, who was busy behind the counter. I ordered coffee and lit a cigarette. I turned to my book and began writing from my heart. I had always loved writing; writing at home when I was young, with colored paper stuck clumsily over light bulbs, that would render smoky atmospheres; writing poems on tiny pieces of paper – poems that came from my heart and inevitably found their way to those of others. I was so engrossed in my writing that I was shocked out of my reverie by a deep voice that suddenly broke through my focus, with an extremely strange sentence.

"I had a dream," the voice resounded all around me, "that I had to come here and order a coffee. Make it a double!"

I looked up and smiled. I had never ever heard of someone dreaming about having coffee. It was all so dramatic! I saw a very attractive, tall, dark man run a hand through his disheveled hair and almost instantly caught his eye as he ambled over to ask me for a cigarette. Introductions made, he identified himself as a metaphysical writer, who needed desperately to go back to sleep.

Coffee in hand, he asked me where I was staying and promptly arranged to take me out that afternoon. I was pleasantly surprised and had already noted he was my age. I skipped back to my room an hour later and sat on my balcony sketching. I was not used to having a siesta, so was a little taken aback when I began to feel drowsy. I packed up my pencils and went inside to lie on my bed. Within a short time I was deep in sleep where I began to dream.

A young girl is sitting at the foot of my bed. It takes me some time to realize it is me, looking back at myself. For what appears to be eternity, we sit gazing at each other. Once again I listen, communicating, but can recall nothing at all.

The afternoon had worn on and, unbeknown to me, my new acquaintance Constantine was knocking on my door. I was mesmerized by myself still looking at me, when suddenly I heard a rustle of paper and shot up on my bed. I saw a note on the floor in front of my door. I jumped up, opened it and read,

"My lady, I came to find you. If it is our destiny to meet, we will."
It was signed Constantine.

I wrenched open the door and ran down the path. I could barely see the top of his head when I called out. He turned back to me.

"I'm so sorry", I said almost choking, "I was asleep. Please come in. You can sit on the balcony. It won't take long for me to get ready."

I could almost hear desperation in my voice as I spoke to him, but then I became too involved in picking out something dazzling to wear. I cherished thoughts that raced through my mind. Perhaps this was the birth of new life. I could already see myself walking down the aisle with a beautiful satin gown, and I hoped he was the man of my dreams. As I looked across the blue water at the volcano, I felt a shiver run down my spine.

As the past comes to an end, there are always new beginnings. I felt warm, as I walked arm in arm with Constantine to Melissa's bar, overlooking the volcano, and ordered coffee. Constantine told me about the books he wrote, and I shared the many visions, that had taught me so much, with him. We had a common purpose and this made everything seem so pleasant. However, something was definitely not right! Although I tried hard to be as attentive as I could and truly wanted to feel excited about my new acquaintance, I began to feel shivers run down my spine relentlessly.

"It is full moon tomorrow," I said quietly and yet passionately. "Can I watch the moon with you?"

There was a plea in my voice, sharply spiced with my dreams of Eros that is never exstinguished once passion has been shared, but rather becomes a solid flame in which all light and love remains constant.

"We don't know if we will be alive or dead by tomorrow! If you really want to watch the moon with me and I am not there, you can pretend I am."

Constantine's words hit me with such a force I hardly understood what he was talking about. For a moment my life flashed before me. I had rocked the lives of my in-laws and my ex-husband's life with my affair that broke my heart, because I did not know what tenderness was. My second affair had left me bereft when he announced I was in a sea of emotion drowning and desperate to hold onto any raft that came by, even if the wood was rotten! In all my endeavors to meet with a replica of the love I searched for, I kept meeting men who inevitably could never give me what I wanted. I still did not really know what I wanted. As I looked at the man sitting opposite me, I tried to ignore the eyes looking back at me, and yet could not help but feel myself drowning in them. As the sun set and the moon rose in the sky, I ached all over. I wanted him to wrap his arms around me and to live a million lives in one. I couldn't understand why I began to feel empty and as though I were being rent in two!

I tried to focus on the conversation we were having, whilst recalling his reply that I kept on repeating over and over again in my head, like a mantra. Why had he been so brutal about life and death? What were the possibilities of death coming so swiftly?

"Come on," Constantine said nonchalantly, "let's go and eat, I'm starving."

We walked to a small tavern called Mama Africa and I tried to slow my needs down and relax. My body, however, was tensing up. When we arrived at the tavern, Constantine introduced me to the owner, who began to play African music. The sound of gumboots pounding in the dust sent me out over the seas and back to the hot sands of Africa. I thought about the citrus trees at the farm in Middleburg. Part of my soul had always remained there, so I thought back to the magnificence of the land I loved walking through. The farm was beautiful. It was 365 hectares and at the bottom it bordered a nature reserve. I had poignant memories of Christmases spent there, with fresh, frothy milk, sticky *koeksisters* and sweet Maroula plums. I could not easily relate to the feeling of parallel living.

The red wine was dulling my sensations and I poured out my story in between the firm notion that I was in a parallel dimension and probably finding truth at last. I may have been sitting beside Constantine drinking wine and tasting of the local dishes, but I was, as well, walking in the grass at our farm. I told Constantine about the place which appealed to my poetic heart. I had memories of watching the sunset and listening to the noises of the African bush. As I looked out blankly at the horizon, not seeing the place I was in, but rather the big sprawling farmhouse, the dusty roads and the beautiful trees, rustling in the breeze, the emotions of romance made me feel heady.

We finished our meal and walked slowly back to my room, arm in arm. It seemed obvious we spend the night together, perhaps only because we had shared so much.

When I woke in the morning he had gone, and my head was pounding. I got up and went to sit on the balcony, trying to relate to the evening's events. I wanted to recapture the sense of emotional freedom that comes from new romance, but could not. Instead, I felt heavy and an icy chill swept over me, making me shiver, although the temperature was well into the thirties.

I tried to read although I was feeling very listless and, as time passed, I felt as though my head was in a vice. I went back inside, got dressed and went out for a walk. Nothing whatsoever seemed to make sense. I was agitated, uneasy and my mind clouded. My headache was turning into a migraine and I felt sick. I went back to my room then suddenly began to shake. As though losing all control, I pulled off my jewelry, put on a pair of black jeans and black top and started crying. I had no idea whatsoever what was wrong with me, and it was as though something was pulling and pushing me at the same time. The only thing that came to mind as I struggled to make sense of my experiences was the need to find solace and protection. I decided to go to church. Pulled by an unseen force I ran to the church of St Mary, desperate now, trying only to find my guide and the balance I needed, so desperately.

My guide was St Nicholas. I had seen St Nicholas in a vision, approximately two years before, when I had gone to a seminar, led by Bob Nejemy, to find my purpose in life. It had been just after my son talked about being older than I was, and I had surrendered completely to the divine. As I lay down to follow the meditation I was truly open to experience and was shocked by my vision.

An old man with a grey beard stands looking at me. The love in his eyes is the love I have experienced, as a young child. The love is what I know exists and has, for some unknown reason, been extinguished by everyday life. The symbolism is so powerful I begin to cry. Tears flow and fill my ears, as I lay there, in ecstasy.

"What is my purpose?" I ask from the depths of my heart, unable to hear Bob any longer, for my ears are completely blocked with tears.

"To learn to love unconditionally," is the reply, gentle and filled with love that runs through my body and into my soul.

I recalled sitting up later, filled with despair for the difficulty that faced me. I did not know how to love unconditionally and yet my guide knew I was sincere in my pleas. Unconditional love meant I could no longer blame others for hurting me. It meant I had to open my heart and mind and that, in opening my mind, I would see the world exactly as it was. The world was filled with wounded souls and no one was without wound. The only reprieve that could come to men, women and children, was to overcome suffering and see Light through Love. This love I knew to exist, for I had experienced it, but it was not human love. Rather, it was Divine in nature and touched on the symbolism of the archetype – the Father-Mother image that was translated into the need for a Creator, someone that would accept me, exactly as I was. It spoke of compassion, and letting go of all else; I needed desperately to find an icon of St Nicholas and pray.

I reached the church and stumbled in! At the time, I thought I was possibly having a breakdown, because I could not stop crying and my head was pulsating. I found myself standing suddenly in front of the icon of St Michael and Gabriel. The archangels looked down on me and I tried to connect with them. Reaching a crescendo, the pain in my head exploded and I could not reason. Deep inside my soul a voice cried out "be strong", and it was then, as I made my way towards the door, that I saw St Nicholas. As I looked at the icon of him, I saw tears streaming down his face. What was perhaps a mirror image, I took to be a sign I was perhaps mad, but Divinity within my soul would not abandon me. Like a child, I asked him if he was crying because I had gone mad. Feeling terribly alone and confused I went outside.

I sat on a low wall just beyond the church, hugged myself and cried, until I heard a voice.

"What are you doing here?"

I turned around and there he was. Thoughts exploded through my mind and I found myself in my wood. Amidst the looming shadows an angel had appeared. Constantine laid a hand on my shoulder, and although I wanted desperately to jump up and settle in his arms, I remained seated. The dreamer was standing behind me, pragmatic in his insistence that the moon was affecting my mood, determined to send me down the path that would free me from despair.

"If you feel poorly, go and have a meal. There is a nice tavern," he pointed. "Go and eat!"

He left as suddenly as he appeared and as though sleepwalking, I followed his advice to sit down and order food. The tavern filled up and a while later a waiter asked me if I could share the table with another girl on her own. I nodded and welcomed her, introducing myself. A little later, another young woman would sit at our table, an iridologist who would ask us to meet with her the following morning, bright and early, for a reading. I had no time to think about the events but simply accepted them as they came.

That night I fell into a restless sleep and the following morning woke up and walked to the mini-market to buy some milk. I never drank milk in the morning, but something urged me to find milk with a straw, but to my despair the cashier had no straws. I threw the milk down and called him a fool for selling milk without a straw! I began to observe myself and yet something was leading me on, and I was following. This is how I left the supermarket to go to the travel agency and call home – home which was a house, the house in the Epidavros of my dreams, where my ex-husband was spending summer with my sons. My eldest son Dimitris answered the phone.

"Hello Mummy," he said in a serious voice. "Daddy wants to speak to you."

Suddenly, I was enraged. A surge of energy ran through me. What did my ex-husband want from me? I was sure he wanted to spoil my vacation! He came on the line. Time separated and I entered the void.

"Hello," he said curtly. "Why are you phoning?"

"To speak to my children!" my reply was equally short.

"You don't know I am looking for you?" The question was heavy.

"No! Why should you?"

"So you don't know I have been trying to find you through the radio and the television."

"Of course not – I don't watch TV or listen to the radio when on holiday!"

We were spitting at each other, words that had no meaning.

"So, what is it?"

Perhaps my question was too cold, too angry for him to respond to. Perhaps I will never know, what exactly prompted his answer that hit me like a knife in my gut.

"I have bad news for you! There has been an accident! Your brother is dead and your parents are in hospital. There was an accident on the way back from the farm!"

I dropped the receiver. Moaning, I clutched my stomach! Moaning I walked back to a coffee shop, where I faintly recalled a tall man asking for a double coffee he had dreamt about. I repeated over and over again.

"Oh, my God, my brother is dead! Paul is dead!"

Two Swedish ladies, trying to help, followed me, but I was beyond help. Driven only by Spirit-Soul, I walked back to the coffee shop, crying and begging for the owner to find the man who had had the dream, for I could no longer remember his name. She found him and he took me back to my room. He packed my bag, took me back to his house to give me a sedative.

"You have between now and when you arrive in South Africa to cry," he said, "because when you get there, you have to be strong!"

All the way to the airport in Santorini, I rehearsed his words; and during the flight; but first I had to get back to my apartment. In a daze I got out of the taxi and went to the first floor, to knock on my neighbor's door.

Aspasia was a police woman who I had befriended. Our children often played together in the beautiful garden surrounding the apartment, as we spoke about our lives. When she opened the door, I blurted my story to her and she took me upstairs to my apartment. She called Philip, only to be told by my ex mother-in-law, that he had gone swimming with my sons.

The pain in my heart was choking me, as I stumbled around. Aspasia called the airport, found out there was a flight that evening, and I began to call my friends, trying to find someone who could help me, because I had no money to buy a ticket.

George was someone I had met months before at a South African Embassy function. We hardly knew each other, but the moment I told him what had happened, he came to pick me up with his Diners card to take me to the airport. George tried to get me a ticket with Air Zimbabwe and to pay with his card; the airline announced they couldn't accept the card. He asked me if I knew of someone who could give me a cheque. My mind worked furiously; who could afford to pay for my ticket and who would be available on the 24th of August when everyone was on vacation? I was in so much pain and yet it seemed as though a part of me had gently detached itself, and was giving me exactly what I needed, to deal with the physicality that had been so abrupt and tragic.

The only person who came to mind was my gynecologist. Spiro had been the doctor who had facilitated the birth of my children. He had been instrumental in finding me a lawyer when I wanted to divorce my husband, and had been a friend. I knew I could trust him. When I called him, he promptly promised to come to the airport, and give me a cheque, but the ground hostess mentioned someone had to guarantee the cheque. An unknown woman watching us, as George ran back and forth carrying messages, promised to be the guarantor. As surreal as everything was, there was a constant and firm presence all around me. At exactly the right moment, the manager of Olympic Airways just happened to pass. He promised to accept the card and nonchalantly spoke to me.

"We will accept the transaction, but just pray the plane doesn't crash because you won't be on the passenger list! You will be listed as leaving on Tuesday."

The moment he had spoken, he realized the enormity of his words but it was too late. I suddenly realized how responsible I had to become and, tearfully, I clutched at George, thanking him profusely and went to board the plane that would take me to Jan Smuts Airport. I had become an unknown citizen, bereft of name and address, to make my way home to a hell I was being forced to enter by circumstance that had to do with a full moon of 1991 and the death of my beloved brother, Paul.

CHAPTER TEN

Traveling on the road to freedom, we are never alone. Spirit holds us gently and souls meet us, as we struggle to know which road we must travel on. In the darkness there is never really darkness. There is light that begins to slowly brighten and twinkle like a star, bidding us good journey.

Spirit

As I stepped off the plane, I had completely ceased to be myself. During the flight I had wept, but now became something else, some-one else. I stepped into my brother's shoes. Paul was a strong man and yet he had become an enigma to me, because he was so weak whenever it came to love. Mother had often manipulated him over the years because he reminded her so much of herself. She had taken advantage of him, whenever she tried to explain her sadness in her marriage to my father. He became a scapegoat for the lies that kept her sane as she struggled to forget her past. He constantly reminded her of her failings as a mother, and constantly reminded her of her weakness as a woman. Paul had been a doormat everyone stood on, in the hopes of finding another dream and another gateway to success and freedom. Always contained, he had paid for my excursions to the stores to buy clothes; he had bought my first car, paid for my university, trips back and forth, and a maid to help me when I was in need. He had clothed Mother and bought her shoes. He had tried desperately to be whatever we wanted him to be, at the expense of his own soul and spirit, and I knew I had to take his place. He had been the only person in my family I had connected with and I loved him very deeply. I was conscious that this love that had been appreciated because he had always loved my wandering soul, and answered its call. He had arranged for me to go to Woodside Sanctuary, bought me The Prophet by Kahlil Gibran and the Rubaiyat of Omar Khayyam.

no one else had made the effort to understand my heart.

It was not easy, but his silent suffering became the strength that took me to hospital to see my parents and the strange apparition of a woman, who claimed she had been going to marry my brother. Detached from the drama slowly unfolding before me, I gave my parents the support they both needed. Mother had lost both children of her past, and Father had been the driver of the vehicle that brought death and injury. My parents had been lucky in that their injuries were minor and then were discharged the following day, but their souls had been damaged beyond repair. They were locked in the jaws of an insane world.

I insisted I had to go to the scene of the accident, after I had put them both to bed with broken collar bones, to dig in the sand and find my brother's chain and medal of St Christopher. The Africans who came with me were shocked by my almost gruesome strength that had me groveling in the sand, insisting on taking home a bloody pullover I said needed to be washed. I was blessed by the fact two neighbors, who had been friends of the family, stepped in to help, in whatever way they could. I demanded to see the body before its burial and went to the cemetery to arrange for the funeral.

Paul had flown out of the car on impact. He had hit a rock that opened his skull just before the car landed on his face. Simon, the African house boy who had been sitting beside him, had also flown out of the car but his body was intact. When I had managed to persuade the neighbors, who were African and White to take me to the morgue, I was only conscious of a tiny voice that kept on repeating itself, over and over inside of me.

'*The message is in the box.*'

Paul had been mangled in such a way his face was totally obliterated and he looked like a horse. I had no more doubts his corpse was just a body – a body that had been left behind without spirit and soul. I understood the value of my brother's life, because I knew his soul-spirit had flown, but he was also snuffed out in one moment of destiny, before vultures came to peck at what had remained. For a moment that lasted a lifetime, I stared at his mangled form, and then, with hand shaking, placed a monkey and Greek worry beads in his coffin. As I stood looking down from a great height, I saw the remains of Simon, the houseboy, elflike but still intact, lying in a coffin besides that of my poor brother, white material ruffled at his throat.

The so-called 'fiancée' likened him to a file on her desk! Paul's former business partner walked off with a hefty amount of money from the insurance company, and people came and went claiming to have loved him, but taken up by the hand of self, which would play a macabre game of worth, as each became embedded in their own drama. Black and White would lay in the church side by side, their coffins identical, apart from the scales of justice on my brother's coffin. The double grave my brother had bought when we buried my sister Jackie, now belonged to me. This would be the first piece of land I owned.

The Catholic priest who buried my brother would later leave the priesthood to marry another girlfriend who also claimed she was to marry Paul. From above I watched destiny play its hand, recalling my priest friend from my youth, as I sat in the same office reliving my moments with another Irish priest who had dark hair and would leave the priesthood to marry Manola, the young Spanish girl who took me away for a weekend that I needed so desperately, to remember who I was. These events stained my mind and heart with a destined mark.

My brother's death took a toll on us all. He had cancelled all the insurances he had taken out in Mother's name three months before his death, and died bankrupt. He had left behind him no papers or photos, for someone had made sure that personal effects were safely removed from his cottage, the day he died. All I found was a piece of paper that talked about death – a poem written anonymously about Spirit that joined with Soul in another dimension.

When I left my parents to go back to my job in Athens, I had tried as much as possible to hold onto the memory of Paul amidst chaos. People had come and gone, and yet nothing whatsoever had remained, apart from the memory of Collette, the wife of a client of Paul's who bought my cigarettes and took me to a spiritualist church in search of answers to the macabre death that left my parents exposed to the reality of their truth and only their truth, for they had nothing whatsoever left to hold onto.

I took some comfort when the clairvoyant doing readings suddenly announced she could see a young man, his face and head bandaged heavily, who was looking for his mother. Mother had lost her children and subsequently her heart and soul. All she could recall was the fact she and Father were now penniless, poor in spirit and mind, for the pain of losing him was too much to bear. Neither could look back at their lives and their actions. Instead they focused on the money that had disappeared in a cloud of conspiracy, because no one could explain why a black car had reversed across the highway, forcing Father to swerve and lose control of the vehicle he was driving, and why a partner would collect insurance money, when there was no partnership agreement.

I mourned deeply and shuddered to know the only piece of land I owned was a double grave that housed the bodies of my sister and my brother. I shuddered because I had been led to their grave by destined circumstances that reminded me so clearly of Carl Jung's synchronicity. The events however, could never be erased and fell heavy on my heart. They appeared to fulfill a prophesy that spoke of unconditional love, that drew me away from the pain and into a power that allowed me to witness a cold and brutal reality, that had no reason other than survival of the fittest and the shrewdest – that part of life I had never, ever wanted to recognize. It would take a number of years for me to see a tiny light in my experiences that led up to Paul's death. I would always wonder if I had been prepared by the figure that had visited me every night whilst in hospital and whether or not the sheer brutality of death had finally stamped out the evil that had haunted our family for aeons. It became important to me then, that the story of our family always remain in the annals of time. The only thing I could give the world back was what I had been given, and this gave reverence to the story I knew needed to be told.

I became responsible for Paul's life. I wept and cried sobs that wrenched the child-like aspect of my being out of self, until she existed as one with me. I tried to believe the universe was with me but I lost sanity, watching a woman refer to my brother as a file on her desk; I lost sanity when she asked if she could still marry him, even though he was horizontal and she vertical; I lost sanity as I watched the business partner walk off never to return again, richer and colder for his gain. I lost sanity as I recalled a black knight demanding a book from my heart I knew to be mine. I lost sanity as I tried to make my parents remember soul rather than the body and lost sanity, as I recalled how an undertaker had not placed white material around the head, sure no one would look at the body. When eventually I was to learn that Manola married the priest who buried Paul, I had nowhere else to run!

I went back to Athens. I paid back the money I owed to Constantine and George with the help of my ex-husband. I began to delve into the metaphysical and access memories through my power. I flew to exceptional heights and began to see this power of thought manifest in my life. What I wanted I got, even though I knew it was not for me. I began to live, not from heart but from mind, determined to find out why the universe had abandoned me by taking Paul away from me, and why it had flung me to the ground?

Of course the power made me stand tall. I recalled past lives as though they were present. I travelled to Egypt and Morocco to find power in their symbolism and so became more and more clairvoyant. I began to diagnose illness with little effort. I began to foresee the future and to recall the past. I found myself travelling back and forth in time, content on healing my mind of the trauma and oblivious to the inner choking that hurt me, and sent me back down the mountain until I no longer listened to my inner voice but became that voice. I was arrogant in my knowing and yet I had never really given up my quest to love without condition. Perhaps that is what saved me, I really do not know.

What I do know is that the pressure sent me to hospital with yet another hemiplegic migraine and then again with a cyst on my ovary and yet again with another deep vein thrombosis. I used power to heal myself but was moving back and forth in a dimension where I lost the most important parts of my self in such a way, it was inevitable something happen.

I saw past lives come and go. I met people who mirrored my

emotions and who taught me I was nothing at all, apart from a grain of sand in a vast expanse of sky. I was unable to recall my childhood dreams; rather I became obsessed with the vision of a dying world and a dying consciousness, that could not free me from the net I was creating for myself. Like my dream of the fisherman who had caught a dead fish, I allowed myself to be driven by the power of ecstasy that no longer became humble, but rather challenged my birth. I knew I had come from the stars, but the stars had abandoned me.

My mentor St Nicholas became an enemy. My universe had deprived me of the one person I had truly understood, for he had reminded me so much of myself, with a difference: whereas I had blown up my circumstances and shouted them from rooftops, my brother had remained silent. Whereas I had wanted to become real, my brother had wanted to become anonymous. Whereas I had never succeeded, my brother had left this world in such a momentous act he had stifled the ingenuity of love before it had a chance to express itself.

No one really mourned the death of a great man! Rather, they focused on weaknesses instead of strengths. When they spoke about him, it was to reprimand his actions. And I, totally sublime to the act of grace, could not understand what they wanted, what they needed, until I lost myself one day to a realm of Divine madness that was so real, I recalled each and every moment of it.

My first spiritual vision and breakthrough into the Transpersonal that I could not easily integrate had to do with my children. I had spent the weekend with my son Andrew and awoken early.

I go out onto the balcony to see a figure standing in front of me. I understand it to be the Virgin Mary, and I see she has a blue veil, wrapped around her. She takes the veil, folds it up and gives it to me. I tell her in my vision I cannot accept it, because I am a foreigner on this land. I have always been a foreigner. From the day I can recall a knight in shining armor, I have ceased to be an Earthling. I cannot understand why there is so much pain on the planet I am asked to call home. Home has never ever been my physical home! On the contrary, I know a realm exists, where only Love resides, and yet it is totally alien to my mind.

My forefathers in another time and space appear to me, tall and angelic in countenance, filled with love and only love. When I see the veil, I do not only see love. I see duty of love, as a deep destiny to free myself and others; duty to free those souls that were trapped in my near-death experience; to bring light to the world, for receiving the veil means I must take a vow to try to heal the planet and its people, for only then, can I truly heal. I raise a sword in my mind's eye, to pledge allegiance to a place of seven hills. It is easy for me to accept the veil, also as duty to bring solace to the family I have been born into. I begin to relate to justice as well, a little while after I receive the veil. Justice has to do with the scales of Archangel Michael and inadvertently, it means bringing myself into balance. I also see it as bringing balance to the world.

The vision was so powerful that I prayed daily and asked for insight. A week later, a friend of mine casually mentioned she was going to a church, to see the veil of *Panageia*, as Mother Mary was called, which had come to Greece. I understood that something deeper and wider than my personal being was playing a role in my life, and as I went to the church with her, I was greatly humbled.

I identified with the loss Mary had gone through, because she had lost a Son, and I thought about Mother, who had lost two children. I found my life changing rapidly, when I was invited by a friend to go to Egypt. I had another symbolic vision, when I stood staring at a black wall.

I see Arabic writing above a picture of a saint that appears as St Francis, with a bird on his hand, an angel that holds the world in his hands and a pregnant woman in between. What I see on a black wall, is not seen by anyone else. I have no affiliation with the Arabic language, but I copy the writing, which I am told translates as the most Holy words in the Quaran – There is only one God.

I struggled to integrate my visions, but it was not at all easy. I could not relate to the power of a calling that went beyond reason. Although I knew I was being initiated, I disregarded myself and tried to find truth through the outside world. The outside world appeared as a duality of good and bad, and I needed to go beyond them both. Going beyond meant leaving this world behind me which was impossible, for unless I could accept this world, I could not accept the other. My body had begun to resonate with my visions and I became completely absorbed by them. A stream of esoteric symbolism took me out and onto a path where I walked back and forth, learning through vision. I tried desperately to integrate what I knew about spirit with what I knew about the world, and they did not match. The pain inside of me that had been buried in my unconscious began to seep through, as I struggled to find the boundaries between the world of spirit and that of reality.

I do not know if it is really possible to express union that comes through spirit-soul and the division that comes through life with words. Perhaps the only solace I can find is through the words of Carl Jung when talking about his experiences.

'*It is impossible to convey the beauty and intensity of emotion during these visions. They were the most tremendous things that I have ever experienced. And what a contrast the day was: I was tormented and on the edge; everything irritated me; everything was too material; too crude and clumsy, terribly limited both spatially and spiritually. It was all an imprisonment, for reasons impossible to divine, and yet it had a kind of hypnotic power, a cogency, as if it were reality itself, for all that I had clearly perceived its emptiness*' (Jung 1961).

It took me two weeks to find balance and although my experience was truly a breakthrough as it had all happened so swiftly, I understood the contents in the depth of my being and yet not in my mind. I experienced symbolism that came through sacred geometry, Masonic and Rosicrucian tradition. At the time, I knew nothing about the esoteric world but experienced it. I was on leave from school when I experienced this flood of knowledge that welled up inside of me and when leave was over, I still managed to give of myself entirely during the day as a teacher, able to cope with a demanding job. The pressure however, was severe. Exhausted, I tried to sleep at night but then the dreams came, bringing me back to my childhood where a dark figure demanded a golden book from me and I began to choke. Startled by the speed in which things were changing I tried to understand what was going on.

I realized something had happened to me when I was very young so I decided to take myself back in a form of hypnosis to my birth. I was a big baby, who struggled to breathe when I was first born. I recalled having fallen into a rockery, of being punished by my grandmother and of having been left to cry in a high chair. I fell into a state of shock. Had I not studied Psychology, I do not think I would have ever come out of it.

All I was conscious of was that I projected onto the cupboard, whilst I lay in fetal position. My world was about the size of a plate; rabbits, birds and butterflies occupied it. An inner voice told me I should get up in two hours and have a shower. This is what I did and the following evening when I went out with a friend for dinner, I tried to tell him what I was going through. He asked me what I wanted.

When I had gone back to Athens after the strained events of Paul's death, I had gone back to Santorini for a weekend. I felt it was my duty to close a cycle and when I had gone back to Melissa's bar, we had spoken about Constantine. Melissa lent me a book called 'The Pole Shift' by John White that I read soon after.

The morning after my very painful experience, when I woke up, it was with one word on my mind – Findhorn. At first I did not pay attention but then it began to nag at me. I had no idea what Findhorn was, and then recalled the book I had read. In it, I found a short passage describing the spiritual community.

The enormity of my breakthroughs warranted a visit to Findhorn in Scotland, and so I asked my friend if he could get me a ticket for the following week. Catherine lent me some money for my stay there. I tried to talk to Philip over the next few days – he told me I reminded him of a thriller on television.

I arranged to go to London first and went to stay with a colleague who had left Greece. When I told Anna I was going to Scotland I had no idea where I was going. We looked at a map and I located the area.

"I'm going there," I said nonchalantly. "I am going to knock on the door and tell them I came, because I had a calling."

I could not see the turmoil I put Anna in, who caringly made calls, ascertaining it was a spiritual center and that it was safe. She booked me a bus ticket and I left. Findhorn was a dream, come true. I found beauty in nature and like-minded people who understood me. I enrolled for Experience Week and sobbed uncontrollably for the tender support I had never had, and the caress of understanding that brought pain to my body. In the throes of discovery, I shared my inner-most being with a young German girl called Birgit.

Birgit was a beautiful, cheerful spirit who reflected me when I was fourteen. We danced late at night in the woods and laughed deeply. We spoke about our experiences in spirit, but the pain was still locked in my heart. When it was time for me to leave Findhorn, I sat sobbing on the grass and it was Brigit and another girl from Zimbabwe, who decided to pay for me to stay another week. I was eternally grateful for the love that enveloped me, and so began a course on the Science of Intuition with Norman Shealy and Caroline Myss.

We began to explore the concept of control and I shared that whenever I wanted a man in my life, I found him; that he treated me terribly and I persuaded myself it was all right. Intellectuality and intuitive diagnosis had all the answers for me – I had to forgive my parents and ex-husband for breaking my heart. Intellectually it was easy, but deep down inside my heart I still held on to judgment, as I became a case study in a classroom, where Caroline told me I would get cancer of the uterus if I did not forgive. I was in extreme pain.

That week I went to a healer who tried desperately to give me relief even though I was in physical, mental and emotional pain. The relief was temporary and I switched into an intellectuality that kept me smiling and eager to learn more.

One day during an afternoon meditation, I see myself as the leader of an Amerindian tribe. The tribe cares deeply about me and they look up to me. I see myself meeting up with the Red Shirts and making a peace treaty which will be broken. My tribe is slaughtered and as I die, I realize I have not learnt to love, because I hate what the white man has done to our tribe.

My interpretation of the vision was that I had failed my people. At no time did I consider I may have been betrayed through circumstance. On the contrary, I internalized the fact I had betrayed my tribe, and was therefore responsible for everyone's soul that had suffered through this betrayal. I was also filled with hatred for the man who had taken everything away from me; he reminded me of Father. When I left Findhorn I knew I would return.

My cup of love I had absorbed as a child was the measure that kept me sane but it was inevitable that the pressure become too much to bear. I released a lot of it travelling back and forth to Scotland over the next year, but the wounds had begun to fester.

When I reached the Transpersonal, the pain had not been healed and this kept me from truly breaking free from the past. There was much I had not dealt with, especially the shadows lurking inside of me, and I could not even consider the dangers of entering a spiritual path without a physical teacher, because I trusted the universe, no matter that I thought they had betrayed me. When I needed to ask for help, help came. It came in the form of visions and I was conscious they were teaching me a lot. What I failed to realize at the time was that I could not ignore my inner turmoil. I had to face it because pain was tightly woven in with the spiritual, and this was detrimental to my well-being. I had also failed to listen to my inner voice.

I had, in my sorrow, forced doors to open and although I knew a sacred marriage of split selves within me was possible, I refused to look at the possible dangers involved. When my inner voice clearly told me to slow down, I did not. I wanted to understand everything at once, which was completely impossible. So when I lost focus on my inner voice that clearly told me not to go outside but to stay indoors, four months after I returned from Scotland, I entered the land of shadows that threatened me continuously. There were negative thought patterns that swirled around in the unseen, eager to weigh one down. There were inner voices that reached a crescendo and then only one clear voice that began to soothe. The more negative my thoughts were, the more negative my experiences. I learnt through it all that there are two kinds of power.

The one kind comes from the intellectual mind and the other comes from the heart. The intellectual power, almost like a laser beam, can burn holes in the psyche. It is what we use to make dreams into realities and for psycho-kinesis and it is dangerous. Due to the magnitude of its power, it works with a vibration that can destroy as easily as it can create.

The heart is, and therefore has no need for power. As long as there is clear intent, it follows a different law and brings results that are equally powerful, as long as they are aligned with purpose. There is a flow through love that allows self-preservation and without love, we simply become machines. There needs to be a fine balance between body, mind and spirit, as they are entangled. Once spirit is set aside and only body and mind function, we become alienated from our true nature.

In the world of duality, there is always a cost. My first trip to Scotland cost me more than I could ever imagine. I had called Philip to tell him I was staying another week, and that I was in pain. He could not understand me or had chosen not to, because he went into denial. I was a threat to the perfect world he had created for himself, where he always seemed to be in control. The problem was that he gave me an ultimatum; either I return home or else he would take the children from me.

As fate had it, when I had obtained my divorce, I had signed a paper to say I had no claims on my husband's estate, that if I remarried he would take the children, that he could see them whenever he wanted and at the ages of nine and eleven, they could choose where they wanted to live. My sons were exactly nine and eleven when, broken and sobbing, I told my husband I could not return. One week's grace was all I asked for, but perhaps the universe had other ideas in store for me, for when I returned to Athens, my children left to live with their father.

I had come to the end of a cycle and had lost so much. It broke my heart and my spirit so much to lose my sons that I decided to move to Scotland. I sold my furniture at an auction to fund my move, gave paintings my father had painted away to friends, as well as some of my jewelry. This giving away of material goods was an exercise in letting go, but the items I could not sell were my bed, fridge and stove. I accepted it as a message from the universe; I had to stay and become a weekend parent. My sons were pupils at the school I worked at and initially they stopped speaking to me, which drove me almost insane.

Locked in a no-win situation and almost desperate, I resigned from my job, got another and tried to draw my children into my life. It was not at all easy but somehow I managed. When I returned home at night, I sat in front of the fireplace weeping. It was no wonder that the pressures of so many changes came to a head through another spiritual breakthrough. In order to integrate the events that had occurred, I found myself taking to pen and paper. The pressure inside broke free and I began to write as though I had discovered a treasure in my inner being. Reams of paper and words exploded from within, taking me into the heart of esotericism and the dark night of the soul. It was a never-ending process. By day I taught and by night I wrote. I became each and every word and experienced each and every thought, as I found myself traveling through the dimensions between nothing and everything.

When I decided to travel, money appeared from nowhere to fund me and people knocked on my door to support me. I became embroiled in the life of Akhenaten and Nefertiti. I traveled again to Egypt and stood in the pyramid, only to find people around me paying homage to the energy that fuelled my every action. Under the sphinx I saw a secret room in my mind's eye that held history in its hand. On walls I saw pictures others could not. When I returned, pages unfolded from my hand about karma and chakras until I innocently tried to find where I belonged, in all that flowed from my pen. I began to fear what I was writing but nothing could stop the flow, until fourteen manuscripts later, I began to access a strange reflection of myself, desperately in need of finding truth etched in the sands of time. I believed wholly I was writing truth, but never realized there was none to be found, apart from my own subjective ravings, as I dipped and soared between ecstasy and reality.

I tried to be a good mother. I tried to bridge the gap between my pain and more enlightened moments, but it was becoming more and more difficult to integrate. My books ruled me to such an extent I became completely entangled in them. As I wrote about the Universe and my Personal Universe, I lived in the forest I had found as a child, with access to an open door, but how far can one go with no true boundaries? The question of boundaries never entered my head. They had ceased to exist the day I entered this world, and although I was a Phoenix rising through my own ashes, the pain still tore at my being, until I became a keen observer of the signs and symbols exploding from my unconscious. I tried to balance but it was becoming so difficult to lead two lives I was only conscious of one thing: a spiritual marriage of sorts beginning to emerge through my desperate attempt to find balance.

My soul was beginning to manifest itself to me and yet the pain was so severe, I was unable to truly listen to my voice, my inner voice that began to warn me of crisis. Somewhere along the path, I was beginning to lose contact with the danger and began to feel invulnerable. The day my inner voice told me explicitly again, not to leave my house for three days, I lost control and walked outside. Totally open psychically, I began to pick up a cacophony of images that were so real and impossible to integrate, that I learnt how to balance through imbalance. As I walked around, trying to cleanse my space, I began to lose balance. Philip had contacted my parents, but seeing my parents only made the pain worse. Every time they walked towards me, a sharp pain would pierce my solar plexus. Desperate to escape, I left my apartment late at night to walk the streets of the neighborhood I lived in. A group of motorcyclists caught sight of me and began to circle me, threatening to take out condoms and rape me. I desperately asked the universe to help. An inner voice or Higher Guide answered me.

'*You will see two women in the distance, walking on the pavement. You may take energy from them and raise your vibrational level.*'

I saw them, and began focusing on raising the vibrational level around me. I refused to see monsters and think negatively, although dogs were barking furiously around me and the motorcyclists were coming closer. Something snapped around me, and I watched them drive off. Not knowing where I was or how I would get home, I called out to Sai Baba and to the universe. Exhausted, I found myself in front of an apartment block and saw a beautiful tree in the garden. I went in and lay down to sleep. When I awoke, I looked across at the night sky. There was a flash and I clearly saw the face of Sai Baba. For a split second I knew that what he knew, so did I, and as I got up, I spoke loudly to the sky.

"I don't know how to get home!"

There was no longer desperation in my voice and the answer came clearly to me.

"Follow the brightest light in the sky!"

My reply was perfectly normal, because I knew I was talking to my higher self and to my guides.

"You guys have got to be kidding! There are stars everywhere! How can there be one light?"

That is when I saw it. One star was moving. I began to follow it and see geometrical shapes all around me, giving me some semblance of sanity and, in my crisis, I made a breakthrough. Somewhere from within, I began to see the patterns of support I was receiving from the universe, through spurts of understanding that had to do with quantum mechanics, but then my brain would overload and I would become exhausted. I managed to find my way home and when I emerged from my breakthrough, I was filled with fear. The following day I went to see Bob Najemy.

"Please," he implored me, "do not be afraid. Your Dharma is what you are experiencing. You are traveling into many dimensions. Trust the process. You have not done anything wrong. You keep on telling me as you have been traveling, so have you been doing healing on the planet and Mother Earth. Accept this is your Dharma."

Too much had happened and even though I had been lovingly guided, I could not take it anymore. I resigned from my job, gave up my apartment and moved to the south where I could be beside the sea.

I got a wonderful job at an international school, worked hard and buried my manuscripts and my memories under a pile of papers, deep in my cupboard. I became a down-to-earth teacher and mother, acutely aware I was too afraid to touch the spiritual dimension again, and yet aware it was a very major part of my life.

Can we really ever walk away from who we truly are? I do not think so! In fact I know we cannot, because once we have awakened, we can never go back to sleep. The call of soul is far greater than the world of matter and may contain the remnants of life within it, but inevitably will always return to its original blueprint.

Five years of earthly existence passed me by! They were years filled with learning and yet I slowly began to wilt under the strain of trying to be what others wanted me to be, but not myself. Time and time again, an image of my brother found its way into my heart, and time and time and time again, I saw how similar we were, in the way that I was becoming a citizen on the planet I tried desperately to call home. My parents came and went. I tried hard to communicate with them but it was becoming difficult. My intellectuality was beginning to wear away, as I continually faced their inability to recognize my brother's worth as a human being. I tried to find excuses, but at times they were impossible to find, because my parents had stopped growing a long while back and were stuck in a victim and persecutor role of suffering. I tried to talk to them about spirit because I wanted them to open up to it; if they could, then so could I, but it was impossible. I tried to convince my ex-husband that spirit was within, but he denied me as I was denying myself. I tried to talk to my sons, but they had their own paths, and I felt torn in a way that was almost indescribable, because I knew I was losing my self – my spiritual self – but was trying desperately to persuade the members in my family they had to wake up first, in order to give me the courage I needed to walk again on my path. I was fighting a losing battle and yet I tried desperately to heal myself through healing Mother.

I had unintentionally told Mother the previous year, as we sat on the balcony looking out to sea, she had water in her lungs and that she had to go and see a doctor. Mother told me I must be mad and yet, Mother had lung cancer and soon after her return to South Africa, she was told she had to have chemotherapy. She refused, as if by accepting this sentence of impending death, it could take her back in time to deal with the true death sentence she had supposedly been given in absence, due to her love for a German officer, or so I thought at the time. Mother carried her cancer with her as a protection to be used every time I tried to open my heart to her. Every time I tried to speak to her about her life she would begin to cry and tell me to stop because she was ill. I tried to heal her as was my duty, but I knew she was shutting a door on both herself and me, and this was a memory that took me back to my childhood days, when I had desperately needed a mother, but instead had been made to play the role of parent.

However, Mother's illness brought me back to my soul. Every night I sent healing light to her but, oblivious of what I absorbed through healing from a distance, I found myself in hospital again. Determined to heal, I carried on praying for those members of my family who were in pain and began to reach out again towards spirit. Yet again, I began to move beyond boundaries and once again found myself in crisis. This time, I went to hospital for a week and was treated as though I were an animal – not a human being.

Spiritual crisis is in essence a warning of imbalance. As long as there is a store of pain, guilt and suppressed emotions, it interferes with spiritual, religious and mystical experiences. Those who deal with patients and who have no background knowledge of spiritual crisis treat it as a psychosis. Those who do not understand what a person is going through use violent means to bring them back to reality and this hurts them even more.

I was sitting in my living room, healing Mother. I had no idea I was opening myself more and more, as I entered her space. I did not protect myself, and so began to have flashes of war and disaster. I wanted to go for a walk and my inner voice clearly told me to stay at home. My reply was that I was old enough to take care of myself! How come every time I went into an altered state, I insisted on going outside when, each time, I was warned not to? Would I ever learn?

Clutching my keys in hand, I left my front door open and walked down the stairs. My keys were very important to me because I had, in my last experience, left them in front of a church, exchanging them for the key to the door of universal understanding. It was ironic because I had truly surrendered to the universe in this way, but forgotten completely I existed as a body. As I stepped outside, visions streamed forth and, conscious of the need for safety, I began to walk up and down outside trying to balance. A kind neighbor came over to walk with me and I struggled to explain what I was going through. He was just managing to calm me, with a very beautiful gentleness, when a police car drove up. Unbeknown to us, another woman, who lived on the second floor and always complained about everything, had called the police. Although I was doing nothing at all, apart from walking up and down, they made me get into the car and took me to the police station. The young policeman sitting in the back next to me held my hand, whilst the older driver spoke aggressively to me. It was he who pulled me out when we arrived at the station and pushed me roughly into the station. Most of the policemen on duty were young, but no one dared speak up for me. I kept on asking why they were so weak and why they could not tell this brutish older man to treat me with respect. Laughing, he literally threw me into a cell, locked the door and left. The pain began to soar.

Looking around the cell, all I can see are the many Bulgarian, Polish and Russian girls, who have lain on the dirty mattresses, crying. In my vision, I see policemen playing backgammon and then their threats late at night. Blow jobs, or quick sex against the desk will ensure the girls are released the following morning.

I began to scream!

At the apartment I had just left, my landlady who lived on the second floor realized something terrible had happened, when the kind young neighbor knocked at her door. A deeply caring citizen, he had taken the time to ask questions about me, and had ascertained she lived in the apartment. My landlady was furious with the neighbor who had called the police.

"Why couldn't you tell me?" she implored. "I would have calmed her down and she would not have been taken to the police station. Are you mad?"

My landlady rushed upstairs to find my door wide open. She knew she had to let someone know what had happened to me, so she began to search the apartment. The fact my handbag was on the kitchen table escaped her completely. As though the universe had thrown an invisible cloth over it, it remained silent and still, unable to give her the number of my ex-husband that was written as an emergency number in my diary. In my bedroom, my landlady found a piece of paper with telephone numbers on, that my eldest son had left there. She phoned a friend of his, who called him. Dimitris called his father who immediately rushed to the police station.

Unfortunately Philip had never trusted me and his fear and hidden aggression towards me only made me fly even higher. Desperate to escape, I prayed continuously and only realized something was terribly wrong when I was forced into an ambulance and my ex-husband was looking at me in despair, but not with compassion. I tried to apologize for my erratic behavior that had not been damaging to anyone other than myself.

I had gone into spirit with no desire to be connected to the past that suddenly appeared to me exactly as it had been. My children had been wrenched from my heart; my husband had been unable to love me and his parents were so cold; I had lost my siblings in tragic circumstances and tried to love parents who were deeply troubled. I had longed for love and had not found it; I felt so much guilt inside of me for the broken marriage vows, the lack of conviction to talk to my sister before she died and the inability to express the love that had eluded me in the garden of my visions, in the presence of a catholic priest and with a man I had chosen to spend my life with. So when the ambulance reached a stop outside the hospital that was waiting to admit me, I fought, promising to be 'good' – to stop crying and behave like a 'normal human being'. My pleas reached deaf ears. I was dragged down to a room, tied to a bed and left in the darkness. I tried desperately to break free; I tried to call on the spirit world and when the light came through the tiny window in the morning, I was whole. A nurse began spoon feeding me with water. I spat it out, my words ringing in my ears,

"I am not an animal – I am a human being!"

Perhaps having at last recognized my value as a human being saved me, because the resident psychologist entered the room and told the nurse to untie me. I sat up and meekly took the medication I was handed. For the next four days, I stared with eyes full of compassion at those people who were locked in between the worlds I knew so well. I was equally aware the staff had no idea what I had been through, and had simply abandoned us all, to tragic labels. When I asked to be allowed to go into the garden, I was refused bluntly. I stared down at the trees knowing nature would give me strength and so it was, as I was standing and looking outside, that a young nurse came to tell me I had a visitor. I walked slowly towards my father who sat in the visitor's lounge with a small suitcase.

"I've brought you some clothes," he said. I tried to smile.

I asked him how Mother was and took the case to my room after he left. No amount of medication could have blunted the reality of taking out a bikini, an evening outfit, a small make up case, a brush and a blue denim skirt and shirt. There was no underwear, no money and no nightgown. I wore the bikini under my denim skirt and shirt and two days later when I was discharged, I asked my ex-husband who came to fetch me, to take me to a lake in Vouliagmeni for a coffee. I looked at the water and then at the man who sat opposite me, who understood nothing whatsoever of the ordeal I had been through. Three days later, I went back to my job, only to take sick leave two weeks later because I was so exhausted.

I slowly began to heal as I sat in my living room trying to put the pieces together in my shattered mind. This was how I learned about the importance of balance; how the mind can be healed; how spiritual crisis could become breakthrough rather than breakdown. I did not like the fact I had to accept how little those who were in positions to help me knew about spiritual crisis. I had required those around me to give support, unconditional caring and understanding. Instead I was hurt both physically and mentally. I had to find balance on my own, reconnect to spirit, and connect to Gaia because I knew that pills could not cure my bleeding heart. Pills as they had in the past, stifled me completely and made me a zombie. So when a friend answered my plea and gave me the name of a psycho-analyst I could start therapy with, I truly believe that the universe was yet again involved in my destiny.

CHAPTER ELEVEN

We are born alone and die alone. However, we are never truly alone. Across the web of the unseen we are drawn to those earth angels who will help us heal, no matter how hard that healing may be. It is of utmost importance we not lose sight of who they are and what they represent.

Soul

I had stopped taking any medication and knew that in order to find peace I had to go on a journey of self-discovery and heal my inner child. I was aware that if I wanted to help others I had to have helped myself, and it was with great relief that I found that the therapist I would see was well aware of spiritual crisis and was on his own path of self-discovery. My expectations were clear and I wanted to focus on the lessons I had learnt through my experiences.

It was September of 1999, two days after an earthquake in Athens, that I sat talking to the young psycho-analyst I had made an appointment with. After introducing ourselves, I gave him a summary of my experiences and he told me he was not really sure I needed therapy, because I seemed to have understood and analyzed a lot about my path. Then I told him about the young child who had been raised in a family where there had been no boundaries. The psycho-analyst inclined his head, took a deep breath and told me to look around his room, to make myself comfortable and that he would do what he could to help me with my past. I looked around the room. Time had slowed down and as I looked at the pictures on the walls of his office I felt comfortable. I noticed a stand with a piece of music by Handel behind my chair, and it held a certain atmosphere of mystique for me. There was a beautiful stone statue of a young woman on the floor and I smiled. My gaze gently rested on the picture behind his desk, which was a picture of the Virgin Mary and Child when suddenly, as though from far off, I heard his voice and brought my eyes back to his desk only to freeze as I watched my new doctor move some pieces around on it.

"Nothing at all," he said softly, "is here by chance."

No amount of dreaming could have prepared me for such an inexplicable way of introducing me to my inner being. On the desk were five items he had moved to the centre of his desk! Unbelievable as it may appear, one was a knight, made out of wood. I stared at it mesmerized as my eyes darted back and forth. There was a beautiful wooden horse with gold and ivory inlay, a small book with gold lettering and a clay cup in which a feather lay. I was totally shocked.

I focused on the feather. I had written about a feather that represented freedom of heart. It had fallen to the feet of an Amerindian called White Star, who I had felt in presence, when I was completing a story of my life and who had become a guide when I had written my second manuscript, I had called *Mahanavita*. White Star had been a presence behind me, and I had begun to channel a number of books after that. I looked at the knight, horse, book and cup and silently cried out to the universe.

"What does all this mean? Who is this man you have led me to?"

I got no reply at all, so I looked up at the man sitting opposite me, shocked by what had suddenly sent me back to my visions and dreams of childhood, expecting him to carry on talking. My eyes kept on darting to the objects so carefully placed on the wooden desk; how could they have manifested in front of my eyes? Why had he chosen them and moved them around on his desk? I tried desperately to focus on the man who sat in front of me.

The man in front of me had salt and pepper hair, brushed back, that haloed a handsome face that was part of an equally well-proportioned body. He looked kind and gentle, but I was unable to relate to his presence because it seemed as though I was slipping quickly back in time into the past. Had I at last found the soul mate I had lost in the wood of my childhood days? It was all so much to take in, as I focused on the practicalities of booking our next appointment, even though I seemed to be soaring to the heights of an altered state of consciousness. When I left, I stumbled out of his office and it seemed time had frozen. I managed to find my way home and sat shivering. I was pleased it was a Friday and that it was not my weekend to have my sons. Thoughts raced through my mind and that night I fell into a dreamless sleep. I had hoped for some insight – something that would explain the connection between us, but there was nothing!

I tried talking to the universe in between taking long walks in the sunshine and sitting in my living room, tears pouring down my face, that weekend. At last, I thought, he had come to me. On Sunday morning I woke early and sat on my couch, in a dream state. I closed my eyes and began to meditate. I began to watch a mind movie that would last three hours – a film of life that was haloed in light. What appeared to be all my psycho-analyst's past lives began to stream across my mind's eye vividly. I dared not think! I dared not dream! All I could do was watch and believe fully I had at last found my angelic friend and knight all in one. There was no pressure and although I felt simultaneously great sadness intermingled with incredible joy, I was able to fully connect with what I was seeing. The following Monday, I went back to his office and sat awkwardly in my chair.

"I saw your past lives!"

I blurted out the truth because I could not contain it any longer. I was taken aback when he asked politely.

"What did you see?"

Each word held the image and I began to feel a cold sweat break out, as I struggled to contain my shivers. My voice was low.

"I saw many, many lives. Most of them were soldiers who had been wounded in battle. Some were more gruesome than others. They spoke of deep betrayal and yet I could connect with the light in each and every one of them."

At the time, I appeared to be literally describing events rather than listening silently to the messages I had been receiving. I could not help projecting each and every vision onto the doctor, who suddenly became everything to me. This change of events was more than overwhelming as I realized I had found my heart and my soul through the vision, that probably had reflected my inner being as well – something I had always needed to do. This feeling was not intellectual but rather was born from a knowing connection that had occurred because of the significance behind everything that had happened since I had met him.

The universe had literally become visible to me and in that universe I saw the beauty of my inner self. I found myself twirling gently in a ballet that followed the notes of a rare piece of music that played in each molecule of my body. I was slowly pulled into the deeper aspects of my wounds that had never had a chance to heal, as I spoke about my past.

From the time I was conceived, I had not particularly been made to feel welcome. Feelings of pain had passed from mother to child and those of anger that passed from husband to wife, I had also absorbed. Years of suppression and guilt must have taken their toll on the tiny sperm and egg that would come together to make a body for my soul. However, my soul-spirit itself must have held an incredible amount of suppressed memories as well. A mixture of emotions needed to be freed; not only for purification of form but also for purification of spirit. I discovered that spirit and soul were related much like siblings in a family; but they appeared to be unique, the latter much clearer and brighter than the former.

My understanding of spirit is that it is an inner body of memories that are not only our own but those of our ancestors; they always remain spiritual memories. Each and every one of these memories could heal as I deepened my understanding of them and learnt about consciousness. Soul belonged, as I saw it, to the realm of guardians and keepers of a temple of light, where I was like a priestess. As I had incarnated into material form, I was part of the soul body as well; my challenge was to purify those aspects of spirit that blocked the light from my soul. At the moment of conception I had realized my bond with the universe was breaking, and this had brought fear into my life. I was afraid I would not succeed in re-building a temple of light within me and this fear became my rational mind. My psycho-analyst was also afraid.

He had been raised in a home where his mother had always been the centre of everyone's lives. A mountain climber, a socialite and someone who believed in the balance of life, she was a powerful figure. To get to the top, you had to carefully calculate all the moves you had to make and measure the distance between your every step, and this was something he did not like. He wanted to break free but couldn't because deep inside he knew he was not ready to plunge into the unknown and experience union. He was also ethically bound by the Hippocratic Oath he had taken. To him, union meant losing a major part of his inner being he himself had not yet contacted. It was imperative he not lose his sense of soul in a union where there were no boundaries and, he had taken on the commitment of helping me.

At a deeper level he may have forgotten what it meant to be united, not to each other, but to soul-spirit as well, because he was still learning about his inner world. Soul-spirit was the ultimate edge of all being for it implied surrendering to heart and soul rather than body and mind. My perception of soul was not only everlasting but also incorporated those aspects of self that had remained hidden from view. He seemed to have a sense of innocence and so did I. He believed firmly my soul was in need of retrieval and tried not to focus on his own as well. His job was not easy because often he had no idea where I was traveling. All he could do was follow and hold the energy as I had visions of my life and as I struggled to contain the emotions that came from within. Sometimes he was brusque and I would get very upset and at times he would get angry because I kept on insisting he was my soul mate.

My soul had drifted in and out of my conscious, but I had never lost it. On the contrary, I believed it had always been my protection and yet I had, in my past, thought it had left me. It was so important for me to I hold onto it, as it emerged reflected in the eyes of my therapist, who I firmly believed was my soul mate. What I needed to do of course was to plunge into the depths of my unconscious, to heal the dark shadows that lurked there not by fighting them, but rather by embracing them with light. I did not embrace them. I sent light to them but held onto them, afraid that if I lost them, I would lose sight of my soul and I was so intent on holding onto my soul I forgot the universe behind that soul.

I did not want to be an idyllic child but rather a challenge to my parents. I wanted them to realize their fallibility and to work with it. I had always seen my children as reflectors of my divine self and believed they were older than me because they had come to teach me something; something about myself. I wanted my children to be proud of me, but was unable to see they would love me no matter what, simply because I was their mother, but that they would not necessarily like me, for I had also broken their spirit. These are bonds that cannot be broken no matter how much we hate our parents for what we think they did to us.

Two weeks after I met my soul mate, I bought an angel medallion for him. I found myself sinking into a spirituality I had never experienced before. Visions of him and his family were clear and precise; visions of past lives or parallel lives were equally strong, and I had no other reasoning apart from a very strong feeling this was destiny. As a therapist, he tried hard to follow as I dipped and soared, slowly trying to unravel the pain and the spiritual messages that streamed forth. When I told him I was falling in love with him, I also told him of my fear. The fear urged the act of falling totally and completely in love with him, and inadvertently, this helped me trust the process I was in.

I became fully committed to my healing process and, although our relationship was totally platonic and that of therapist and client, I believed we would be together based on the union I was experiencing. Although he continuously told me he wanted me to go beyond him, I would not listen. Our spiritual connection was so profound it very often took precedence in my perception of him as a therapist. Although I tried to find reason for the objects on the desk, I hardly understood what a major paradigm shift had occurred because of those symbols, because there was no way he could understand how much they really meant to me. He was never able to give me an answer as to why he had moved them around and eventually he simply said they were symbols, and that it was obvious we shared a similarity between them. Although it was a valid argument because of the extent to which they had played their role in my life, it was impossible for me to accept things so simply.

One day he gave me the knight and I felt touched beyond physicality, but could not erase the fear that he had chosen deliberately not to become a knight but rather a man who would logically take a decision to leave the spiritual connection behind him, in order to help me find order in my life. I failed to realize then, he was reminding me that both knights were aspects of my own self. My shadow wanted to destroy the beautiful book I carried within me, and yet I had been clearly given the support of Love to find my way through the labyrinth and into the Light. I took the wooden knight home and placed it on the table in my living room and it nurtured me. I lived in a safe space for approximately two years, dealing with my shadows until the fated day he told me he was getting engaged. I knew there was someone in his life whom he had met four months before he met me, because he had told me and yet I did not want to believe I would lose him. The pain was almost unbearable because I needed to move beyond the pain I had felt as a young child, when my angelic mentor had left me.

My therapy had not only been one of visions but also dreams – dreams of giving birth to his child, dreams of dancing with him, of living a perfect life with him so that it was as though life was a dream. Reality however, was totally different. I could not believe the Universe could have brought him into my life, only to take him away. I told him I thought he was mad to get married and that he wouldn't be happy, because I truly felt he was denying a major aspect of self – his and mine. My pleas fell on deaf ears and so the man I believed truly to be my soul mate began to plan for his wedding.

I went on holiday to Cyprus for a short while that summer and became heavily involved in healing the planet. It was just prior to 9/11 and I knew something terrible was going to happen. I called him to tell him I needed help because I felt I was to have another crisis, but he went on holiday with his fiancée and never called back. I suffered as I was drawn to heal what I hardly understood and wept because I needed support that would not come, but had to get through this momentous time, for what I knew was my innate ability to receive. For ten days I lay on a couch, connecting with the universe, healing, as much as I could, the planet I had refused to call home, and those who walked on it.

I managed to heal myself and cope although I was hanging by a thread. I had finally broken through the veil of the unseen, managed as much as was possible at the time to maintain balance, and got myself home, not wanting to listen to him tell me I had to be alone. I gave him back the knight he had given me and he threw it away. I pleaded with him to give it back to me, but he refused. I was no longer sure what role he was truly playing. Was he simply relieved I was safe? Did he truly trust his own behavior or did he simply know I had had the strength to deal with things, as I had the strength to accept his pending marriage because of my deepening understanding of my inner world? My learning process brought anger and despair every time we reached critical moments. A cyst on my ovary burst and I was rushed to hospital. I begged him to come and see me and he charged me for the visit; the visit that culminated in him saying:

"I have just realized I am everything to you. The friend, the lover, the husband, the brother, the sister....!"

I felt the blood draining from my face.

I began to lose faith because of the extremes we were in. No matter what I had told him about my visions of him, he always told me I was wrong. When I had called him up concerned about his father's health, he told me I was mistaken. Often he became cold and distant then he would be warm and emotional. At times, tears fell from his eyes and he moved me with his understanding and yet I was no nearer to the ultimate understanding, that as long as I relied on someone else for my peace, I could never truly be happy. Once again the darkness began to fall and three times I came extremely close to shutting the spiritual door forever but something stopped me each time. I was convinced the energy and focus of love that flowed unconditionally from me was the energy that made his relationships become stronger. I used my intuition to protect myself for I knew I was slowly draining and he was growing. This is when I began to learn about the need for boundaries and protection. Something had to give way and although there were times I wanted to break away so finally and with anger and despair, I also knew I would only be harming myself. I had come so far on a very long and painful road that it did not seem fair to myself to do so. I prayed constantly for the universe to guide me and learnt to detach as much as was possible. Four years had gone by and I nurtured my breaking heart when he finally took his vows, to send a beam of healing energy to him and his wife because I knew he was a part of me.

I sent prayers of goodwill to his family who had become in a way like my adopted family. I cared about them all, even though I knew them not and gave at last the love I knew to be my purpose, without conditions. I worked hard to extinguish the flame between us without damaging my spirit. We would do seven years of therapy and I would struggle to contain my feelings and not long to dream, as I had when I first met him, but during these years and those that followed, I would finally learn the true meaning of unconditional love.

The dream was for a life without struggle. It was a dream for the intimate and the joy that comes when we realize life is sacred and those people who touch us even more so. My soul mate had touched every fiber of my being. He had given me reason to live because he had fulfilled my unfulfilled dreams; and yet, my being was filled with the joys of the spiritual and not the physical. They were the dreams of a child wrapped up in innocence and the dreams of a child who has stepped beyond time and space in order to find a temple few knew to exist. The temple of light was not a figment of my imagination. It was something that had been given to me as a gift – it was a memory that found its reality within the beauty not only of the sky, but the earth as well.

Whenever I connected with nature it was with the essence of the Mother and Father figure as one component. It was with a greater order that had begun to flow as a seed to a perfect flower or tree; my life was found to mirror those aspects of godliness that others found mundane. Connecting with this space, I had finally connected with that part of me that Earthly life had threatened on a daily basis.

So when he decided to come to see me for biotherapy, some years later, I had detached completely and truly wanted to connect with his inner being. He told me during his first session he had a confession to make. All that I had felt during the seven years I had been his client, the concerns, the visions of his father's ill health were true. I stared at him aghast. In his nonchalant way he said he didn't think it appropriate to have said yes at the time, seemingly oblivious of the fact I had come so close to leaving my spiritual path.

This was when I began to see the man rather than the soul. It brought some kind of balance to our liaison but I felt the pain of this balance as something that dulled my senses and brought with it a sense of tragedy. I was still connected to him though, and one evening I had an extraordinary dream.

In my dream I am sitting next to him. A woman is sitting next to him and she keeps on telling me to leave. Exhausted by her insistence I finally give in and tell him I am leaving. He asks me to follow him into an inner room where I see his mother dressed in black. She is receiving condolences from her friends. I tell him I have to leave but he askes me to look at the horizon and at the miracle taking place. I try to look at the miracle but instead I see three young boys who I believe to be his children. They are standing in the shadows but I notice their heads are bigger than their bodies. I tell him I have to leave for a third time and ask him who the woman is that insisted I leave. He tells me it was the babysitter of his children and I tell him a fourth time I have to go. I begin to shake as though there was an earthquake and as I reach out to hold his hand, he has gone.

Our spiritual connection had been severed completely, and it was as though I began to live in a parallel life. He had reminded me of God. In one of my previous experiences just before the motorcycles had encircled me, I had seen the Christ light shining in the eyes of a student of mine and had denied it completely then. I would not make the same mistake again.

When I told him about the dream he became quite angry. Much of the symbolism in the dream related directly to his life at the time but instead of seeing the beauty and extraordinary contact between us, he only saw the fact I was once again exact in knowing the most personal aspects of his life, as he saw it. At the time I was appalled at the lack of wisdom on his part and the fact he had never taken as sacred my visions that came spontaneously to me, suddenly and without warning. However, it was so difficult for him to break free, knowing I was always aware of what was happening to him. I could not see the fear that was radiating all around us because he had to remain firm, no matter what I did. The profane and the sacred, side by side they came, and even though he may have entertained thoughts about his life with me, he had to remain faithful to the little child that hopped out and around him every time I bared my soul to him. I realized that perhaps after all I had been through we had been sentenced by life, no matter how powerful our bond had been. It was through this final moment of realization that I could break the pattern I had got so used to, of giving him all my power.

I took a vow to be a friend to him because of the magnitude of what I had experienced but I would let go completely and never, ever return to what had once been so real to me. He assured me that nothing whatsoever would be lost but at the time, I believed he was wrong. I lost the beauty of the emotion that had taken me out into the transpersonal space of union. I lost the woman that had finally emerged like a butterfly from a cocoon. I lost the child who had dreamt about love and felt it flood through her and I lost the sacred spiritual marriage of heart and soul which was an even greater weight to bear. I lost them all and I knew that they had gone and this realization brought the memory of the fear that had flooded through me when I told him I was falling in love. Desperately, I tried to stem the landslide by asking him if he would have an affair with me. I had played every card I had and so had nothing whatsoever to lose. When he politely said 'no', I accepted my fate and could do nothing at all, apart from hope I would be able to pull myself up from the ashes and become a phoenix. My hopes would blind me for another four years.

When I look back at the symbols he had on his desk, I realize this was something that connected him to me and me to the universe. I was struggling on my spiritual path determined to work alone and only with the universe as my guide. It was almost impossible for me to distinguish between the spiritual and the everyday, because I had tried so desperately to make the everyday realm of human existence part of the spiritual. I could not see there were millions of layers of being, all spread out and entangled with each other. I could not comprehend the importance of being human in the realization that the spiritual and soul planes of consciousness could be accessed, but only that. I wanted to shift the spiritual, to move it into the physical only because I hankered after it so much. In spirit I was free – in physicality I remained in bondage no matter how many times I felt free. What I did not realize then, was that I had to gain my freedom in physicality in order to free myself from the illusion that I was alone and abandoned on Planet Earth.

Unwittingly, I had tried to make the spiritual become physical, not content to accept that each belonged to its own realm and that the knowledge of the spiritual could help define evolution. My release from him came only when I severed the tie between therapist and client and learned to love him as a very dear friend, and reflection of my inner being.

CHAPTER TWELVE

What gives us joy gives us sorrow. Nothing whatsoever is permanent in this realm of existence. To live in the past is to regret and to live in the future is to control. To live in present time is to unravel the secrets within and to become mindful of the fragility that we are, in our earthly existence.

Yin and Yang

My life had changed radically. Conscious I needed to keep busy, I enrolled with a university in the United Kingdom to do a long distance master's course in Western Esotericism. I needed to ground my experiences in academia. My course filled me with joy and I arranged to travel to Exeter for my first conference. I felt a surge of power run through my veins as I stood in the lecture hall. The universe, which had always been on the sidelines trying to protect me, drew me into the heart of wisdom. I met soul sisters and brothers. I was content and the moments shared filled me with joy. I met with spirit-soul as it had been given to the human race through the ancient past and man's everlasting search to find truth. I gently balanced with my new-found friendships and went back home to study hard. I took my power back and decided I had to leave Greece. I wanted to look for a job in Italy because I had always loved Rome, and was ecstatic when I got an interview at an International school. I packed a bag and flew to Rome.

As I walked around Rome, feeling like a woman, I was convinced I was taking a new road that would support me. I was conscious of the growing spirituality that I could be a part of, so I went to an internet café to send an email to my new friends. To my delight I found a second interview invitation for another school in Rome. Everything was falling into place and I was starting to feel happy at the turn of events that were giving me a break. I had lost twenty kilos,

198 A SOUL'S JOURNEY

looked attractive and was confident I would be moving to Italy the following summer. What I had not considered was that I might not like the schools I would visit.

Two days later, I sat crying in Barberini square. I had been offered both jobs but did not like the schools at all. I was shocked! My heart had always played a vital role in all the decisions I had ever taken. I knew that unless something felt right, I could not do it. So that night I took myself out for a lavish dinner and said goodbye to the dream of Italy. When I returned to Athens I threw myself into my work. I taught avidly during the day and did my assignments at night. I looked forward to my next conference in Exeter and was happy to meet up with my soul family. However, I began to feel stifled. Our course was purely academic without any experiential work, and I began to realize something was lacking. I needed my balance and realized my course leader was very close to snuffing out the spiritual in me, with his rather austere rules of academia. On the last day of the conference I told my course leader he reminded me of a big fish that was about to swallow me, a little fish. I could not tell him about the struggle I had been through not to lose my spirituality, so for once in my life, I decided to wait before taking any decisions to drop out of the course I had already completed the post graduate certificate for. When I returned to Athens I tried to remain open and balanced in looking towards a future that would enable me to do what I loved best. I looked for courses on the internet and one day found an advertisement for a Master of Science in Transpersonal Psychology. I no longer dreamt, for dreaming was futile; I decided I needed to fully immerse myself in the studies that would allow me to discuss what I knew to be true and others just laughed at. My life had certainly come together after the great upheavals I had experienced. The upheaval that had emptied me was not the only upheaval I had been through.

Mother and Father had, whilst I was still in therapy, decided to move to Greece. My parents had struggled a lot since their loss of Paul. Intent on holding on to some semblance of sanity, they knew their salvation lay with their grandsons and their only living child. Soon after Paul's death, my parents sold the farm in Middleburg for a very low price. They used the money to survive and carry on their six month visits to Greece until there was none left. They then sold a piece of property in Cape Town and when that money was gone they sold the property they had bought in Greece. I trusted their judgments and tried to get both of them to talk about their lives.

Mother had lost all contact with her family since her father's death in 1978. When the US bombed Belgrade I asked her why she was so detached and how she could not worry about her family. She told me there was no family left. Mother's father Mihail had died of a heart attack and her cousin Risto had let her know only three months after his burial. Although Mother had always been wounded by her upbringing, she had remained faithful to the memory of her father. They had started corresponding after his return to Belgrade and subsequent divorce from my grandmother. Perhaps the pain of loss was too much to bear, so Paul had taken it upon himself to write a letter to her cousin, severing ties.

I was upset my grandfather had died, feeling connected to my ancestors. I could not understand Mother's pain, continually asking why the spiritual realm was so inaccessible that people chose to live with their wounds rather than heal them. Mother had longed for love her entire life. She had longed to have a family and be happy and yet she had turned her back completely on them.

Father had done something similar as well, and Grandmother Johanna had cursed him and his children, when he enlisted in the army. This was the tragedy that had brought so much pain into our lives – the curses and closed doors that had brought additional pain through lack of insight and understanding.

My parents knew time was running out and so they decided to sell the house in Johannesburg. They moved to Greece and because the value of money was so different, they only managed to survive for four years. When they had no more money left, my parents were eternally grateful to Philip who arranged for a monthly sum to be deposited in their account. I, who had squandered my money on trips abroad and psychotherapy, was not a daughter, Philip relished in telling me. I explained why I had to do what I did in my life to Philip but he could not understand me; had he, we would still have been married.

When my parents and I went out for dinner every now and then, I drank too much wine in order to speak up! I inevitably went home with guilt because I was killing them, as they told me. In a way they were challenging me. I could sit back, feel sorry for myself or I could grow stronger and place very firm boundaries into place. I chose the latter and when, three years later, Mother fell ill again, it was the universe that gently came to stand with me, for I had tried to let go, see their point of view and realize it was impossible for them to understand me. I did not even understand myself fully!

Mother's health began to deteriorate and she started having pains in her uterus. They were bearable but nagging. One day however, she collapsed and the doctor was called in. When he arrived to tend to Mother, Father fell down the stairs dislocating his hip. These events were fully synchronistic, because had Father not fallen, he would have spent the time with Mother in hospital and I would not have been there for her, because I had to work.

An ambulance brought them both to Athens. My youngest son took his grandfather for X-rays, whilst I stayed with Mother, who was admitted into a different hospital. Father was discharged, but had to stay in bed, so I moved into the room I used for therapy, in between visiting Mother in hospital. I knew Mother was dying and tried to prepare Father for this event, but he was in total denial. I called into work and told my headmistress I could not come in because Mother was dying, but she told me I had to.

My headmistress had been as supportive as she could, but it was a natural process for her to think of work rather than the dilemma I was in. I left Mother who was pleading with me to stay with her, because I had to go back to work. I tried once again to be what I was not and thank goodness by the evening I had taken my decision. I called the deputy head, told her they could fire me but I would not come in! I had to be with Mother. It was something I knew from the bottom of my heart I had to do!

Money had always come in bursts and then had dwindled. It had been one of the main reasons for the sorrow and pain that everyone in my family had felt. It had blotted out the heart and demanded revenge whenever it reared up in life. I could not let it be the dividing line between love and life any longer.

For ten days I nursed Mother, conscious of the bills I would have to pay and the constant reminder from Mother that Philip would help her, because he had promised. For ten days, I held Mother's hand and tried to prepare Father for what I knew had to happen. Mother held my hand tightly. She became a young child in need of strength, and finally she began to tell me some of the details of her life. The child I had once been, who had lost her heart, slowly began to emerge from the place she had gone to.

Soul retrieval is an amazing capacity of the shaman and I had become a shaman of sorts. No matter how hard I tried to be a mother or teacher, I was a spiritual warrior. At last, the child in me emerged. Both of us knew Mother was dying and both of us knew she wanted to die in Epidavros. So when the doctor told me Mother had sarcoma and that nothing could be done for her, I arranged for a nurse to take her back to her home in Epidavros, when she was discharged. I found a Polish lady to look after her and five days later, Mother told me in a hoarse voice she loved me. The following morning at six thirty, Mother's spirit left her body. The call came a minute later.

"Your wish came true!" Father's voice broke through my sleep state. "Your mother's dead!"

Father was not going to make the passing easy.

"I didn't wish her dead, "I replied dully, but Father was angry he had lost his lifelong companion.

Mother's funeral took place five days later and as I had used all my funds to pay for the hospital and her nurse, Philip paid for her funeral. I was filled with shame. I tried to bridge the gap between Father and the growing awareness within me, but he was a very stubborn man. I explained he had to leave the three bedroomed house they had been living in.

"I'm not moving," Father said over and over again.

"You can't live in a three bedroom house on your own!" my reply was stilted.

"I'm not having that woman you found look after me. She murdered your mother; she gave her soup with weeds in it, poisonous weeds."

Would it ever end?

The following weekend I went to start packing up Mother's life. I was burdened with weight as I tried to untangle the house that had become a museum. It took weeks; weeks where I returned each time, totally blocked by the negativity that surrounded me. Father sat on the balcony, berating me to Mother; however I could not expect more, as he was deeply troubled

"She's selling your things. She doesn't care! She's brought strangers in. She's going to kill me like she killed you!"

I patted his head. I argued about books and things he wanted to keep and I knew had to go. He argued about moving. I pointed out he couldn't keep an enormous apartment on his own.

"You and that woman killed her," he mumbled.

I opened cupboards to find my sister's clothes everywhere. I found shoes Mother had gathered over the years, and felt as though I would drop from the growing weight. I found pictures and letters written in Serbian and became determined to find out why? Why had Mother turned her back on her family? Why had she collected so many things when they had never given her joy? The strain sent me to hospital with a swollen leg but I was not going to fall ill again, as I had in the past. Father moved further and further away from me and became more and more belligerent, holding onto Mother's spirit as much as he could.

"Stop going through my things!"

His words fell on deaf ears. I was determined to find truth.

One weekend, as I leafed through the wonderful library Mother had over the years collected, a nagging feeling made my eye dart towards Father's bedside table. He was sitting on the balcony, so I swiftly and quietly opened the drawer. Beneath a pile of papers, I found a bundle of letters and some documents which I could see had belonged to my grandmother. I quietly removed them, put them in my bag and carried on packing. The following day I gave everything I had found to a Serbian parent of one of my ex-students.

"I think these may be letters from my grandfather," I told her smiling.

Sania was as diligent as a detective and driven with a true desire to help me in whatever way she could. Piecing together pictures and names from different documents, she found Risto's daughter Zorana. Destiny had ensured her telephone was still in the name of her father and so Sania made the call. My 'aunt' was overjoyed to hear from someone who had news about Mother. Zorana had always remembered her father's words.

"Kaya saved our lives."

Risto knew the details of Mother's life and so had fully understood that part of Mother's bargain to leave Serbia behind her had been sealed with a promise of safety for the rest of the family. Zorana told Sania that she, her sister Brana and brother Branko had played with Paul and was devastated when she heard about Jackie and Paul's deaths. They chatted for an hour and Sania was ecstatic.

"I found your mother's family," she shared excitedly one week later when she came to my classroom.

She told me all about Zorana and about her son Darko.

"All three children are alive and have children. I also found pictures of them and your brother Paul when he was little. Look! There are also letters from your grandfather but I haven't finished looking at them all; especially the papers from your grandmother."

Three days later, Sania came to my classroom again during recess. She looked subdued and her eyes filled with tears. We sat down at my desk and this is when she told me about Dragan.

Dragan had been Mother's first love. Mother at sixteen had met a young man, who was one year older than she was. She had gone to a dance where he had been playing music. She had shyly looked at him all night and after they had danced he had arranged to meet her the following day. Amidst the violets growing by the side of the river Drina, Mother and Dragan had shared what was to prove to be true love, because it was so innocent.

Innocence is something we experience when we are children. As we learn about the environment, our innocence escapes into another dimension especially when it is threatened. The soul holds onto it because it is the face of love. When we lose our innocence we can only find it if we find the part of our self that has withdrawn. Without soul retrieval we remain empty. Information exchanged with Belgrade, I began to correspond with my nephew Darko. We tried to catch up on time and I arranged to go and meet Mother's family.

Going to Belgrade was a pilgrimage. I walked down streets Mother had, and firmly felt in my heart that I had to place flowers on my grandfather's grave. I walked into a home where I was warmly welcomed from the moment I arrived in Serbia. My cousins Branka, Zoran, Branko and Lubitsa opened their arms to me, and I fell into them. As though we had been together for years, we sat up late at night talking and drinking pear liquor. They took me around Belgrade and I went to the cemetery.

Grandfather had been buried with his second wife and I laid a wreath on the grave. I felt like a warrior who had finally returned home at the end of a very long battle.

The following day, I left with Darko for Zvornik where his mother Zorana lived. At last I was to see the town Mother had frequently visited, with her cousin Risto. Zvornik was beautiful and Darko's mother perfect. In my broken Serbian and her English we communicated as well as we could and the following day, arranged to visit Loznitsa, where Mother was born. Unfortunately, a friend of Darko who was to drive us to Loznitsa had to cancel. The woman who had been a child when Mother was sixteen, but remembered her and who we were to visit, also had to cancel. I had only two days at my disposal, and truly wondered why this was happening. I had also asked Darko to arrange a meeting with Dragan, who was eighty-five years old.

Sania had told me the letters he had written to Mother were the most poetic writing she had ever come across. The letters had been written when I was four and when it seemed Mother had been thinking of visiting Serbia. Dragan had written to tell Mother she would be safe if she returned. I felt broken by the tragedy, more so because Mother had never spoken about him. It seemed to me it had been too painful, but something had prompted me to write to him. I needed to thank him for loving Mother so deeply.

It was an intuitive move like the many I had experienced without logic. I did not know what to make of the possibility I might not make it to Loznitsa, so that night I gently spoke to the Universe. I thanked them for my path. I gave up my desire to control things, and slept wondering what would happen.

Giving up to the universe is an exercise I learnt as a child. Like any child, I wanted a happy home. I wanted to feel love and to be happy. When circumstances do not give us what we truly desire, we have a choice. We either become bitter to dwell on our loss, or we accept and surrender; to surrender is a move of strength. That night I surrendered. I slept, grateful for the all that had been found, and with a prayer that that which was incomplete, could become complete.

The next morning I looked out of the window at the houses of Zvornik and made my way to the kitchen. Darko was still asleep but his mother was awake. The phone rang and suddenly we were busy getting ready. The obstacles were no longer there, and soon enough we were on our way to Loznitsa. I was excited. I looked out of the window at the passing landscape and chatted away. It was a glorious day and Loznitsa was getting closer. As we rounded a bend, the small village was still out of sight, apart from a church that could be seen on the left. My intuition was strong.

"I have to go to that church," I said firmly.

Darko replied pleasantly, "Ok, on our way home."

We were cordially and warmly received by the woman who had once held Mother's hand, whilst taking Sunday walks down the street. At the time, Mother had been in love with Dragan and she had held a young six-year-old's hand. I could not believe I had opened a door that had remained closed for so many years.

Time passed as we drank coffee, ate pastries and chatted. Darko was translating everything as best he could, but I was getting agitated because I wanted to go to the church. I pulled out a notebook and wrote Darko a short message. He translated my fears of the church closing, but the woman replied warmly.

"Even if it is closed," she said understandingly, "The priest lives next door, so you can ask him to open the church."

A short while later we were on our way, having hugged with promises to meet again. We parked in a space close to the church and I stepped out of the car cautiously. As I walked into the church, Darko and his mother stayed at the entrance. I went slowly down the aisle. Then, I stopped and stared, conscious of the sound of music in my ears. A young boy, who had stood in the entrance to greet us, had put a tape on with a priest chanting.

In a dream state I stared down at the icon that was placed on a wooden stand in the center of the church. Time had ceased to exist because it was a Greek icon of a saint. The saint, who looked like Mary, held a veil across her hands, the veil I had accepted in vision, even though I still considered myself to be a stranger on the land. I was conscious of a need deep within my heart not to lose focus, as the veil was held over hands, as if telling me I had arrived at last, to a place I had to be in. I turned towards the right, my eyes darting. There was a tapestry of the Last Supper – a tapestry that was hanging in my dining room at home in Athens, that Grandmother Maria had embroidered. I carried on walking. There was an icon of St John the disciple of Christ and one of the Baptist. My mind was racing, for both played major roles in the books I had written hidden in my cupboard.

I made the sign of the cross and walked towards Darko, Zorana and his friend who had driven us to Loznitsa. I could not speak and they, understanding something was going on, chatted about visiting a hotel where Mother had had her reception after her marriage to Masha. It was close to the main square and Darko suggested we have coffee there. Suddenly my story poured out as I knew I had to return to the church.

I couldn't believe there was a Greek icon in a church where I was told Mother had been christened and where she had had her wedding. We raced back to the church only to find it was closed. However, the assurances of the woman we had visited had been enough for Darko to go with his friend to knock on the door of the priest's house.

Roused from his prayer, the priest explained the icon was on loan that month from Mount Athos in Greece. No, he did not know who the saint was but, he could look it up. After, pulling out a number of books he found the story.

The Virgin Mary had appeared to a group of people who had sought sanctuary in the church of Belvedere during the Turkish occupation. Two priests who had seen the apparition had felt both awe and fear. Awe because a veil had been placed over the church to protect those who had sought sanctuary and fear of the enormity of

such a vision for the incredible responsibility that had to do with
protecting not only those who were in need but the earth and its
peoples. The saint was Aghia Zoni – saint of the Veil.

When Darko emerged to recount the story, I felt relieved of a great
weight I had carried for my entire lifetime. It was as though I had
done something for those lives that had been lost, over generations
of painful struggle and I knew I had partly come home.

Love in all splendour began to envelop my soul. It began to hold
onto my heart as I tried to integrate the enormous realization that
spirituality was my uniqueness, and that I had not failed in trying to
bring the past to rest.The following day, back in Zvornik, I went to
meet Dragan.

Dragan was a short, delicate man in his eighties. Blinded through
glaucoma, he peered into the distance with a beautiful smile as he held
out his hand to hold mine. His wife graciously accepted us into her
home and his son, in a low voice, warned Darko his mother did not
know his father was communicating with Mother when I was four.

Zorana chatted gaily to her whilst Darko translated all that Dragan
could remember of his love. Tears unchecked fell from my eyes. For
some reason, all I could dwell on was the tragedy of lost love. My
soul mate's face kept on coming up and I cried. I cried for the empty
space in my heart and the apparent emptiness in Dragan's. I cried for
Mother, who had been in so much pain she could never share this
highlight in her life with me. I cried because we had passed each
other in life and never really been able to connect, apart from the last
ten days of her life.

I cried for the rose bushes of my youth that had all withered in
the garden of my dreams. I cried for the book I had written about my
life and my heart. My heart broken, I had placed it in the pocket of a
grey coat, to hang in the cupboard of my dreams, until one day I
buried it because it had grown so heavy. I recalled my sessions at
Findhorn when I had realized my spiritual heart and my heart as a
young bride were buried under the sands of time. I chokingly recalled
the arms of a white knight that had held me so warmly. My dreams
had shattered but dutifully I had followed the advice of Caroline
Myss who had told me I had to dig up my heart and in ceremony,

place it back where it belonged.

Later that afternoon, when we were back at Zorana's house, I sat in the living room looking out at the sunset. I realized I had been given a very special gift. I did not know what I had done to deserve this gift. Although I knew this was something profound, it wasn't only for me. I realized I had been taught something very special and that I could not find peace within myself, unless I held the gift in my heart and shared the gift with those who wanted to learn.

Later that night sitting at the table where we had eaten dinner, Darko began to translate some of Dragan's letters. In one of them, Dragan had told Mother.

"I do not know if you have told your children about me. If you ever share with them this great love, then tell them, you will always be my only love!"

I had sought Dragan out to thank him for love, not knowing what he had once written to Mother. I had acknowledged him and perhaps set the record straight for on my return to Athens, I wrote to tell him Mother had died poor. Was it destiny's hand that had carved out her ending; was karma a clear aspect of the balance needed in order to point out how love must always be of paramount importance? Had Mother turned her back on love to bring my brother, sister and me into the world? These were questions that would not find answers. Who was I to judge Mother, or to wish she had married her first love? I became smaller and smaller through the incredible vastness of the universe and the sky. This time, as I became a dot in an immense expanse of sky, I had no fear.

The events that had taken me to Serbia were events that gave me strength. Strength came because I needed to satiate the hungry ghost that walked across my heart, the day I touched a unique feeling in a dream that filled my heart with knowledge, because I knew what Divine Love felt like. I had also paid homage to my ancestors and wondered when the time would come for me to go to Ireland, to pay homage to my Irish ancestors. However, it is not enough only to feel this love. This love has to be integrated. It needs to find its reflection for it to become real. Reality cannot only be on a spiritual dimension. Reality must be part of this life as well. As I understood how great life was and how small my personal being, I began to ponder on my trips to Egypt.

Egypt had symbolized for me the union of Divine and Soul, through the vision I had of a woman, pregnant, a saint who held out his hand for a bird to peck at the crumbs, and an angel who held the world in hand.

My mind exploded with questions about the burial customs of the Pharaohs. Were the food and tools buried with the ancestors who went to the other side, reminders of the need to recall this earthly life? Was Egypt a perfect place that symbolized heaven and earth through its Sphinx? Was the message clearly etched in the sands? The message blazed in my mind!

Perhaps we are animal in strength – lion in body and god in mind. Is the mind capable of overcoming the body in such a way where the animal nature becomes one aspect of being, divine nature the other? Are the pyramids in Ghiza a reminder of the body, mind and soul paradigm?

All I knew was that there was only one moment in time, when the universe as one, separated into distinct parts that held the following message:

Contain the physical as part of the spiritual. Learn to balance the two as the left and right side of the Nile. Learn to acknowledge both life and death as stages in the transitional period that will lead to unity. Respect that each stage you go through is part of acknowledging the never-ending cycle of events. Contain the body for it is your vehicle. Bury your silver and gold for they will only help you in your physical life; respect they are your tools to help you whilst in your physical body, but never make money your priority. Beyond the border of time and space, Spirit shall rise and this spirit will take you into the arms of your soul – Ka. You must remember both! Money and body are of the material but the spiritual is your true freedom. As your body is buried, so shall your money be also, and all that will remain will be for you to face soul-spirit. Each must be given the acknowledgement they need. Neither is more important than the other. This is your balance.

I recalled the lessons I had learnt through my soul mate's fear of union. I understood how he had faced both selves. Perhaps the universe had truly separated us, so I could finally accept both worlds and also the respect union had given me. I could not move forward and free myself of the past until I truly understood, and I would not understand until I had worked further with myself. Working only with my reflection was not enough.

I returned to Athens and told Father about my trip to Serbia. Father was not willing to open his heart. He could not open up his being and clear out the debris from within. I could not blame him. I returned to Epidavros where he lived to move him into a smaller flat and he began to curse.

At eighty-two, it was not easy for him to let go of the physicality that had been his mentor. It had rewarded his victim and persecutor roles. It had supported his ability to blame the outside world and his personal God, for he was being forced to live alone, without his companion in life and without the economic means to carry on believing. Father was angry and his anger, which masked his wounds, culminated in a stroke. Once again, I met an ambulance and once again went to hospital to try to take care of Father's needs.

Father was a wounded man and this had always interfered with his ability to love freely. In any dysfunctional family there is always some kind of abuse. Sometimes this abuse is verbal, emotional, mental, physical or spiritual. Although, in my classes at Findhorn, we had been told a child does not feel abused but rather sees it as a form of love, and that this is an adult perception, I do not agree with this. A child knows something is penetrating the veil that cocoons innocence and boundaries are being transcended. A great amount of sadness follows and this pain is locked away in the psyche. I believe thoughts penetrate this veil, and that what a child feels is what marks a child until such time that wounds can be dealt with. We tend to move from one abusive situation into another until we regain our dignity and honor but how can we truly know what this dignity is, unless we know its opposite? We go through tremendous hardship and yet this is an aspect of living in duality. One has to walk through pain in order to walk through joy, for they always come together hand in hand.

What I had done was bury my pain which exploded every now and then. I did not understand Father's lucid demands on me for financial support when any form of emotional support had been non-existent. Memories of my childhood days had been frightening; Mother was continuously under tremendous pressure; most of the time she spoke to Grandmother Maria in Serbian and I refused to listen to them arguing, as I tried desperately to understand what they were saying, secretly hidden away behind a door. My parents spoke to each other in Italian which always excluded me. Deep down I almost hated my father and yet I loved him too. So as I folded his pajamas in the hospital, I was angered when he said in a low voice, "You owe me!"

Something snapped inside of me.

"Owe you," I shrieked. "I owe you nothing at all. I owe my dead brother who bought my first car and sent me to university, and my mother, but I don't owe you."

I was startled with the words that flew out of my mouth but even more startled when I grabbed hold of Father's pajamas, flew to the bed, held them across his face and hissed, "Shut up old man!"

My inner voice reached my ears.

"Back up at once or you will kill him."

I backed up. I burst into tears, grabbed my bag and left. On the way down in the lift, my shadow self, whispered softly,

"Kill yourself and don't tell a soul what you are planning to do. Your life is worthless."

Struggling to contain shadow, I got into my car and drove home weeping. I went to bed.

On one of my trips to Scotland, I had again met with shadow self. I had felt a different power, similar to what I was feeling now. I had stopped off in Bath to visit a publisher and discuss my books with him. I knew I could desire they were published and they would be. There was also an attractive young Italian man I wanted! I knew if I desired him, I could have him. I was invincible and knew that, at that moment, I could move beyond physicality and be safe and sound in the process. At the time I had felt the power surge through my body and simultaneously recalled a story I had read in my Bible about the temptation of Christ in the desert. I had turned to my friend Birgit and said in a tired voice, "I'm going to bed!"

I did not believe in crossing the borders of time and space when I lacked the clear knowledge of what was best for my soul purpose. I also did not quite know what kind of energy I was tapping into at the time and there had been enough shadow in my life. If I was meant to have something, I got it, but... I wanted to surrender to this unseen thread rather than to my own power.

I had a choice then. I could have turned away from Father forever, blaming him for my childhood. I could have lost control perhaps and killed him or I could have committed suicide. I chose to forgive and to try to reach this man who was so blinded and deafened by his own anguish, realizing this outburst had probably been the one thing that would free me forever.

Father was discharged a few days later and I returned to his apartment with a nurse to look after him. I did not stay long for the atmosphere was strained. Back in Athens, I went out with a friend of mine for lunch. I tried desperately to answer the question that had been pounding in my head for most of my life. Why? Why did we have to go through so much pain in this life? What was the point of so much pain and what had we done to deserve it? The result of my questioning was that later, at home, I walked to the kitchen and literally fell on my head, slicing it open on the marble floor and cutting an artery.

I was rushed to hospital, where I wailed continuously. Once again I had made a mistake. The shadow was as much a part of being as was a deeper self. Both had to be held, and I had to trust that I could not find all the answers.

Father had always been a challenge. When I was young, he had initiated me into the ways of the Amerindians. As an adult he withdrew the spiritual blanket that I held abruptly. For the ten days that I needed to recuperate from my fall, Father called me every day, content at last to play the role of father. A day before he died, I called him and told him I loved him and the day he died, close to Christmas, I managed to ask for my Christmas bonus to bury him. With dignity I reclaimed the power I had lost when Philip paid for Mother's funeral and with dignity, I let go of my pain because I had to acknowledge that Father was a wounded human being. The months after Father's death, I was haunted by dreams of both my parents, and the tragic circumstance that gave me another double grave in Epidavros.

They came often to tell me I was mad – they were alive and I was dead. Once they came to tell me that they had prepared a room for me and that they were waiting. Their shadows loomed over me until I began to pray frequently for their souls, sending them love and light.

In my dreams, I deflated their egos and their shadows. In my waking hours, I sent healing light to their souls. I faced my fear of dying and demanded life instead. Slowly, I lost sight of the shadows to carry them over the bridge and into the light. As I did, I noticed Mother was wearing my shoes and that they were golden. I was wearing her slippers and they were grey. I asked her to give me my shoes and to take hers. As they left and smiled at me, I realized both reflected parts of me I had finally dealt with and understood completely. I could no longer blame them for anything they had done in their lives because I was capable in my human weakness, of doing exactly the same.

It takes a lot of courage and honesty to look into a mirror and to realize what we are capable of becoming. The fact we choose not to, is tied to the aspect of accepting who we are. It is not enough to have thought about it only; if we have ever thought about it, then we have to go deep within and work with this wounded aspect, if we are to release ourselves from this shadow that may hide and emerge under stress. I began to learn more about healing and started working as a therapist. The universe, as always, came to teach me about healing. Amerindians came during lucid dreaming to teach about protection, about healing the planet and healing the wounded spirit.

My experiences were leading me slowly but surely to a balance that required of me to close a major cycle, and open a new one. I decided to ground my experience and leave for the United Kingdom where I planned to do my master's and PhD in Transpersonal Psychology. I would not give up. I knew I had to complete my own balance, if I were to ever become a true facilitator of those in need. I slowly returned to my initiation that had allowed me to experience

Divine Love.

I began to realize the black knight was a shadow self. This shadow wanted to reign and demanded innocence. My innocence was the golden book held to my heart. My white knight I take to be my spiritual self that held me safely and when I drank from the golden chalice, I carried my spiritual self with me. When I saw the path in front of me, I felt my entire being challenged as I parted from my angelic friend; knowing that he was my guide and would be with me always, had been a kind of insurance; a solace for the difficulties that lay ahead of me. I finally accepted the higher order that was protecting me, and recognized myself in the angelic spiritual self, and the earthly other.

I knew that, somewhere between my conception and my initiation, I had remembered something that had existed prior to my material being. Perhaps it had been an awkward moment in my childhood when I had lost my innocence. What remained was the memory of what could never be lost. Perhaps when I lay, trembling and wishing fervently for the tender touch of the man I had chosen to marry, something snapped when I realized no one could give me what I needed to desperately find within. My priest friend had said so in words and even though my soul mate had taken me into the dream, pulling me back into the space of the Divine, I had to walk away without malice.

Naked we come into the world and when we die, we face the afterlife, naked and bare, with nothing to measure our personal gains in this world. I was stripped naked, having lost so much only to recall what I held deep in my soul; I had carried blame for having betrayed a tribe and having been betrayed. The only freedom I could gain was through my understanding of the pain we all carry in order to forgive and in forgiving the persona, befriend the shadow and learn to love without conditions. My life was about to begin.

CHAPTER THIRTEEN

As we descend into the unconscious so must we ascend to the heights of the super conscious! As we struggle to integrate experiences we realize that beyond the physical lies the mental and emotional spheres of our existence. We must travel beyond these, if we are to find the true Self.

Re-birth

When freedom comes, it comes in many different ways. One of the ways it manifests is through the heart; another is through the mind; yet another is through the spirit-soul. In my case, it was through a discontinuation of one lifestyle and a step towards another, but perhaps it included all of the above.

Selling furniture yet again and boxing belongings, took me back to the time I had left South Africa and yet I was as brave as I had been then. I could recall the difficulties in trying to settle down in Greece. I had faced so many hardships and yet no thoughts at all settled in my mind. Only my heart pushed, as it had in most cases, giving me the assurance I was doing what I had to do – there was no logic. If I had used logic, I would have shuddered at the thought of leaving a good job, a beautiful apartment, friends and clients who trusted me for therapy in order to go and study.

I had done a course in Biotherapy, with a doctor who had brought the system from Italy to Greece. My hands had been photographed with Kirlian photography and measured, the results showing Dr. Brillakis that I had above normal energy flowing from them. I had started working with Mother, and although she had been diagnosed with lung cancer, tests had shown five years later that the cancer was no longer in her lungs. I had worked on a colleague, who had a tumor, and the tumor had shrunk, but I had never documented my work, or really taken any of it seriously. Logic was something Philip had tried to teach me, and yet, I could not think about my decision to leave it all. I would have laughed at my foolishness, finished my master's in Esotericism and stayed where I was. The magic, however, took me flying over the waters of life.

How can the beauty of spirit, which is ethereal and never ending, be boxed and labeled into physicality? There were no thoughts – just movement and this movement took me to Northampton, where in three days I had bought a car and found a lovely apartment overlooking the River Nene with the help of a friend, Stella. In a flow of events, as I was left alone in my apartment, I bought furniture, my boxes arrived and I set up home.

Outside, the river flowed, carrying with it tins of beer, reeds, ducks and swans. I had dreamt about the riverside apartment approximately a month before leaving Athens. It seemed incredible at the time to tell people I had flown down to the water and found someone who told me he had apartments for rent overlooking the river. The apartments had balconies which surprised me and I distinctly saw beer cans floating in the river.

My apartment block was opposite a brewery and there were different flats for rent, some with balconies The universe had always supported me but what exactly did this mean when, a month later, I looked at the grey skies and wondered why I had left my comfort for a land that would prove difficult to settle in. Like my out-of-body experience where I was a dot and space vast, the fear crept in as I tried to make Northampton my home. Fear came as I drove through the town and onto wide roads that led off into the unknown. I was afraid of getting lost and got lost on more than one occasion.

I had been offered a teaching job as an A level Psychology teacher for eighteen hours that suddenly became six. Forced to do substitute teaching to make up a salary, I found the work trying and different from what I had been used to. Students were both challenging and rude during substitute work, which made me realize I had to stand up for myself. The school I worked at was a Catholic school which took me back to my days in Johannesburg, and the warmth of belonging somewhere was so important to me. Had I ever really belonged anywhere apart from the space I had tiptoed in, as I once danced amidst the stars? I realized my challenge was to belong to the earth and its peoples.

University life was a dream I had cherished and I was not disappointed. At last, Transpersonal Psychology gave me a more holistic view and I loved going to lectures and studying. I made friends with a young Belgian girl, Rachel, who understood me as I understood myself. This was a beautiful process of connecting with the spiritual and the reality of the times. We talked until the early hours of the morning on occasion. We played the Transformation Game I had got in Findhorn, and found solace in the growth that began to take place deep within. Time began to extend as we meditated on Wednesday afternoons with our course leader, and then went into group practice later in the day. Exhausted, we would be avid in recalling the experiences that began to reflect the soul's journey, rather than the physical journey alone that held momentary glimpses of pain and suffering. The soul was clear.

One day, as we sat on a tree trunk that lay across the green grass, I began to tell Rachel about a dream I had forgotten about.

"I once dreamt about my youngest son, Andrew" I told her. "He was seven months old when he climbed up a chair and fell behind it. He shrank into a bottle with his dummies and I saw his spirit walk off and wave at me."

I knew then I had not dreamt about my son, but rather an aspect he represented. Somehow, as a very young child my spirit had remained, even though I had shrunk from physicality because it was harsh. My parents had struggled with their own problems, but I knew deep down in my soul that they had loved me and we were connected no matter how difficult our earthly connections had been. This was an opening that could only occur in my heart and as my heart began to open I saw a different beauty in the changing seasons and my struggle to work and study what I had known to be true in experience, but now had to integrate into a more academic approach. As my heart opened, and because it was a requirement for the course, I began to keep a journal.

Mystical, spiritual and religious experiences had come to me when I had needed them the most. The face of science had continually challenged those subjective experiences, trying to label everyone and put them in a box. The work of scientists had done so much for evolution and yet it had tried so hard to deconstruct everything. I knew I was finding myself in my work at university and that at last I was learning to say something of value and that there were people who were prepared to listen.

My journal was filled with the critical thoughts of a researcher and yet I finally found the ground to support what I knew to be real. This was what began to untie the knots that had been created after my therapy and in my search to truly experience freedom. I could no longer blame other people for what I thought they should have done because I began to realize life had its own agenda.

The Transpersonal is a study of religious, mystical and spiritual experiences that lead to a study of the higher aspects of the unconscious which is, according to Roberto Assagioli, the superconscious and the spiritual self, although it is called Tranpersonal. The reality of the superconscious is Divine experience and I realized there had been a continuous exchange between my conscious mind, my unconscious and the Divine superconscious. It became a release to realize that my breakthroughs into the superconscious that had occurred so frequently in my life, were those moments when I had been inspired and my centre of consciousness had been raised.

I often thought about my therapist's mother, who had spent so much of her life climbing mountains. My psychological mountaineering had, no doubt, been prompted not only as an escape from the painful reality of everyday life, but had primarily been spurred by the unknown and the mysterious I had believed in so totally. The moments when I had faced my most fearsome trials had been sacred moments when I glimpsed the altars of mysticism from afar, and reflections of my Spiritual Self. I was slowly able to see how I had not only descended into the darkness that St John of the Cross describes as the 'dark night of the soul' but that I had ascended in order to find a mirror that reflected a Spiritual Self.

To find the Spiritual Self is not easy. Many times the ego thwarts this process, rather hanging onto blame and an external cause for internal pain. However, no external pain can really be the onset of internal pain – the pain must already be there.

The Spiritual Self was a reflection of all I truly believed the figure of the man called Jesus had given, as a description of freedom, through the Christ principle, and that I tried daily to live, through forgiveness and healing. On Wednesdays whenever we meditated, I would clear the space from the shadows of lower energies in the room and would then enter silence. Many times I had clear and vibrant pictures of Eastern deities that brought a deep sense of peace to me and yet I managed to encompass Western thought as well. I did not want to be tied only to the Christian belief system, but honored all those who had sought the transpersonal. One of my greatest experiences had been in Egypt when I had seen words written in my mind's eye that when translated were the most holy words of the Quaran – there is only one God. I no longer wanted to use the word God, because it had proved to be a word that led to the division of nations, but rather clarified my belief in an essence of which I called Source, in order to encompass it all.

I let the scientific side of what I was studying threaten everything I had experienced simply because I knew it so well, and the mechanics of Quantum Theory helped me so much in integrating what I knew to exist in my subjective world with what I knew as well to be objective. Science had failed to prove meaning in nature but it had not disproved it and this was at last a reprieve for me. I began to see myself as a therapist but truly wondered about the healer that was reflected back at me through my Spiritual Self. It was almost as if I saw a number of the doctors who had touched my life when I had been in need as having failed completely to respect aspects of their medical profession that had probably inspired them to become doctors in the first place. It was only by reading books written by Dr Larry Dossey and Dr Daniel Benor, that I took heart.

The area of alternative medicine and Transpersonal Psychology was still in its infant stages, and yet it opened up a completely different way of perceiving the world, because I did find there was enough evidence for those who truly wanted to further research areas of mind and consciousness. Although I wanted desperately to research my work as a hands-on therapist, circumstances clearly pushed me into writing my final dissertation on integrating the Transpersonal into everyday life.

I was lucky enough to find twelve subjects for my qualitative research from different traditions including Shamanism, Buddhism, Sufism, Christianity, Orthodoxy and the Kabala. My research showed me it was difficult to integrate those experiences that gave people a glimpse of the Transpersonal and the Spiritual Self and I became deeply involved in the depth, internalization, ascent, path, enlargement, development, empowering and awakening that these experiences gave.

Having found my niche, I was surprised when I began to seriously think of leaving the United Kingdom to go back to Greece. I was unable to find funding for my PhD and our course leader was making plans to leave Northampton. Rachel was going to Germany and although I had left Greece to settle in the United Kingdom, I realized it was not my home. Although I had seen my friends Susan, Jane, and Brigitte who had once lived in Greece and moved to the United Kingdom and were settled and happy, I had to go back to Greece where it had all begun. I knew I would miss the people who I had met in England: my boss Kent, who had been a perfect boss, my friends Maureen, Kathy and Jim, Giordana and Marie and many others who had truly touched my life, and made me feel welcome in England.

A different home was beginning to emerge and that was when I realized I had always belonged to the universe and therefore it was inevitable I finally embrace my human body and mind as well as my spiritual self. I also knew I wanted to live close to my sons, whom I loved with all my heart.

In order to free myself from the burdens of the past I revisited the concept of 'spiritual crisis'. I have always had a problem with labeling and although I understand that we need language, I do not think it helps. The language of symbolism is far more effective, because there is no connotation to the words. These supposed 'crises' were experiences that were the most enlightening experiences I could ever have imagined to know. They were experiences that taught me about life, about the human race, about the extremities of fragmentation and how blind we can become. They filled me with light and opened my mind. They showed me that ultimate reality is affected by the observer and that I was my ultimate reality.

I wrote my own guide book. There had to be caring and love – love of a detached universal kind that supported a person's process of learning that was unique, and did not have a need for labeling. I had gone through severe initiations into shamanism and yet I was being excluded from the mainstream because I was different. I began to realize I had chosen to climb the mountain I had seen hovering in front of me; it was almost as though I had lived in arid and dry conditions at the base of the mountain and been one of the few who set out one day, oblivious to the threatening weather conditions and only with a small back pack and some tools, to climb the mountain no one wanted to climb because it was steep and rugged. As I climbed up, I often fell back, only to try again. It was as though those whom I left behind could not see where I was going and I was sure many of them had felt fear. They had urged me to come back down and live as they did, satisfied, at the base of the mountain, with what they knew and had some measure of control over. I had ignored their pleas and plunged on, simply because I had once seen what lay at the summit and beyond it.

Once again I identified with my therapist's mother and thought of her often because once I had reached the top of the mountain I always needed to climb more. I remembered my children at Woodside Sanctuary and appreciated that each one of them had a message. I realized that free will was one of the most important gifts I had been given. I could truly surrender to a greater order in my life, thus freeing my insane attempt to bring about a perfect world when there was so much imperfection around me. In the end result what I became in my struggle for freedom was what I had always been – a spirit-human-soul on a Transpersonal mission through life. Of course, I had broken all barriers in search of that essence that brings ultimate joy and honor, because I began to realize that I had a perfect higher or deeper Self inside of me that had always been and always would be.

This higher Spiritual Self had come to me in the dream about my son, to tell me that no matter what I had been through in my life that had shrunk me and thrown me into a bottle, my spirit was free. It had come to tell me clearly my brother Paul had not been reduced to an animal in form, but rather that the spirit had moved on and was in need of spiritual healing having completed its cycle on earth. I had come to value the lives of my mother and father, no matter how hard I had struggled to make them love me as a child needed to be loved. My Spiritual Self had held a mirror up to me, promising me that the perfect and sacred image I saw reflected back at me was what I could gain by embracing my shadow self.

My two years in the United Kingdom brought balance to me as nothing had ever before. I lost fear in standing up for my rights; I accepted I was worth my weight in gold and gave up the role of victim, persecutor, rescuer and warrior to settle for the role of advisor, not only to others but my very own self. My life changed in hue and whereas it had often been grey in tone, it became a vibrant pink. In order to show compassion to others, I had to have compassion for my little self and to embrace the everlasting challenge my Spiritual Self gave to me in my everyday interactions with others.

At last I began to feel happy and content with the way I had chosen to build my inner world. I was unable to say it was the best choice – on the contrary I paid homage to the growing wisdom inside of me that continually brought me peace. Peace was something everyone wanted but it had a high price. It was worth it, setting off to climb the highest mountain for the sheer magnificence of the view that changed perceptions. Eventually though, I began to realize that it was perhaps not something everyone wanted to do and this realization plunged me into the pain I had felt after my birth.

I think I had always assumed that all people wanted peace and would work to achieve it. Perhaps most of my pain came from understanding that, although there were simple solutions to complicated situations, some reveled in making others unhappy and were conscious of what they were doing, but unable to stop. I began to read a lot about Carl Jung's concepts of 'shadow' and came to the following conclusion:

Many were those who had lost their way and succumbed, probably even unaware of this, to the more base and negative energies of self.

This shadow self, greedy to feed the ego, had no limits and to hurt others simply meant that more power was gained. I realized that the entire history of the human race was based on this selfish gene that seemed to be predominant in life. It was a tool to enhance the self and produce a pseudo power and this is where I understood my own despair, because as long as people clutched at their lower self and believed only this aspect of the 'I' to exist, there would never be peace on the planet and this was something that hurt me deeply. It took me a long time to learn that I should not worry about how others chose to live their lives and all I needed to know was that I was learning how not to be so lost in the physicality of a deconstructed world, where men and women played roles of victim and persecutor. In a way, I realized that as long as I was playing the role of rescuer, we all belonged to the same realm. Every person had a path and if asked I could give advice, however, I would dedicate myself to clearing my path, planting my flowers, weeding my garden and maneuvering big rocks around my garden. This was what I could do to make a change in the world because if there was someone out there who wanted to learn and adapt, they could.

I had to break free no matter what the cost and suddenly I began to truly appreciate the fact I was not tied to someone who was insecure and unable to see the beauty I did – a beauty that began to unfold that was beyond words. Perhaps only a poet could have sung the song that began to make its tune known to me; it's beauty was so rare that I could not describe it at all. To have tried to describe it would have confined it, and therefore all I could do was surrender to this knowing feeling that drew me closer to my personal God and further away from my ego, until I lost sight of it. Only the silence greeted me and it was in this silence that I first saw it.

It was not easy to give it form, time or space. It was impossible to define and yet there was something comforting that came out to greet me as I stood alone, wanting to connect with it. My life had almost come to a standstill and yet there was a flow of energy that had its own life force and own energy that swept me up into its arms and held me close. I knew then that I belonged to it as totally as I had searched to find it, and what was the most arduous of journeys into the twilight and beyond, became what I had always been and what I had always thought I was not.

The gentle wash of emotion is something that can only be felt and it is something that is earned. It cannot come to us unless we are ready to truly surrender to a greater aspect of being, for it carries with it a memory of integrity and honor that goes completely beyond the personal and into the transpersonal, which vibrates at its own pace and within its own laws, that expand way beyond anything I could imagine and therefore went beyond form. It was a moment I wanted to contain, for it meant that somewhere in my life I had managed to achieve what I had longed to achieve since I was a child. The joy I felt was not joy as I had known it, but instead it was an awe-inspiring experience that lifted me up into a state where consciousness became me and I became it. This was the grail so many knights had given up their lives for. It was the state of moving beyond all matter and form and into the unknown that suddenly afforded me the breath I had known as a young child, before the fear robbed me of all. Suddenly, everything I had experienced and everything I had lived became a blessing that was no longer a curse and I slowly found myself lifting off from the material and into the Spiritual where I gently met with my Higher Self.

Integrating these experiences was easier than I expected, because it became apparent to me I was completing an enormous puzzle and that, with most of the picture to use as reference, I could look back at the visions I had had over the years and reconsider their meaning. What immediately came to mind were the beautiful evolved souls I had seen; effervescent beings of incredible beauty standing tall, thin and radiating a love that encompassed all of humanity; these became my angels – my guides and reflections of a transpersonal self that had the capacity to love in such a way, that even a glance of compassion sufficed to bring their energy radiating. This discovery led me to contemplate on the vessel that was my body and was slowly 'becoming' and I began to appreciate the complex nature of physicality, as a law that brought together elements into form and structure. I realized I could correlate this perfect dance of creation with the many sub-personalities that were hidden in my unconscious. I began to dream about friends I had met over the years and those few people who had differences with me, and whom I had left on the path. In my dreams I met them on another level and began to see the incredible reflections they set up, thus finding release, as I slowly eliminated those aspects of my inner being that no longer served me.

This burst of enlightenment gave me the understanding and wisdom that nurtured a sense of freedom inside of me, and for perhaps the first time in my life I realized I could begin to choose what kind of person I wanted to be. It was as though my understanding became a conscious effort to focus more and more on my Spiritual Self and in this way to surrender to it, safe in the knowledge I was surrendering to something that was inside of me and not outside.

Over the years I had very often done therapy on others without taking the time to wrap myself in a protective cover; I had opened myself to different vibrations on numerous occasions when sitting in a restaurant or whilst having a drink, and it was clear to me this had often blocked me and confused my intuitive flashes. I no longer saw the extraordinary but rather saw the ordinary as something that held symbolic meaning. Of my visions in Egypt, I began to realize that the saint who reminded me of St Francis and the angel who held the world in hand were nothing other than aspects of my higher nature that were represented by the woman who was pregnant; this was the extraordinary gift creation had given to being, and this brought a deep feeling of peace to my heart.

I had undertaken to bring circles to a close in the best possible way and whenever I thought of the veil I had been handed, it seemed I had been given the opportunity to change not only my perception of life but those perceptions that would make a lasting difference in the lives of others. When I had located my mother's family and Dragan, I had made a difference not only in their lives but mine as well and I could not help but hope this had freed Mother, as well, of an unnecessary spiritual burden. Suddenly I could see that had I not had such clear dreams of my parents waiting for me I would not have tried to send light to them and that in fact their consciousness could have been waiting for release through this.

I had spoken to my ex sister-in-law about my dreams. When she had stopped talking to her mother Vaia, after a series of events that had hurt her, I told her about the importance of forgiveness and that she would feel so much better inside, if she bridged the growing gap between them. Athena took my advice and even though there were difficult periods that came and went, she also felt the surge of release through this. I had forgiven Vaia, and often visited her until her death.

The ego was often a difficult aspect of personality that appeared as a frightened child, insisting on using the more negative aspects of dealing with a situation. It was clear to me that the ego had a perfect way of trying to protect the self, but this was a personal, much denser aspect of being than the True Self, and I still could not easily understand why people chose rather to become trapped in the ego's manipulative character, than to surrender to the potential within them for freedom. I was reminded over and over again of the fact it was a power trip that allowed someone to play the role of victim or persecutor, because this gave a sense of control, that of course would always remain pseudo-control. I began to feel sorry for people who could not let go and this brought a certain amount of compassion to my heart and yet I was always conscious I needed to work continuously with my weakness of judging others; slowly I began to detach and focused on observing and learning through the process, but it was also heartbreaking at times. I could see the pattern of despair from my childhood days pitter patter across my mind and realized that part of the sorrow I had carried with me came from the ability I had nurtured to see beyond appearances, and notice the games people liked to play when wanting to find control.

Although I felt inspired by the wisdom gained through studying, this was not all that I felt at that time. Joy was never fully present in life because there was always a portion of sorrow that came from deep inside of my heart. Northampton seemed to bring me into the awareness I had a heart and that my heart was a wounded heart. Although I had all the answers to the philosophical questions, it was never enough. The pain of loss was always present, reminding me of how things could have been and if they had been different, how much happier I would have been. If I had not lost so many people and if we had been truly happy then I would never have felt so alone. Looking through a spyglass, I tried to imagine things as though they were different, but this did not help. On the contrary, it seemed as though my only freedom would come when I decided to stay in my emotions, which were deep, and face my darkest memories and reality. My aloneness was too difficult to handle, so I tried to hold onto those whom I met and whom I really cared for. They were present in a way, but were also absent because my life style had always included meeting people who eventually left to live somewhere else. I thought of those people that I really had bonded with – my friend Vicky who had left Greece to go back to Australia to marry John, was forever in my heart; Birgit who had gone back to Germany to find her soul; Rachel who would leave Northampton for Berlin; my friend Thalia who had shared moments of joy and sorrow with me, but who had never opened her heart. Thalia would fall ill and die when I was still studying and I would be left with the memories of how I had tried so hard to reach her, as I had my dear friend Margaret. People had died around me and had left me to live in remote areas and yet they were so close to my heart.

Although it was difficult to deal with, I realized my attachment to them had something to do with my struggle to maintain an everlasting picture of life without change. Instead of seeing they had come into my life to give me something and then moved on, I stayed with the pain rather than the joy.

I knew I could no longer live in England and that I had to go back to Greece. When I finished my dissertation, I collapsed from too much stress and decided to take advantage of the medical system in Britain. I had an operation to alleviate a chronic problem and packed whatever I could in boxes yet again, to make my debut as an initiate who would try to complete all circles.

I left The United Kingdom in April of 2009 and landed in Athens again, with a promise of a new start. It was not an easy time for me. Although I was full of enthusiasm, I knew things had changed since I had left Greece. I was coming back to people who had mostly stayed in the same place; I had definitely changed, so returning to a place that held so much mystery and charm for me was not easy. My children found it difficult to relate to me and Philip was cautious, although he gave me a lot of support.

The universe suddenly became a set of cycles of which I was part and it no longer mattered whether or not I would make it on this earth, but rather whether or not I would make it every single morning I looked in the mirror to see a reflection of myself. At the end of the day, I needed to be able to accept that everything I had done, I had done because I realized I was free and that my will was my own. No longer attached to the universe, I could decide who I wanted to be. I decided to open a Transpersonal Association in Greece and dedicate my life to furthering knowledge of the Transpersonal by accepting to host the XVI EUROTAS conference in Crete, and started my PhD.

CHAPTER FOURTEEN

The clock on the wall chimes and the hand begins to move. The silence every now and then is broken by the harsh sound of reality. The sound of nature begins to remind me of the gentle silence that I once revered. I must soon begin to live my life with no one to guide me, apart from a number of people who are trapped in their own confusion.

Self-realization

Outside my window, the cicadas noisily flutter their wings; a car goes by and someone hoots; a bird caws noisily and people's voices reach my ears. I have been given grace through a friend, Dimitris, to spend two weeks in his holiday home on the island of Kea. There is absolute silence and yet none whatsoever, but I welcome it.

Traveling back in time, I realize that lying in my cot I can hear people arguing and doors slamming. The fear begins to tighten inside of me and I begin to wail. My crying only seems to make matters worse because when I am finally held, I can sense tension in my mother's voice and I can feel it in her arms that are trying to protect me but cannot, because I am perceiving things in my very own, unique way. When I finally begin to focus my eyes, I see the tears falling down my mother's face and the angry scowl in my father's eyes. Sometimes they look at me with love, but most of the time they seem to burn holes into my entire being.

It does not take long for me to block out the sounds and sights because I discover a way to escape into another space where, idyllically, I begin to feel safe. I do not want to be alone. I want to be connected to what I see, because I recall the umbilical cord that once connected me to my mother's innermost being. I realize that perhaps it was this being that I felt so completely at one with, and that perhaps I did not have any other recollections. As I begin to explore my new surroundings I discover the world is sometimes safe and at others terribly unsafe. My realizations are the projections I take with me as I begin to explore the realms where I feel safe only to see that nothing whatsoever is completely free of duality, because I have been unable to pass through the door I now presume to have represented death. Unable to move beyond this door, I decide to re-live it as though it were a part of my life when I was born. I look at the effervescent light, realizing it is light without form. If there is form, then surely I would still be in duality?

Using my imagination, I begin to explore this light. Perhaps there are figures there and perhaps they belong to a different vibration, but when I begin to move through this layer of spirit, I find a spiral staircase that leads to another level and another and another. It seems that as I reach up into infinity the light becomes more transparent and the figures translucent until they disappear all together. I begin to lose a sense of my personal being and to become part of the light, absorbed in all being. There are no words, for I have gone beyond time and there is so space because it is beyond space. In some way it is as though I no longer exist and yet am what I have always been.

Coming back down the spirals I reach the denser aspects of being and yet they no longer appear to be dualistic. On the contrary they seem to be of the essence I have experienced beyond time and space. This essence is what encourages me to go back down into my body and when I open my eyes, I perceive a subtle change. No longer drawn to parts, I begin to see the whole. Bursts of light like a million stars move around me in a dance and although some of them shine brighter than others they are all made of the same. When some of them go out, there is dark space but even this darkness is not unfamiliar, because it seems to have absorbed the light. It isn't bad and it isn't good. It simply is!

I slowly realize I have projected my fears that probably came through my birth where suddenly I was being forced out of the darkness in my mother's womb. I realize there are no figures that threaten me and that the space is one in which I can be asleep, because there is only the dark and all the lights have been extinguished; all I will know is silence and I will have been absorbed by this silence, until I become it. Content to stay there, I realize it too becomes a safe zone. I ebb and flow and as I do so, I lose all sense of being. I seem no longer to be conscious at all and this peace reminds me of death.

I am aware I have left a part of me behind as I finish this exercise, and I feel my heart has expanded. My logic drives me to conclusions. I see myself made up of both dark and light which are no longer different apart from a sense that should I awaken, I would become the light and should I sleep, I would become the dark. I become aware that the darkness still brings fear into my mind and this I equate with my experiences related to the dark knight who wanted the golden book I held to my heart. I remember a book written by Alan Paton called 'Cry the beloved Country' that I loved always and I recall a few words:

'Cry the beloved country for the unborn child that is the inheritor of our fear. Let him not love the land too deeply or smile too gladly, when the setting sun makes red the veld with fire, for fear will rob him of all if he gives too much.'

I do not remember more, and I am too lazy to find it, because it has moved me into a place where I need to ponder on what it means to me. I realize that loving the Earth too deeply and that being moved by a mountain or a valley will inevitably rob me of something I feel, because it will never be mine and there will always be a threat to whatever I attach myself to so completely and fully, to the exclusion of something else. I realize I have loved the sky too deeply and that this love has been part of my pain all along. In essence, nothing whatsoever has changed and yet I can see life has changed it all because my experiences have been instrumental in my fears. For a moment I want desperately to wipe the slate clear and to look through the eyes of innocence and wonder what kind of life I could live if I trusted completely. In a way, I see myself again as a star, amidst other stars, radiating light, and I choose to explore this realm a little more consciously.

Without form, lights dart here and there and begin to have no purpose because they have purpose in their being. I smile as I realize how desperately I have been trying to make them swallow up the dark and suddenly I wonder really, why the darkness and light cannot simply be. Why does the one have to be more important that the other? Why should being awake be more important than falling asleep? I decide I need to honor both and to see how wonderful both are but I also realize I want to detach from both, in order to continue my journey of contemplation.

My logic draws the following conclusion. What if there is no purpose in either dark or light and what if I have been mistaken all along in believing there has to be a purpose in everything? The only conclusion I can draw is that physicality must of itself be a state a consciousness striving to perfect itself. I am pleased I do not touch the notion of 'athanasia' because I suddenly realize that believing in an elixir whereby the form is so perfected it never dies, is a constraining thought to have. Having grown fond of the idea there are so many mountains to climb and so many aspects of being to learn about, I want to think of Earth as simply one station in a very long line that may never have a destination or an act in a play that is so vast, my mind could never contain it. I also realize I don't want to know it all, because what then would be the purpose of journeying in the first place?

I begin to sense a growing feeling of excitement because my universe is beginning to expand in such a way as to incorporate all form, all time, all space, and so on. I want to explore this universe that appears to be never ending and I am deeply grateful I have opened myself so much to experience. For the first time I fully realize that, by working with my inner being, I am freeing myself to work more with the outer space that no longer appears as a threat to me, but rather as a reflection of me. My inner daemons are suddenly important to me as they are my friends, and I realize that many of them have grown up overnight because I am slowly acknowledging them.

In shamanic style, I can see wild animals ready to fight for their territory and the meek and mild as well. I can see nature perfectly reflected inside of me and I realize that to have a pretty garden, where the wild roses bloom and the scent of nectar is heavy, I have to weed that garden and realize that just like in any garden, as the weeds come out, that this is a lifetime of conscious living that will never end. My entire perception of life slowly begins to change. Being a healer of self becomes one of the most exciting jobs. I see my inner world as being so rich and so complex it becomes an awe-inspiring task to undertake – not to get to know how others think but to get to know how I think, and what I am doing each and every moment of this precious life, to enhance my inner world. I know I am wild in my nature as well as tame, and that my wildness sometimes harms both me and my outside world. I want to learn to play with those aspects of my inner world that appear as a threat to me, to nurture their wounds that make them wild and love them for their beauty. I know I have the means to tame those that are threatening, and I love the symbolism that comes to me where the lamb and the lion lie side by side.

I cannot not see purpose in this change of perception but rather see the brilliant balance of life where home has no longer country or nation attached to it, but rather heart. I had been looking all the time outside of me for what I had inside of me all along. I want to think that as long as I have been weeding my internal garden I have also been creating a universe for myself that will become a part of the universal consciousness, and a part of my personal being, because it is a noble thought that carries with it the honor of a knight and a horse that has been me all along. I feel self-sufficient in a way, and yet still want to draw other knights to me, so we can share things and experience union. I know I am truly blessed by the realization that gives me a wonderful sense of union with all those people who I had once criticized and judged, and who left me because their lives had ended. Mother and Father are the most important of them all because they gave me life, and have been instrumental in me facing my own shadows. I move beyond them then and into the space of realizing union with all the experiences and spirit-souls of my past which is a perfect close to my book and a perfect start to a new way of living. I gently recall Jackie and Paul, Grandmother Maria, and days at school, longing for true friendships with faces that are engraved in my heart, and no longer feel regret for lost moments. Rather I release the faces and dwell on the souls of my classmates, who shared a space with me and who could not easily understand my soul as it wandered through the different veils, searching to find love. The past is behind me and it has healed me. The future is not known, but I am no longer in fear of it. The present is full of potential because I am fully aware I know nothing at all and yet have glimpsed something everlasting inside of me. It does not matter if there is life after death, because this means I am not fully immersed in understanding that my life is everlasting each and every moment I am conscious.

When death comes, if I become conscious of something else, then I will truly be conscious of it because I am not shutting doors on anything any more. I wonder for a moment whether or not I created the door myself in another time-space continuum as a child, because I had not fully understood the beauty of my inner world and the freedom I had to explore it. I am aware of the fact I do believe in reincarnation because I have had so many experiences not only with my own memories, but in my work with others. I know that eventually one day the Earth will probably cease to be, and the known universe will dissolve to start all over again, but this continuing cycle simply makes me realize that the possibility of a new cycle being an improvement on this one is up to us – it is simply a matter of choice.

Maybe, in what I call God's living room, we all meet in our different stages of growth and plan to meet each other and facilitate each other's passage to clearer waters. Maybe there are evolved souls in other dimensions that help us when we need them most, and when we surrender not to a personal will but to a transpersonal one, only then we find true freedom. I can no longer see the point in trying to prove these dimensions exist, as I can no longer see the purpose of trying to disprove their existence. It is nice there are other people who are dedicated to research, but I fail to see that proof of any kind will actually serve a purpose. There will always be questions that will not be answered, because this is the true nature of our universe. It seems far more important to find a way to still a churning heart and find inner peace, to become the strength that can lend a helping hand to others who are on a path through life. I realize we are all on this path and that eventually we will all awaken to this fact.

Somehow, having gained some clarity, I choose to listen to the one voice I have never fully listened to – the voice of my heart.

Having become so entangled in the drama of my life, I have failed to look at my heart and listen deeply to what it wants from me. My heart has its own story to tell.

Ever since I had not looked at my heart I believed we were apart. I had tried to get closer and closer to it and in its physical form, recognized it was part of my body, in that it pumped the blood around it to keep me alive. In its spiritual form, however, it had wounded me continuously and it was as though it was separate from me.

It was to a large extent what I was inside of me but it could not be like I was. In a way, its entire existence was based on another level of thought and this was a place I could not visit, not even in my dreams. Perhaps it helped me to think of it as the record keeper of all I held inside my memory bank – a deposit of all time and space as only it knows it, and far beyond as well. In order to communicate thoughts, the pain reminded me of who I can become, rather than who I am. It is so easy for me to say I am a product of my environment because even when I refer to past lives, I am an outcome of them. This is the part of me I can recall – the shadow aspects of myself being reflected in my daily life every time I meet someone.

In essence, the spiritual heart can never be hurt because it is beyond emotions and beyond time and space. It is an extraordinary aspect of being I had yet to meet with fully and learn about. It was capacity and depth; it was all things I could become but most of all, it was my protection. When I was in danger of losing my self to the outside world, it would pierce the fabric of illusion I carried with me. I could draw on my wisdom and learn from it but I could not become that wisdom. There were times when I pulled at it as though I wanted to consume it, and although it existed as part of me, it was not me. I existed as part of my brothers or sisters in life but we were separate entities. My existence went beyond form, just as theirs did and therefore this was a separate part.

I was aware I had a pain in my chest – a dull ache, as though I was taking my spiritual heart and throwing it from me. I knew I needed desperately to focus on what I was feeling and yet could not. I wanted to hold onto my thoughts and hold onto it and yet I could see how I was smothering it. I wanted to control it, to become master of it and to protect myself from it. Could I really let go of everything and simply wait to see what would happen if I did? Had I really projected even what I thought a spiritual heart should be onto it, so that I had almost strangled its existence? I realized that maybe I was only communicating with it because I truly wanted to let go and reach my potential but I had not realized that it may know more than me and could become my guide or friend without me becoming one with it. Suddenly it made sense. How could I possibly know what it knew? How could I possibly judge it and how could I presume it was on the same level as I was? Surely it was capable of so much more than I was? Surely it was unlimited in its scope of feeling? I no longer wanted to be wounded by it and yet I guessed it had wounded me to remind me it was there as my protector. That was when I realized I also had an emotional heart.

Talking to my heart was not easy. I seemed to have all the answers to what I thought would make me happy but I realized that unless I could see these separate parts of me, I could never be my true self. I knew I had stopped trusting my spiritual heart because I had forgotten about my emotional heart. Did I really have so little faith in it? I knew it would always be with me and that in silence, I could trust it would guide me as I had never been guided before. I had to trust there was a part of me that knew better than I did and an essence that went beyond me. It reminded me of Buber's 'I and Thou' because I suddenly saw my spiritual heart as 'Thou' – an aspect I did not know and had never really wanted to acknowledge; perhaps this was the part I had always projected outside of me but had never understood was within me. I was not sure whether to call it my heart or not. I did not know if this was cosmic consciousness and could not bear to find a name for it other than Thou. It reminded me of the Beloved I had read about in the Sufi tradition and all I could do was acknowledge that it was there, inside of me and that I was ready to accept this aspect of me I could learn from but never become.

This realization took me far out, away from the mundane activities of daily living. I could see clearly I had never truly mourned the loss of my youth and my innocence. I had always believed in my own responsibility but in a sense blamed myself for the difficulties I had been through and this was the pain that inadvertently changed my perceptions and called for diving into the depths of my unconscious to embrace the child within me and walk her out of the past. I had never really been compassionate towards my inner being and it was an education to suddenly become aware of the fact I could look at my spiritual heart as a wiser aspect of self and that I had to heal my emotional heart. This brought to me a sense of balance.

My emotional heart had always been prompted by the wild dreams of the past and the knowing feeling that things could have been different. Perhaps I could finally draw on my spiritual heart to heal my emotional heart. I came from a semi-dysfunctional family and for the first time in my life I could see that explaining things away through the spiritual approach also had a darker side. Emotions were scrunched up and left to fester within. It was not enough to believe that the angelic world held and supported me because I needed this from the physical world as well.

I was aware that often the spiritual became a reason not to look deeply and mourn for the emotional losses that come and go, putting so much strain on the mind and body. I still longed to feel the closeness in a partnership with a man and I had to admit to myself this had to become my priority before all else. There had to be balance between both worlds. It wasn't enough to only live one and not the other. Spirituality had to be grounded fully if I was ever to come to the point of release – something I truly desired.

CHAPTER FIFTEEN

The time comes in all our lives when we have an opportunity to break free. In order to do so we need to surrender to that greater aspect of being in order to touch the light. When we are ready, the light manifests to draw us within.

Peace

I find myself expanding as I listen to music and look out at the calm sea. I suddenly find myself separating from my body although I am fully aware of what is happening to me. I am rushing past the stars of the night sky and the clouds of day until I am in the arms of the Overseer. The Overseer is an energy that is completely Transpersonal and is therefore un-identifiable. The Overseer is where I feel safe and I am conscious that I feel again what I felt as a young child. I realize fully that the love I felt for my soul-mate could never be in this lifetime as I would have stopped with him and never gone beyond him. This conscious realization frees my soul from its burdens and I can at last look forward to a great friendship with him. Some-where deep within, wounds are miraculously transmuted and I am deeply grateful and in awe of what is happening to me.

The Overseer is radiant and the light I have known and have always believed in is part of me. The world is exactly as it is and I no longer have the desire to change anything because I realize that in order to know the darkness and the light, mankind must experience it. The Overseer is gentle and the light is a love that reminds me of all the times I have been in need. I realize that where I have thought the universe to have abandoned me, it has been my fear manifesting to me, for I have never been alone. I feel ashamed I have been so blind and that I have got stuck at people and events, rather than going beyond them, but my shame dissolves. Whereas I had imagined a little boy as an angel, he is now the Overseer and the White Knight, one and the same, and I realize how continuously I have met with the Overseer, every time I have been in turmoil. I feel, and in my feelings I understand I am re-connecting with what I believed I had lost. I see mankind on a continuous cycle of birth, death and re-birth and this continuity persuades me we are all on a path and that eventually we will all have walked all paths, if we are to experience peace. Life has suddenly new meaning and in this meaning is the struggle to know everything about the nature of being human. It incorporates all those feelings that have to do with the dark and the light. It is obvious to me that in order to know the light we have to know the darkness as well. Understanding of this inner shadow that manifests without is clear. The darkness is so much a part of us that we have manifested it outside. This outside realm can only harm us if we entertain thoughts that vibrate at this level of consciousness. It is not strange at all to realize I am creating my life and this process has enabled me to see how weak I can be and how strong. Strength does not draw on the shadow, but rather touches the light, and the light is what remains as strength.

In detachment, I find compassion and when I see other people struggling or facing the dark, I remember this is where I have once stood. I realize that perhaps it was another lifetime that spirit was lost but I also realize how precious every moment of life is, because it gives me the opportunity to change my perception. I awaken from a sleep state and realize a veil has separated me all along from what I have so desperately sought to find. I know that the veil I received closed my eyes for a while and this was my protection rather than my damnation.

I look out at the world and it is different. I do not see with the same eyes I did before and I am conscious that even though this elation will subside as I enter again daily living the bond that has been created with the Overseer can never be lost. As a therapist, I know I can never heal anyone at all but that all I can do is walk beside the client, reminding them of the dangers they need to face and embrace if they are to lose their fear.

I am conscious the music in my ears is a music that is being played in the different spheres and I recall my experiences, respecting *them even more than I ever have. I feel warm and safe, even though there may be trials still on the way. I have union inside of me to face these trials and that union is with the universe and the Overseer rather than another single human being. The Overseer can be my father, mother, sister, brother, friend and Beloved because this only is everlasting and everything else is transient.*

At last I have goals and know that as I dream about them, I am giving them up to a higher purpose and if they manifest then they are part of my path and if they do not, they are of no service to me. Although I am able to smile and greet other people, I am also aware of the growing need for silence and this inner silence is what brings me strength.

I know unity not only as an experience but also as something I understand with my mind as well as my heart. As they become one, I realize I am fulfilling my soul purpose. I am deeply grateful for this extended state of consciousness and at last this light becomes my guide; I can reconnect with everything I have experienced in my life. My days are touched with knowledge that the higher I fly the worse will be my sorrow and yet they are finally of the same and once I realize this, they no longer appear as great highs and lows.

Language no longer serves me, but expression does and it this that begins to shine from my eyes as I gaze at everything around me. I want to finish the work I have been assigned as part of this great union, and am filled with inspiration for a new year that will bring change to my life and the lives of others. In a sense I have done very little with my life and yet have done so much. I know I will do even greater things, but am also totally aware of the reverence I will feel for each and every new experience that comes to me. I realize that what I tried so hard to find has always been with me and that in actual fact, I have lost nothing at all.

As I reach down to pick up a stone from the beach I am walking along, I connect with the universe and all those my human brain can conceive of. In essence I am united with my Creator and in essence, I have united with my Soul. This is the peace I have and that I can share, because it is peace that is everlasting. My heart and soul, mind and body are at last free.

The peace brings with it a healed past. It is as though I never lived life that was difficult, because I realize it did not change my inner being. I am extremely grateful for the warm feeling of love that surrounds me, as I realize what a wonderful gift union brings. The past no longer is shadowed but rather has gone completely; all that remains is Love and I remember my son's words about purpose and love. Perhaps in his teaching is his learning, because I know it was my purpose to learn to love and I owed that love to everything I experienced. My own shadow is not only my shadow, but a universal shadow that makes me feel even more humble.

I understand that although I have stumbled and fallen many times I no longer feel weight on my shoulders and that I carry the Overseer with me. I think fondly of my family and connect with the sea and the sky as I begin to grow. There is a deep calmness in my heart and I realize I have moved beyond joy and sorrow. I know what the Transpersonal means and this unity gives me a sense of well being. I can no longer sense the shadow and I let myself slowly fall into this ecstasy.

I am surprised when I wake up the following morning, because I still have this warmth radiating from my heart and I gently gather to mind the people I have loved in my life. I connect with them all and smile gently as I make my way to the sea. I bathe in the waters of life and greet the sun as it rises in the East. I watch it set in the West later on that day and when the moon comes up, it is an August moon that fills me with inspiration.

How simple my life becomes over the next few days and weeks because all that I can recall from my life is the sense of connectedness with everything I have experienced. No longer lonely, I do not mind being alone; in fact it is necessary for me to fully integrate my experiences. As I stand on the bridge that crosses over from this world to the next, I see a brilliant star reflecting back at me and I know I have finally come home. In this state of bliss, I have nowhere else to go and this feeling of security becomes my strength to face the rest of my life with dignity and honor. At last, I have touched the light. The light in turn has gathered me forever into its arms. All that is left for me to do is to say 'thank you' to life for bringing me this far.

I greet those souls who have passed before me and acknowledge my ancestors. I enter the dreamtime and become it. I send thanks to those people who support me in this life – to my sons and dear Philip. To my friend Lea, Thalia's sister and to Bilo and Charles, who have listened to me express the deepest spiritual essence. I greet you, the reader, and ask that you find solace when reading my story, and recall the Overseer that lies in you. Sharing my story was not easy, but it was necessary, for in sharing our myths, we encourage others to do the same. Our lives are always entwined, for we belong to the mystery of Life more than we realize.

I look up at the beautiful, white silk material that I have been given by my spiritual family in Moldova, from where I have just recently returned, that I will hang with reverence at the conference Greece is hosting. I know the Transpersonal has given me an answer to the many questions that have haunted me for so long. I think about the veil I took in Vision, wondering what symbolism it has, as I look at the flag I now give tribute to. I understand clearly that each and every person I have met on this path called Life has handed me a piece of the beauty I see before me. It is a beautiful tapestry that has been lovingly embroidered by hand. I know that the 'strangers' of my youth are my blessed spiritual family, as are the many strangers and friends who have helped me walk along this spiritual path. In the now, I know that at last I am free and have fully become part of my life, as my life has become part of me. I know it is not by chance I have brought the Transpersonal to Greece. I feel the song of the ancient mariner sing, as it courses through my veins. At last I can experience joy in knowing life is full of grace and beauty. It is a school of gods and goddesses who once fell from a great height, and who promised to return, to re-learn what they failed to learn before.

Take heart, no matter how arduous your journey may seem, for Light and Darkness bring us into the arms of our dear home, Mother Earth, to recall Father Sky. May your journey into Self bring you into heart where Hope lies waiting, to give you all you need to face the dawn of a new and richer life, connected with Spirit and Soul in the heartbeat of the Universe. No matter how human you truly are, there is a diamond inside of you, of the rarest kind, just waiting for you to acknowledge, allowing its radiance to shine out to all you meet. This is Hope that lies in Heart, that Pandora discovered when she opened the box. A being of brilliance waits to be acknowledged, and it lies in the heart, so it can take your hand and lead you out of the darkness and into the light of true consciousness. May the journey be rich with wisdom, paved with light and full of Love!

'Love is patient and kind; it is not jealous or boastful. Love does not insist on its own way; it is not irritable or resentful; it does not rejoice at wrong, but rejoices in the right. Love bears all things, believes all things, and endures all things.

Love never ends; as for prophesies, they will pass away. For our knowledge is imperfect and our prophecy is imperfect; but when the perfect comes, the imperfect will pass away. When I was a child I spoke like a child, I reasoned like a child; when I became a woman, I gave up childish ways. For now we see in a mirror dimly, but then face to face. Now I know in part; then I shall understand fully, even as I have been fully understood. So faith, hope, love abide, these three; but the greatest of these is love.'

Corinthians 13

THE END

EPILOGUE

Slieve Gullion

The rolling hills of Ireland stretch out all around as I make my way up the narrow footpath, towards the summit of Slieve Gullion. Clouds drift past as I sense the changing landscape bringing the question again to fore.....Who am I? I cannot believe I have at last found my way to Ireland and that a great circle is to come to close.

Battling to catch my breath I stop, to shed the past and empty the cup I hold in heart. Vision comes in the form of faerie folk, who give me a golden scepter and a long white gown. Further along I receive a blue gown and silver scepter. Flashes of a battle fought in another time and place – Dunkirk when my name was Shane – flood my mind. Further up I climb to meet that which is timeless – a king reborn in light; golden fabrics tumbling around me, radiating. I am horse and rider – sky and earth – earthling and spirit manifesting in the shapes of the crags around me. This is the initiation of Goddess mother, radiant in splendor, the maiden and wise priestess of ancient times and the crone, fury of yesteryear urging the final aspect of all life with its shadows and its lights to merge until they are one. A bright light shoots forth to circle the land I have known and must belong to for it is here that my ancestors came from, ancestors I have not forgotten. I can feel their pain as it was my own, for it is a part of me. The land gives and takes, for such is the law of the natural world; without her I realize I am nothing. I shall not make it to the top, where the burial grounds lie, for too much happens at once, taking me back in time. The visions do not stop but I can, for such is the reverence of self, to know when it is too much and there is a need to integrate. I realize in the time it takes to walk back down the mountain, that the vision cannot stop and all life is a vision of birth, death and re-birth. The time comes simply to slow a beating heart and to recall how I got to this place and why I am here. I sit amidst the beauty, wrapped in the Mother's light and reflect on how I came to Ireland in May of 2014.

Ramona was a colleague of mine who I had not seen in years. Her beautiful Irish lilt had always captivated me, as we taught next door to each other for over a year. Ramona and her husband George had contacted me for a therapeutic intervention, and it was amazing to watch ten years go by, as we caught up on the past. I was amazed when Ramona told me she was living in County Down, for this was the birth place of my great grandfather Henry James, and the family link I had still not completed. Grateful when they invited me to Ireland, I marveled at the beauty and grace with which the Source gathers all together, when this is our intention. I set off for my journey to be met in the early morning mists by Ramona, at the airport in Dublin. The fact that Ramona and George lived in part of the beautiful Narrow Water Castle was beyond me. The stately estate took me back in time over the seas to Mother's life in Serbia and then to the beautiful farm where I had walked so many times in the beauty of nature. The small seventeenth century apartment in which they lived with their delightful children baby Lea and toddler Daniel, was the grounding I needed for the expansiveness to follow. On the first day we visited the cemetery in Ballyvarley, to trace my ancestors and found a gravestone that did record my surname, but spelled differently. We had tea with Maggie who excitedly promised to look into the name and who lent me a book on Ireland. We drove to the silent valley and I stared at the beauty around me. Lost in the beauty of the rolling hills, the green valleys and the neat hedgerows I knew I had come home. My ancestors' names no longer mattered for I had come home to the beauty and grace of a land which had given them birth and so accordingly I performed a ritual of bringing them home in my mind's eye. The time flew by, amidst sticky hands, gurgles and cries; glasses of red wine and the time of reconciliation and healing in many ways. There are no words that can easily describe what Narrow Water Castle looks like. Perhaps however, there are emotions that come together when one is privileged to stand in the grounds, looking over the rolling green lawns, the wooden tree house and the lands that stretch forth as far as the eye can see. Walking through the forest, I let the images come forth of tradition and the honour it takes to fully come to terms with the past and present time. I knew nothing about the history of the place and yet partook in its joy and sorrow, as I stared up at the grey stone walls and breathed in visions of the past. The place held deep memories that became my memories and faces that became a part of me, when I found myself walking through the castle to sit in the library. A deep respect for those who were part of its tradition came to me and this respect opened my heart to heal the many sorrows that were trapped in its walls, for such is the work I do.

I learned to look at the land and appreciate the hard work it takes to hold the past in hand and heart to build for a new future. As I healed the castle so the castle healed me, as I found myself drawn towards a new beginning, and one that could not be forgotten. There is much to say about life, when we feel such great devotion and honor for what comes before us and what lies within us, for such is the spirit of the Divine element. This element is what reminds us of the grandeur and simplicity that comes from sharing the laughter and tears of children, the rich ruby red wine shared over a meal put together with love, and the gracious hospitality of a host who loves the land enough and longs to build a strong future for his children and their children. Beyond words we connect to break apart, but each and every memory of the heart and soul remains to remind us of who we really are, and brings the three worlds together in a dance of the spheres that only each man, woman and child can experience, for they are unique.

The leaves rustle in the breeze – the forest is silent and yet filled with a million sounds. The hidden castle, where once there was a dome and a reunion of body, mind and soul, brings a different energy and I close my eyes. The rain softly dusts the top of my head and I recall the books I have touched in the library and the rolling lawns I have walked on. I know I have come full circle and in closing one great chapter of my life, a new one shall open to me. I greet the dawn and the dusk with reverence. I feel the peace that settles in heart for it comes from the land and its peoples. I thank those who have made this trip possible and recall the beautiful smile of baby Lea and the warm hug of her two-year-old brother Daniel. I embody the notion of past and future as I meet face to face with my heart and soul for we are now one and I have come home. United with the land I have so long felt a stranger to, I am deeply moved by the beauty and grace my life has offered me. The breeze blows through my hair and the tears I shed are tears of joy, as I make my way back to Athens. I have lived with Source and have died with Source but in the end know that without the soft touch of a hand and the light kiss of love, I am nothing. The journey of my soul has brought me to a new way of looking at life and, grateful that the Transpersonal has taught me so much, I close this book, knowing that as I do, I render deep gratitude to each and every soul that has journeyed with me and who has played a role in my life.

In the end we are all Divine elements in life, able to awaken to the beauty both within and without when we dare to love and love in all gratitude without conditions.

'An Cailleach Bhearra', Mother Goddess of Ireland, you are Mother, Maiden and Crone as you appear in the highest cairn of Ireland, located in the county of Armagh. Thank you for welcoming me home!